Environmental Risks and Rewards for Business

Environmental Risks and Rewards for Business

Herbert Enmarch-Williams

Solicitor and Head of the Environment – Health – Safety Group at
Lawrence Jones Solicitors, London

JOHN WILEY & SONS

Chichester • New York • Brisbane • Toronto • Singapore

Copyright © 1996 by John Wiley & Sons Ltd,
Baffins Lane, Chichester,
West Sussex PO19 1UD, England

National 01243 779777
International (+44) 1243 779777
e-mail (for orders and customer service enquiries):
cs-books@wiley.co.uk
Visit our Home Page on http://www.wiley.co.uk
or http://www.wiley.com

Other Wiley Editorial Offices

John Wiley & Sons, Inc., 605 Third Avenue,
New York, NY 10158–0012, USA

Jacaranda Wiley Ltd, 33 Park Road, Milton,
Queensland 4064, Australia

John Wiley & Sons (Canada) Ltd, 22 Worcester Road,
Rexdale, Ontario M9W IL1, Canada

John Wiley & Sons (Asia) Pte Ltd, 2 Clementi Loop #02–01,
Jin Xing Distripark, Singapore 129809

Library of Congress Cataloging-in-Publication Data
Environmental risks and rewards for business / [edited by] H.E. Enmarch-Williams.
    p.   cm.
    Includes index.
    ISBN 0-471-96437-9 (pbk.)
    1.   Environmental policy—Economic aspects—European Union countries.
    2.   Industrial management—Environmental aspects—European Union countries.
    3.   Sustainable development—European Union countries.   4.   Environmental
law—European Union countries.
    I.   Enmarch-Williams, H. E (Herbert E.)
    HC240.9.E5E633   1996   96–8733
    333.7′0973—dc20   CIP

British Library Cataloguing in Publication Data
A catalogue record for this book is available from the British Library

ISBN 0-471-96437-9

Typeset in 11/13pt Garamond by Poole Typesetting (Wessex) Ltd, Bournemouth
Printed and bound in Great Britain by Biddles Ltd, Guildford and King's Lynn
This book is printed on acid-free paper responsibly manufactured from sustainable
forestation, for which at least two trees are planted for each one used for paper production.

Contents

Appendices

Foreword

Lord Clinton-Davis

This book – which emerges from a conference *Environmental Risks and Rewards for Business*, which took place in Copenhagen in May 1995 – is very timely. It endeavours to pose essential questions confronting European business interests, their attitudes, their suspicions and doubts, their positive support for environmental initiatives and, regrettably, sometimes the lip service that is paid to these. It addresses the impact that not only European, but also global environmental initiatives will have, both in the relatively near future and more importantly in the long term. It is timely because of the role that the environment will play in the review of the Maastricht Treaty which is taking place in the Inter-Governmental Conference.

As a European Commissioner for transport and the environment, I swiftly perceived on taking office in 1985 that DG VII (Transport) was not conspicuously concerned about environmental issues in relation to transport policy yet, by any token, it should have been plain that the two were integrally connected. I believe that by the time I left office in January 1989 there could have been no room for doubt about this. Indeed, the present transport Commissioner, Neil Kinnock, has underlined this integral relationship in developing transport policy over and over again in a number of Commission communications concerning shipping, urban renewal, the development of the railways and the Trans-European Networks to name just a few.

It was swiftly evident that the work of DG XI (Environment) has been conspicuous for its far-sightedness. It was helped immeasurably by a concerned public opinion, which affected not only the perspective of the policy-makers but also that of much of industry. This public support, which is continuously illustrated in Euro-barometers (or opinion polls), represented that the most popular policies emerging from the European Commission were those in the field of environment. This continues to be the case and it is somewhat surprising therefore that, notwithstanding the efforts of the present Environment Commissioner, Ritt Bjerregaard, the Commission, at the behest of a number of the Member States of the European Union, has tended to put its foot on the brake rather than the accelerator as far as environmental progress is concerned.

It is especially surprising in the light of some disaffection on the part of many people in the European Union with many aspects of policy. In these circumstances one would have thought that the Commission would have been emboldened to support even more initiatives which were more likely to generate widespread support amongst the 370 million population of the Union.

This negative approach is not unconnected with the attempts that were made, principally by the United Kingdom, to repatriate environment policy substantially during the Edinburgh Summit. Although this effort was eventually frustrated the use, or abuse, of the doctrine of subsidiarity has markedly undermined the development of environment policy within the European Union. Instead of posing the question as to how best the environment of 370 million people could be protected, the question that has seemingly preoccupied the Council of Environment Ministers has been how best can we thwart any further activity in this field by enabling the Member States to assume prime responsibility in this area.

As Herbert Enmarch-Williams remarks in his contribution to this book, many non-governmental organisations (NGOs) and individuals perceive the European Commission as a sort of court of appeal from the failures of Governments to implement European legislation for which they had been responsible under the unanimity rules, which then prevailed in this field. Of course, it was an incorrect perception as a matter of law but people are fed up with the constant excuses that were made to disobey or to fudge implementation and enforcement of environment law.

By 1987 the Commission had identified no less than 400 breaches of environmental law alone and its attempts to ensure that the law was enforced were usually accompanied by strident abuse from the Member States concerned, rather than by a willingness to put their house in order. Since in many instances Member States had been given liberal time scales to implement these laws (which so frequently they themselves had substantially adulterated in the negotiating process), I saw this as a deliberate and unacceptable breach of the rule of law upon which any civilised organisation must depend.

Eventually, indeed, under the Maastricht Treaty provision was made to enable the European Commission to recommend financial penalties against Member States found to be in breach of European legislation, with the European Court of Justice being given the responsibility to determine the precise nature of any such fine. I myself doubted the wisdom of this approach, preferring the approach favoured by the Court itself of empowering the citizen to initiate litigation against the Member State concerned in his or her own domestic courts, provided always that it could be established that damage had been sustained by that citizen. Of course, this judicial concept is not limited to environmental issues but it will be interesting to see how it develops over the course of the next few years.

Quite apart from helping to secure more effective implementation of environmental law, European citizens, particularly through NGOs, have played an invaluable role in encouraging the Commission to undertake important initiatives until the recent inhibitions (to which I have already referred) were imposed by the activities of certain Member States. Thus in 1986, reflecting this public demand, the Commission proposed a chapter in the Single European Act dealing for the first time in the history of the Treaties exclusively with the environment. Unfortunately, it was not prepared to go as far as to propose that qualified majority voting should apply, but this was changed, again largely in response to popular demand, in the Maastricht Treaty of 1992, when qualified majority voting became the norm rather than the exception (although frankly there are still too many exceptions contained in the Treaty and hopefully these may be reviewed in the course of the Inter-Governmental Conference).

In relation to these processes I have paid tribute to the work of sensible activity on the part of NGOs, but one must also pay tribute to the more enlightened attitudes adopted by much of industry and commerce.

In the pursuance of good environmental policy – as in virtually all other areas – balance is essential. It is no use putting intolerable burdens upon industry which, even with the utmost good faith, cannot be satisfactorily fulfilled or, indeed, upon the poorer Member States which may not have the resources to enable them to undertake these functions. Sustainable development, which was defined in the course of the conference by a number of contributors, has to be the key to achieving this necessary balance. Poorer countries and regions need special help in the form of incentives and financial resources to assist them to attain these objectives. Such regions are not always to be found in the poorer countries alone.

Help is now being provided, but the question that always arises is whether this will provide to be adequate, especially in those countries in Central and Eastern Europe aspiring to be members of the European Union. Once again enforcement is a question of great moment because unless one has comparable ground rules applying throughout the European Union, inadequate enforcement can so easily become the ally of those parts of industry seeking to obtain a competitive advantage resulting from low standards of enforcement of the law. This is unacceptable to good business interest who want to see ever-increasing environmental standards.

I was never entirely convinced that industry and commerce suffi-ciently utilised their influence in helping to shape European Union legislation to the best effect. All too often representations were not made at a suitably embryonic stage in the development of that legislation.

Invariably, this would be followed by a great deal of criticism about the legislation in question. My experience was that business interests can sometimes be their own worst enemy by refusing to recognise that there could be any point of view other than their own and by refusing to seek a consensual approach if that is at all possible. I recall only too well that originally this was the attitude of the car manufacturing companies in relation to atmospheric pollution arising from vehicle emissions. Similarly, those responsible for atmospheric pollution caused by large combustion plants tended to ignore or diminish the ill-effects of their operations. On the other side of the coin, some environmental organisations would engage in equally unbalanced representations suggesting, for example, that when an accident arose through the operations of a chemical plant (*e.g.* that at Sandoz in Basle) all chemical plants should cease to operate. The truth is that there can be no sensible alternative to the quest for balance.

One can only hope, as is perceived in many of the contributions made at the conference, that there has to be some reconciliation of conflicting ideas, a recognition that rational environment policies can go hand in hand with rational industrial policies, thereby enhancing employment and living standards in a sustainable way.

To achieve this, one must contemplate the use of a variety of instruments, legislative and non-legislative alike, using incentives as well as penalties, recognising that in practice the voluntary approach might be found to be wanting and appreciating too that small and medium-sized enterprising (SMEs) might require special treatment to encourage them to adopt a programme of sustainable development. Of course, large industry can be a powerful exemplar for its smaller brethren but this is no reason for letting SMEs "off the hook" bearing in mind the significance of their contribution to the totality of the industrial effort.

Globally, nationally, regionally and locally we cannot simply transfer the burdens of responsibility to industry alone. We all have a role to play. There must be increased understanding of the problems confronted by industry but equally a greater recognition on the part of industry that, by operating in partnership with NGOs, local government and others (rather than in an atmosphere of mutual suspicion and recrimination), real progress can be made for the benefit of the overwhelming majority of citizens within the EU.

Acknowledgements

The Editor wishes to thank the sponsors, EU-LEX International Practice Group, and in particular its then Secretary General Peter Spark and its Director Ariel Lees-Jones, for their unfailing commitment to this book, and their assistance in getting it published. The papers set out in this book stem from a major conference entitled "Environmental Risks and Rewards for Business" which was held in Copenhagen in May 1995. EU-LEX was the conference sponsor, in association with the Centre for Environment Law and Policy and Foreningen Af Registrerede Revisorer (the Danish Association of Chartered Accountants).

The conference – the main highlight of which (and there were many highlights) was the appearance of the then newly installed EU Environment Commissioner, Ritt Bjerregaard (whose speech appears at Appendix I of this book) – attracted delegates from companies from all over Europe, including a significant number of the world's leading multi-nationals. All credit therefore to the conference sponsors for supporting this attempt at pushing out the boundaries of what professional advisers are (traditionally) expected to be concerned with.

Thanks are also due to:

Brian Riley of the UK law firm Watson Burton, for his work in editing the Country-by-Country Reports produced (in the main) by EU-LEX member firms (see Appendices III and IV);

Dr Glen Plant of the Centre for Environmental Law & Policy, not only for his involvement in and support of the conference and this book, but also for his support and encouragement down the years, and the example he set as an environmental law and policy expert;

Lawrence Werner, an acknowledged expert in environmental disaster management/crisis communications, and his company Ketchum Public Relations, for supporting the paperback edition of this book;

The partners of Babst, Calland, Clements and Zomnir, again for supporting the publication of this book in paperback format, and in particular Dean Calland and Ron Frank, both excellent commercial and environmental lawyers;

The Editor's colleagues and the partners of Lawrence Jones, for their support and assistance in enabling him to complete the task of editing this book; and finally,

All of the contributors, especially those who also spoke at the Copenhagen conference, for their time and efforts given in order to push forward the debate on the role which industry must play in making the concept of sustainable development real.

Although the papers contained in this book have been revised in conjunction with the contributors subsequent to their presentations at the Copenhagen conference, it should be taken that any views expressed in this book are as at 1st May 1995.

List of Contributors

Herbert Enmarch-Williams is an English lawyer, practising environmental and European law, and is a Consultant and Head of the *Environment – Health – Safety* Group at the law firm Lawrence Jones, based in the City of London. He is a member of the United Kingdom Environmental Law Association and Convenor of its Practice & Procedure Working Party. He is a former Research Associate at the London School of Economics Centre for Environmental Law and Policy.

Lord Clinton-Davis is presently a Consultant on European Law and Affairs with the London law firm SJ Berwin & Co. From 1985 to 1989 he served as a Member of the European Commission with responsibility for transport, environment and nuclear safety and (for one year) consumer affairs and forestry. He is also a UK parliamentarian – a member of the House of Lords – and has previously been a UK Member of Parliament and a government minister. Amongst other positions, he is currently Chairman of the Advisory Committee On Protection of the Sea (ACOPS) and Chairman of the Packaging Standards Council.

Mikael Skou Andersen is a member of the Centre for Social Science Research on the Environment (CESAM) at Aarhus University, Denmark, where he is also Assistant Professor in the Department of Political Science. He is acknowledged as an international expert on the issue of environmental taxes and is author of the book "Governance by Green Taxes: Making Pollution Prevention Pay" (Manchester University Press, 1994). He has also been a consultant to the OECD Environment Directorate.

Ian Bird is a US attorney and is currently Vice-President – International Counsel at CH2M Hill Companies Ltd, Denver, Colorado, USA. Until the end of 1996 he was Vice-President Government Affairs at Waste Management International, based in London.

Ritt Bjerregaard is presently the Member of the European Commission responsible for the Environment. She was previously a Member of the Danish Parliament and a leading parliamentarian. She has, in the past, held the posts of Minister for Social Affairs and Minister for Education.

Peter Blackman was formerly Assistant Director of the British Bankers' Association. He has also been at the forefront of the European Union Federation of Bankers' discussions with the European Commission and the European Parliament in response to the European Commission's 1993 Green Paper on Civil Liability for Environmental Damage. He is one of the UK's leading experts on the issue of banks and the environment.

Dean Calland is a leading US environmental lawyer, and is a founding partner in the law firm Babst, Calland, Clements & Zomnir, based in Pittsburgh, Pennsylvania, USA.

Øystein Dahle is Board Chairman, World Watch Institute, Norway, and until 1 April 1995 was Executive Vice-President of Esso Norway, the Exxon Corporation's Norwegian affiliate, and was responsible for the company's downstream activities. He is also Board Chairman of the Norwegian Tourist Association.

Genevieve De Bauw is Director, European Union Government Affairs at Dow Europe. From 1992 to 1996 she was Environmental Affairs Adviser at the Union of Industrial & Employers' Confederations of Europe (UNICE), Brussels, focusing upon the initiation and co-ordination of European industry action with regard to EU environmental policy issues.

Margaret Flaherty is Project Manager and a trade and environment specialist at the World Business Council for Sustainable Development in Geneva, which was created in 1995 following the merger of the World Industry Council for the Environment and the Business Council for Sustainable Development.

Robert Hull is Head of Unit for Policy Co-ordination, Integration of Environment in Other Policies and Environmental Action Programmes in Directorate-General XI (Environment, Nuclear Safety and Civil Protection) at the European Commission in Brussels. Prior to this, between 1990 and 1994, he was Adviser to the Director-General for DG XI.

Olivier Kaiser is a French lawyer and is Counsel at Exxon Chemical Europe, a subsidiary of Exxon Corporation, one of the 10 largest chemical/petrochemical companies in the world.

Richard D. Morgenstern is currently Visiting Scholar at Resources for the Future in Washington DC, USA, a leading environmental think tank. From 1982 to 1995 he was Director, Office of Policy Analysis and Chief Economist at the US Environmental Protection Agency. Between 1991 and 1993 he also served as Acting Assistant Administrator for Policy, Planning and Evaluation at the EPA, and Acting Deputy Administrator from January to March 1993. He was Chairman of the Group of Economic Experts formed by the Environment Directorate of the OECD, from 1987 to 1991.

Dieter Rompel is Executive Chairman of the Board of Hölter Industrie

Beteiligungs AG, Germany, one of the world's leading environmental engineering and technology companies.

Ursula Schliessner is a German lawyer and a Partner in the Brussels office of the US law firm Oppenheimer, Wolff & Donnelly. She was formerly Chairman of the Environmental Liability Working Group of the EU Committee of the American Chamber of Commerce, Brussels.

William G. Seddon-Brown is Director, European Government Affairs at Waste Management International, based in Brussels. He is also chairman of the American Chamber of Commerce EU Committee, and of the steering committee of the European Energy from Waste Coalition.

Elizabeth Smith is a Senior Environmental Specialist at the Environmental Appraisal Unit at the European Bank for Reconstruction and Development (EBRD). Prior to her arrival at the EBRD in July 1991, she worked as an environmental consultant, developing worldwide environmental standards of practice for multinational corporations, particularly in the area of emergency prevention, mitigation and response.

David Stanners is Programme Manager at the European Environment Agency, based in Copenhagen. He was Chief Editor of the Dobris Assessment – published in 1995 by the European Environment Agency – the most comprehensive pan-European report on the state of the environment in Europe ever produced.

Raymond Van Ermen is Secretary-General of the European Environmental Bureau, Brussels, a federation of some 160 environmental non-governmental organisations. He is also a member of the United Nations Environment Programme (UNEP)/International Chamber of Commerce (ICC) Advisory Panel on the implementation of the ICC Business Charter for Sustainable Development.

Lawrence Werner is Executive Vice President/Director at Ketchum Public Relations Worldwide; Ketchum is one of America's three largest public relations companies. He is a leading expert on crisis management and communications, and was one of a team of four public relations executives recruited nationwide in the US to assess the communications and public relations challenges posed by the Exxon Valdez oil spill in 1989.

Contributors to Country-by-Country Reports

Bryan Riley (Editor of the Country-by-Country reports) is a partner at the law firm Watson Burton in Newcastle-upon-Tyne, UK. He has been practising environmental law since the late 1970s.

Austria – Kornelia Fritsch-Vallaster is a partner in the law firm Friedrich Schwank Law Offices in Vienna.

Belgium – Mario Deketelaere is a professor of environmental law at the Catholic University of Louvain and is allied to the law firm of De Meester, Ballon, Billiet & Co in Brussels.

Denmark – Poul Hvilsted is a partner in the law firm *Bech Bruun & Trolle, Copenhagen.

England & Wales – Michael Conaghan is a partner in the law firm Lawrence Jones, London; Lewis Denton is a solicitor in the law firm Davies Wallis Foyster in Manchester/Liverpool.

Finland – Mika Alanko is an Attorney-at-law in the firm *Bützow & Co Ltd, Helsinki.

France – Laurence Rager is a partner in the law firm *Custax & Legal, Paris.

Germany – Jochen Köster is a partner in the law firm Benkelberg, von Stein Lausnitz & Partner, in Halle-Saale.

Greece – Dimitris Zepos is a partner in the law firm *Zepos & Zepos, Athens.

Hungary – Dr Károly Bárd is a partner in the law firm Eörsi & Partners.

Ireland – Andrew O'Rorke is a partner in the law firm Hayes & Sons, Dublin.

Italy – Dr Natalia Barbera, is a lawyer with *Studio Deberti Jacchia, Milan, and was formerly with Studio Legale Tributario Alderighi Rome/Milan.

Luxembourg – Nathalie Gattoni is an economist at *GEDELUX SA and Serge Bernard is a lawyer at the law firm *Etude Roland Michel.

The Netherlands – René Bakers is a partner in the law firm Thuis & Partners in Heerlen/Maastricht.

Portugal – Carlos Matias is a partner at the law firm Antonio Marante & Associados, Porto.

Spain – Felix Vilaseca is a partner at the law firm Bufete Roig Aran, Barcelona.

Sweden – Lena Eriksson is an associate at the law firm Engström & Co, Malmö.

All the above firms, except those denoted by an asterisk (*) are Members of the EU-LEX International Practice Group.

EU-LEX International Practice Group

EU-LEX International Practice Group is a multi-disciplinary, non-exclusive association of professional firms providing high-quality legal, accountancy and taxation services throughout Europe and also in the United States.

EU-LEX Members advise both businesses and private clients. EU-LEX's core philosophy is a belief that both business and private clients today seek personal, responsive and cost-effective assistance in relation to their legal, taxation and accountancy needs, and that professional advisers from smaller to medium-sized firms are best placed to provide such service.

In addition to providing local advice in all major commercial centres, all EU-LEX Members have experience in solving cross-border problems, and each EU-LEX Member firm employs professionals who are able to communicate in at least two European languages. Furthermore, EU-LEX has contacts beyond Europe and the US, enabling Members to provide advice for the benefit of clients worldwide.

Advice and assistance outside the fields of law, accountancy and taxation can also be provided via EU-LEX Members, to cover a wide range of clients' needs.

Regular co-operation via established working relationships, assisted by a full-time secretariat, provides the basis for a truly international service to clients. EU-LEX is not a passive network or a mere list of international contacts; Members meet together regularly to discuss international and cross-border developments, and ways of servicing clients' needs more effectively, and are otherwise in frequent contact with each other.

Consequently, EU-LEX is pleased to commend itself to businesses and private individuals in all areas of the world as the first and best source of professional legal, taxation and accountancy advice and assistance, both local and international.

For further information, please contact EU-LEX Director Ariel Lees-Jones at EU-LEX IPG, Harvester House, 37 Peter Street, Manchester M2 5GB, United Kingdom. Tel: +44 161 228 3702/+44 161 839 9005; Fax: +44 161 839 9006.

Introduction

Øystein Dahle
Board Chairman, World Watch Institute, Norway

Business as usual – not an option

A US Chief Justice was once travelling by train from Washington, north-bound. When the conductor came for ticket control the Chief Justice searched his pockets, his valet, his bag and other belongings, but could not find his ticket. The conductor, who had recognised his distinguished passenger, felt a little bit embarrassed on his behalf and whispered: "Sir, if and when you find your ticket, please just mail it to our office in Washington and that will be fine". The Chief Justice looked at the young conductor and responded: "Son, the problem is more serious than you may think; if I do not find the ticket, I do not know where I am going".

Mankind probably does not have a "ticket" either, but it is surprisingly confident that it will get there. No doubt, the passengers on the *Titanic* felt the same way about the vessel on which they sailed, until that disastrous accident befell them. The ship was a technological dream, and the passengers had unlimited confidence in the ship; they believed that it could not sink. Consequently, when the ship hit ice and, in fact, started to sink, the people on board literally did not believe it. Reports of the tragedy commented that as the ship disappeared into the dark, cold sea, dancing music was still being played on the upper decks. Of course, any parallels with the destiny of the human race is purely coincidental, is it not?

Perhaps rather than subscribing to the concept of mankind being passengers on a ship, one could use the analogy of spacemen and women on "Spaceship Earth". A very useful model of human development mirrors exactly the process of moving from the cowboy economy to the spaceship economy. During the early history of the Earth, the destructive capacity of man was limited, thus providing our ancestors with almost limitless flexibility. Man was small and almost insignificant relative to the environment and the biological system in which he lived. The extreme end of the development path is the spaceship analogy. The remaining flexibility is limited, resource considerations are critical, energy use must be compatible with a sustainable future, and there is much emphasis on human interaction with the environment. Whilst there is a general

1

acceptance of the value of this model, there are vastly differing interpretations of how far along the development path mankind has travelled. The biggest challenge, however, is to recognise that mankind is moving incredibly fast in an unwelcome direction, or rather in a direction in which the final destiny is unknown.

Around 25 years ago some of the most dramatic events in the history of space exploration occurred, namely the launch and subsequent breakdown of *APOLLO 13* on its way to the moon. The famous US news commentator, Eric Sevareid, commented on the dramatic situation on the evening prior to the crew's return asking why everyone was so fascinated by the event. Was it because people identified with the crew? Or was it because people realised that man and technology had created the situation, and that man had to rely on that technology to bring about a happy ending. In fact, the space journey was symbolic of the reality that the problems created by technology should ultimately be solvable by technology.

Forty years ago Albert Einstein said that the world we had created by our way of thinking had serious problems which could not be solved by continuing to think the same way.

The challenge facing mankind has two dimensions: first to identify and characterise our mode of thinking; and, secondly to modify this way of thinking. A simple way of describing this change is to characterise the current thinking as a "masculine fragmented" approach, while the more desirable approach may be "feminine totality". In this context sustainable development is not a distant goal, but a new way of thinking.

Western industrialised countries have increasingly become consumer orientated, anchored in materialism as an ideology. Since materialism does not have any built-in limitations, this concept cannot be sustainable. The modern environmental challenge is no longer merely to clean-up pollution – although a massive effort must still be made towards cleaning already damaged environments – but to put into operation the four key concepts critical for mankind's survival, which are:

(i) sustainable development;
(ii) the precautionary principle;
(iii) integrated responsibility; and
(iv) intergenerational equity.

The potential climate destabilisation and the massive soil erosion currently taking place are just two remarkable examples of how the environmental challenge is surfacing. The environmental challenge must never be marginalised, nor must it be just another thing to worry about, competing with more immediate concerns.

Introduction

The situation can be compared to the trials and tribulations one can imagine might face a single mother when the dog has run away, the children are fighting, the dinner is burning, the babysitter has not shown up, the mother is late for the Parents and Teachers Association meeting and has just spilled gravy onto the carpet. Suddenly someone knocks at the door and announces that he is carrying out a door-to-door survey and wants to know how she feels about the proposed landfill site being planned for the edge of town. "To hell with it!" she may reply. Of course, the timing for the request was grossly inappropriate in the circumstances. But one might ask, when is it ever appropriate?

Environmental harmony is a vision, requiring much analysis, much debate and a great deal of hard work and adjustment. One is surrounded by environmental issues which are worsened by scientific uncertainty. To overreact to any of these issues could be counterproductive, but to ignore any of them would be irresponsible. The cornerstone of the world's future strategy will be the ability to manage risk and to manage change. In this process, industry has to move from mere compliance to leadership. Business as usual is not a sustainable option.

The first priority is not to find the right answers, but rather to ask the right questions, such as:

- Are political systems designed to cope with the impossible process of prioritising long-term issues relative to short-term concerns?
- Are current economic models sufficiently sophisticated to cope with physical expansion within a closed, limited system?
- Are existing models for management training adequate as a preparation for the unprecedented change process ahead of us?
- Can human needs be redirected towards choices and provisions in line with sustainable development?
- Can the concept of sustainability be packaged so as to make it attractive?
- Is the difference between policy and politics fully understood and mastered?

In other words, what does one imagine our future will be when man's commercial system conflicts with everything nature teaches? Adam Smith introduced the idea of the "invisible hand working towards the common good". Imagine now the "invisible foot" of environmental irresponsibility and vandalism kicking the "common good" to pieces and trampling it to the ground.

The concept of sustainability is a concept of optimism and hope, offering quality of life rather than just quantity. It is a moral obligation and pursuing it is a fascinating task. However, contrary to what many people seem to believe, mankind cannot change without actually chang-ing. Very little remains of this century, even this millennium. There is much work to be done and not a single day to waste. If the future is to provide any hope for the human race this momentous task must be started in earnest, and it must be started now!

Chapter 1
Environmental Risks and Rewards for Business in the 1990s

William Seddon-Brown

Director, European Government Affairs at Waste Management
International; Chairman, American Chamber of Commerce
EU Committee

The theme of this book, environmental risks and rewards for business, is a particularly appropriate theme for our times, since many of the unresolved issues relating to the European Union of today – particularly with respect to the environment – involve questions of "balance": for example, centralisation versus decentralisation; national legislation versus EU legislation; regulation versus market mechanisms; fines and penalties versus incentives; and cost versus benefit. Many aspects of EU policy and of the EU legislative framework involve balance. The theme "risks and rewards" is therefore very pertinent.

Fundamentally, environmental policy and action must reflect the importance of *sustainable development*, a concept which is discussed in various ways by many of the contributors to this book. The concept of sustainable development is a wonderful idea. However, ideas are plentiful in this world, and it is only when an idea is turned into reality that it actually begins to make a difference. Therefore, a great concept – sustainable development – now exists, but something still needs to be done about it, to put it into effect.

The concept of sustainable development is of course (at least in theory) the driving force behind the development of the EU's environmental regulatory system at the present time (see *Towards Sustainability*, the European Commission's Fifth Action Programme on the Environment (1993) (COM (92) 23 Final). However, it is interesting to pause briefly and consider the more concrete forces which, in reality, drive the various environmental policies and movements currently evident in Europe. These forces might be categorised as:

- science: the facts, the risks and the standards;
- public perceptions and behaviour;

- economics and employment;
- political and social policies and their effects; and
- the legislative and regulatory framework.

A brief discussion of three of these aspects will act as an initial challenge for the reader before he considers the issues highlighted and discussed in the chapters which follow.

First, the issue of public perception. Awareness of environmental issues has, it is generally acknowledged, risen over the past few decades. Recently, the major question being asked has been, "has this concern faded?".

Taking the United Kingdom as an example: in the 1970s UK citizens were asked in a poll carried out by the Government whether environment/pollution was a key issue. In response only about 1–7% replied that environment/pollution was a key issue. In the early 1980s the response level was 8–10%. By 1989 the figure had risen to 30%. However, the latest polls carried out in the early 1990s show a reduced figure of 22%. As a result, some sceptics conclude that the concern has faded. Whilst public environmental concern does appear to have reduced somewhat, nevertheless it must be pointed out that public opinion polling has shown that the environment is still the third most important concern out of all public issues, including education, economy and social security. Therefore, there is a strong argument that the concern is not fading, but has perhaps suffered a degree of adjustment relative to other, more "recessionary" concerns.

In late 1994, there were some interesting poll results surfacing in the United States and in Europe. In the United States, people were asked, "who is to blame for the pollution and the environmental problems we have today?": 44% blamed companies; 27% blamed apathetic citizens; and only 18% blamed the political leaders. A similar study in Europe asked, "who should solve the environmental issues that are being raised?": 46% answered that individuals should solve such issues; 39% answered that companies should be responsible; and 70% answered that central government should be involved. With respect to the question of who actually is to blame, respondents apportioned blame on the individual and on the government to about the same degree, but blamed business more so.

The second aspect to be discussed is the issue of economics. The environment is a major cost item. In the United States today, 2.2% of the annual gross national product is spent on environmental protection. It is expected that by the year 2000 there will have been an increase to 2.8% or $178 billion per annum. That figure is enormous. There are also considerable spin-offs: for example, the top 20 national environmental groups in the United States are now reckoned to spend more than $400 million per annum on lawyers, lobbying and public relations.

In Europe in 1992, the best estimate of ECOTEC Consulting (whose research guides the European Commission's environment programme) was that ECU63 billion or $82 billion was being spent by the then 12 EU Member States on environmental protection. Of that figure, public authorities and industries spent about ECU15 billion, which covers waste management services, regulatory functions and internal environmental management activities. In addition, this huge investment supports around one million jobs, which is 1.3% of total employment in those 12 countries. According to latest estimates, there could be growth in terms of a further one million jobs by the year 2000.

The third aspect is the legislative and regulatory background (which is one of the key issues raised by many of the contributors to this book). It must be appreciated that this backdrop to legislative and regulatory developments within the European Union is developing constantly.

To demonstrate this, if one starts with the 1992 Maastricht Treaty (the Treaty on European Union) which enshrined the precautionary principle, the principle of prevention at source and the polluter pays principle in EU law and policy, the further development of the environmental policy of the EU can be traced along a series of initiatives undertaken by the EU Institutions, namely:

- the Fifth Environmental Action Programme, published in 1992, sets out the proposed direction for EU environmental policy-making as the European Union moves towards the year 2000. In particular, it discusses the most appropriate tools and instruments to be used, targeting certain sectors as priority areas for cooperation between the various actors involved, such as industry, the public and policy-makers;
- in November 1994 the European Commission's environment direc- torate, DG XI, embarks upon what is described as an "interim review" of this Action Programme, to bring it up to date and to take a fresh look at the issues;
- midway through 1994 the site of the European Environment Agency – the newest EU institution in the environment field – is finally established in Copenhagen, Denmark. Its remit is to gather and collate information on the environment in Europe, which can then be used by EU policy-makers as a firm basis for future policy and legislative initiatives. Its first task is to publish the Dobris Report later in 1995, which will be the most comprehensive and up-to-date examination so far of the state of the environment within EU territory;
- early in 1995 the Commission's work programme for 1995 was pub- lished, which contains a section on environmental policy, detailing

proposals for legislative initiatives during the period covered by the work programme. In March 1995 the European Parliament gives its opinion on that work programme;

- in April 1995 the DG XI Consultative Forum on the Environment (an advisory group consisting of individuals specifically chosen on account of their particular expertise and experience in the environmental arena and convened by the European Commission to comment on EU environmental policy) published a policy document setting out 12 principles for sustainable development to guide future EU policy-making.

All these developments are highlighted because it is important to realise that these are part of the framework which has been evolving gradually since Maastricht and will have a major impact upon the direction which the EU environment policy takes for the foreseeable future.

It would appear that a number of vital issues are emerging from the legislative, social and industrial patterns outlined above. It is suggested that these are as follows.

(i) Moves towards the integration of environmental considerations into other policy areas.

(ii) Questions about the effectiveness of environmental policies, including issues of:

- the need for cost/benefit analysis;
- difficulties over the application and enforcement of EU law;
- the role of the European Environment Agency; and
- the role of environmental reporting, accounting and auditing.

(iii) Competitiveness issues, including:

- the proper balance between dealing with matters at national and EU level;
- curbing tendencies towards "over-regulation" and introducing more coherence into environmental regulations;
- introducing producer take-back schemes.

(iv) Trade and the environment conflicts:

- questions of "growth, competitiveness and employment";
- pursuing "minimum intervention" policies, and the reliance on market forces;
- closing the gap between the European Union and Central and Eastern Europe;
- global conflicts and international implications in trade and environment issues – the role of the World Trade Organisation under GATT.

(v)   The issue of environmental liability:

- eliminating differential systems within the EU;
- implementing the polluter pays principle.

(vi)   The debate over appropriate environmental standards:

- harmonisation at the highest or lowest levels?;
- ensuring a level playing-field;
- utilising science, health and risk-based standards;
- conflicts with the standards of new Member States;
- encouraging clean technology.

(vii) Attempts at broadening the range of instruments used for policy initiatives:

- the need for economic and fiscal reform;
- the use of voluntary agreements and other types of instruments.

(viii) Attempts at encouraging behavioural changes:

- the eco-auditing and eco-label schemes;
- environmental reporting initiatives;
- modifying certain fiscal arrangements.

(ix)   Guaranteeing the rights of the public and non-governmental organisations (NGOs):

- access to environmental information, and the use of environmental impact assessment;
- access to justice and recourse to legal remedies.

(x)   The concept of shared responsibility:

- a shift towards voluntary agreements?;
- the importance of consultation;
- solution-oriented environmental advocacy.

Where does industry fit into this picture? The chart set out on p 12 was published in *Tomorrow* magazine in July 1994. The magazine suggested that basically there are four types of attitude gradually being formed by industry with respect to the environment. These are:

(i)   the defensive;
(ii)   the cooperative;
(iii) the proactive; and
(iv)   the preventive.

The challenge to corporate executives and managers reading this book today is this: which of these attitudes typifies your company's reaction to the environment question?

What, then, are the main challenges which are now facing the European Union and which will impact upon business?

First, there is a need to integrate environmental considerations into other policy areas. This is an important issue. It is related to the balance to be achieved between national and EU legislative initiatives. It is also related to the important task of increasing the visibility of the environment as an identifiable issue.

Secondly, there is a definite need for a broader range of instruments to be used in environmental policy-making. Both the present EU Environment Commissioner (Ritt Bjerregaard) and her immediate predecessor at the Commission (Ioannis Paleokrassas) have referred to the need for a greater emphasis on economic and fiscal instruments, plus a range of other instruments. This must be followed through.

Thirdly, the concept of partnership and shared responsibility (again, demonstrating an element of balance), is being emphasised as one of the main solutions to the environmental problems of Europe. It is also related to the so-called "voluntary approach", an example being the voluntary agreements entered into between industry and government in Holland.

Fourthly, the attitudes and patterns of the consumer and of production methods are changing.

Fifthly, there are obvious shortcomings in the application and enforcement of environmental legislation. Ritt Bjerregaard's department has again emphasised the fact that she is very concerned about this aspect. Certainly, industry is very concerned about level playing-fields and enforcement of standards.

Finally, the international dimension of the EU's environment programme is essential.

Which of the above are the "priorities"? Determining priorities is, of course, a necessary, but, nevertheless, difficult judgment which has to be made. It is important, however, that industry and policy-makers do not become so busy attending to the immediate and the urgent that they fail to stop and think about what actually is most important. Serious reflection upon both the practical implications of implementing sustainable development and the proper balance between the themes highlighted in this chapter is clearly the starting point. What has been discussed above is merely the bare bones of the issue. If, however, these important principles and ideas are ever to be fleshed-out, real and practical solutions must be found.

All the contributors to this book are immersed in this important area, and are trying to work out the implications of the legislative, regulatory and policy framework outlined above. The editor and the sponsors of this book should be complimented for having put together a series of papers that provide a perspective which comes from many different (but hopefully complimentary) angles: from the angle of the corporate organisation; from the angle of the consumers and the NGOs; and from the angle of government and international policy-makers. This book may appear to some to be undertaking a difficult balancing act in attempting to present so many different viewpoints. Nevertheless, in doing so it paints a clear enough picture of the environmental risks and rewards which business must now face up to as the twenty-first century moves ever closer.

FOUR COMPANY ATTITUDES

DEFENSIVE

- Only defensive measures considered when complying with accepted standards under government pressure

- Disbelief in environmental problems and reluctance to act

- Short-term thinking

- Limited (internal) focus on profits

- Old-fashioned management practices and human relations

COOPERATIVE

- Working together with authorities to identify environmental improvement priorities

- Realistic approach in trying to comply with standards

- Being a follower – not a leader

PROACTIVE

- Good environmental performance and compliance

- Anticipation of new standards and legislation

- Openness towards authorities and the public

- Integration of environmental performance in total management concept

PREVENTIVE

- Total business concept rethink

- Redesign of products, raw material use and processes

- Acceptance of public reporting

- Environmental protection seen as opportunity rather than threat

Source: Tomorrow, July–September 1994, Tomorrow Publishing AB, Kungsgatan 27, S-111 56 Stockholm, Sweden.

Chapter 2
Sustainable Development: A Challenge for European Industry

Raymond van Ermen

Secretary-General, European Environmental Bureau

What is sustainable development? Can a single, comprehensive definition of sustainable development be given? So far, no single, all-encompassing definition has arisen. This is because, as the Secretariat report to the third annual session of the United Nations Commission for Sustainable Development (which concluded in spring 1995) indicated, the very notion of sustainable development is an evolving concept, with its perceptions changing from one year to the next. According to the UN Secretariat, social development, economic development and environmental sustainability must all be explicitly addressed in developing sustainable development strategies. Consequently, in the ongoing debate about the meaning of sustainable development the evolving nature of sustainable development must always be underlined.

It has increasingly been noted that sustainable development is, at present, the only answer available on the market of ideas at a global level, in the face of the threats hanging over the Earth in terms of development and security. It is also becoming clear that what is required is to shift to another development model as gently and gradually as possible. Furthermore, the implementation of a sustainable development strategy appears to be a powerful element for economic, social, cultural and even political restructuring. In this context the path which the decision-maker must tread is like a labyrinth, complete with a variety of possibilities, obstacles and challenges.

As far as the environment is concerned, the context in which companies must operate has become particularly complex over the last 20 years. A company cannot be competitive without meeting the challenges raised by growing competition between companies operating in the economic triad of Europe, the United States and Japan, to find new processes and new products that can better meet sustainable development requirements.

The goal – based on concepts such as eco-efficiency and the use of assessment methods such as life-cycle analysis – is to design products that might be offered in future to saturated consumer markets in industrialised countries, and might also meet consumer expectations in countries within the economic triad. Successfully servicing these markets in line with sustainable development involves a reduction in the use of raw materials and energy, better ways of control, and a better understanding of the new policies in terms of consumption and behavioural patterns.

However, the drive towards new markets, linked to these new, greener processes and products (and also relying on new marketing techniques such as eco-labelling), has already come up against the charge of establishing new environmental trade barriers. This is a charge increasingly levelled by competing countries within the economic triad (such as, in the case of the EU eco-label scheme, the United States and Canada against the European Union countries) and by countries outside the economic triad, such as Brazil and Malaysia. When considering the potential agenda of the World Trade Organisation trade and environment working group (which will be discussing such issues) it is clear that all national or EU environmental policy instruments are potentially the subject of a wider global debate (and, in fact, the role that voluntary standardisation systems like ISO 14000 are intended to play merely confirms this global dimension).

For non-governmental organisations (NGOs) these new "business-led" approaches fall far short of containing all the necessary democratic guarantees they expect to see. But this globalisation of the market economy, which inevitably strengthens the role of multinational corporations, is, at the same time, accompanied by the rising power of a global civil and consumer society which, in turn, is leading to increasing pressure for accountability falling on the companies themselves (as can, and will, increasingly in future, be seen particularly in the context of environmental reports, environmental audits and environmental management schemes). For the corporation, the weight attributed to its "stake" in this debate will be related to its capacity and willingness for dialogue with the other stakeholders.

Growth at the rates experienced in Europe no longer ensures employment; nor, in an industry deeply transformed by automation, do investments give rise to much employment either. The new economic logic is hard on traditional economic indicators. We have entered a transitional phase between two economic models. As is noted by the economist René Passet, the model which we are leaving behind has reached its limits, and mechanisms no longer work in the same way as they did in the heyday of the old system. Consequently, defining European competitiveness according to traditional quantitative criteria, reflecting the value-system of a market unable to achieve optimisation in the long term, would be very seriously wrong. As Professor Dewoot of the University of Louvain once observed, the logic of the system is going off the rails and it is urgent to take action. Public opinion will therefore increasingly be led to question economic choices in terms of investment policy.

If current growth is more financial than economic and no longer creates jobs, and if it does not bring to a halt the increase in poverty or contribute to sustainable development, the rules for allocating public funds (which now go to a very large extent to major companies in terms of infrastructure, research and development (R & D), public procurement and so on) will have to be redirected towards more efficient companies (as defined in terms of implementation of sustainable development) which are able to create new products and new processes, as well as moving towards other fields of action more conducive to job creation.

Which investments should be given priority? The idea of a global, ecological "Marshall Plan" is slowly gaining ground. As is underlined by the Group of Lisbon in a 1993 report, *Limits to Competition*, unmet basic needs today are the following: *water*, for two billion people (of which millions reside in the EU); *housing*, for 1.5 billion people (of which there are millions in European cities and suburbs); and *energy*, for four billion people. Furthermore, it is hardly necessary to emphasise the huge needs in terms of waste management, rehabilitation of closed down industrial sites and reafforestation.

There is also an increasingly important relationship developing between policy instruments (including those in the environmental protection arena) and the *equity* principle. For NGOs equity is a central principle without which sustainable development cannot become a reality.

The problems of poverty, unemployment, marginalisation, drug addiction and the degradation of suburbs, are eating away at our countries as they do in developing countries. This is one of the elements at stake in the ongoing revision of the European Commission's Fifth Action Programme on the Environment, *Towards Sustainability* (1993) (COM (92) 23 Final). The question is, which strategy will the European Commission use to address the needs of the poor and the unemployed, considering, in particular, that the former are directly concerned by the impact of the so-called market instruments on their low incomes and the latter by the action of the European Union in the area of job creation?

One may think that this is no concern of the business sectors. On the contrary, this would be a seriously wrong assessment. A growing number of industry managers feel concerned by the equity principle and the social dimension of the choices to be made. For example, Sir Alan (now Lord) Shepherd, Chairman of Grand Metropolitan plc and of the Prince of

Wales' business leaders team, Business in the Community, believes that an increasingly vocal, well-informed and sophisticated public expects the roles of corporate power and influence to be balanced by social and environmental responsibility.

Europe must be regarded not only as a regional organisation, modelled in the context of an overall globalisation of the market economy, but also as a source of values. The European Union needs a European development model that would offer a means for Europeans to define their own identity.

The European Commission's White Paper on Growth, Competitiveness and Employment 1994 had the particular merit of considering a European development model and of initiating this process, even if it is clear that this model cannot be defined thus far by the content of the White Paper itself. European participatory democracy, the establishment of European poles of sustainable development, new progress indicators, and an eco-industrial revolution are some of the ways forward proposed by the European Environment Bureau to the European Commission President Jacques Santer for inclusion as part of his 12 initiatives for the new Commission.

The revision of the European Union Treaty in 1996 will be marked by a new major debate on the kind of Europe needed. What Europe is lacking is a blueprint for its faith. There is no doubt that NGOs will want to contribute to this on the basis of the following six criteria: peace keeping; economic efficiency; the response to ecological requirements; the free development of cultures; equity; and European participatory democracy.

NGOs tabled their proposals for the revision of the Treaty in its report, *Greening the Treaty II*. The report determines two directions. First, a more efficient application of the principle set out in Article 2 of the Maastricht Treaty, that the aim of the Union is to promote sustainable development. This approach has led the NGOs to formulate many proposals concerning, among other things, the strategic impact assessment of Community policies, and the Community policy on public procurement. The second direction concerns human rights and a more participatory form of European democracy. It acknowledges that since each citizen of the Union now has two nationalities (including that of being a Union citizen) EU citizens should as such have equal rights and responsibilities, including equal rights in terms of participatory democracy and in terms of the right to a sound environment.

As regards external influences, the policy followed by the Republican majority at the US Congress is bound to have an impact on the debate concerning European environmental policy. As was recently noted by Barry Commoner (who is generally regarded as the father of the US environmental movement) "if the bills that [have] now passed the House go through I think it will literally destroy most of the work that has been accomplished since the 1970s".

In a recent interview given by Mr Commoner, he also explained that it was necessary to change industrial strategy. The approach aiming at a gradual reduction in the accepted level of pollution – for example, for carbon monoxide – has proved a failure. In particular, the increase in the number of vehicles on the road cancels out the impact of the required emissions reduction per vehicle. What should now be done therefore is to move to a zero emission objective. This constitutes a considerable challenge in terms of R & D, developing new markets and, consequently, maintaining competitiveness. Barry Commoner proposed, in this respect, that this should be introduced in the United States without the need for a bill to be adopted by Congress. It could be done, he believed, by a simple stroke of a pen tomorrow by President Clinton without even consulting Congress. The only thing needed to be done was to change specification conditions for public procurement.

What can be inferred from this as regards the European Union? First, the competitiveness of European companies at the global level can only be achieved if Europe is a world leader for sustainable development. Secondly, the zero emission objective should become one of the major elements in the European Union's R & D policy. This is particularly important in view of the scheduled revision of the EU's Fourth Framework Programme on Research and Development in 1996. Thirdly, the European Union has an essential role to play as regards changes in production and consumption patterns. It is also an important opportunity for the European Union to redirect its industrial and commercial projects in order to strengthen its competitiveness. In the view of the European Environment Bureau, the European Union should announce that it will start work on a Green Paper on this issue for changes in production and consumption patterns. The Green Paper should be the subject of a consultation with other (third) countries. More particularly, the Union should set a number of objectives in this Green Paper, amongst which should be, on the one hand, the fundamental redirection of the public procurement system, both at Commission and Member States level, and, on the other hand, the definition of a framework adapted to the objectives of sustainable development in relation to the advertising market.

A further point is that the European Union must play a driving role at regional level. The Union is currently considering various possibilities as regards the establishment of free trade areas, with the Mediterranean area, MERCOSUR and NAFTA. The Commission should announce its intention to draft a Green Paper on free trade areas and sustainable development.

Finally, what role should the companies themselves be playing in the drive towards sustainable development? To assess risks and rewards, companies need, on the one hand, a vision and, on the other, benchmarks. It is vital that they participate in the EU's environmental management and audit scheme (EMAS), which will give companies the necessary benchmarks, first, to assess and compare from year to year their own performance and, secondly, to compare themselves with other companies.

However, companies should consider the issue of environmental management in a broader perspective than simply the EMAS scheme. For example, the European Environmental Bureau is presently in discussion with companies, trades unions, consumer organisations and other stakeholders in the framework of an association launched together called European Partners for the Environment. This has been set up to explore new initiatives and new methodologies in this field, and, to explore ways and means to better involve stakeholders in the EMAS process. The European Environmental Bureau firmly believes that EU companies should now be entering into such a dialogue. In addition, companies may need to begin considering EMAS mechanisms not only at the individual plant/site level, but also at the corporate level in terms of their management approach.

In conclusion, financial, economic and other types of crises make it more necessary than ever to move towards a new development model. The transition no doubt will be long, with many ups and downs. It is important today that all the forces working for sustainable development should take up the initiative. The European Union can show the way, and certainly European companies have much to gain from being, and being seen to be, leaders in this field of action.

Chapter 3
Corporate Winners and Losers in the Race for a Greener Future

Ian Bird

Vice-President – International Counsel,
CH2M Hill Companies Ltd, Denver, Colorado, USA

What follows is, in part, an attempt to make some prognostications about who will be the winners and who will be the losers from high environmental standards. There are some background issues to current regulatory efforts in the environmental arena which make predicting winners and losers difficult. However, there are several trends which appear to be developing, and which may aid in making predictions of those industries and businesses most likely to win or lose from high environmental standards in the future. Or, perhaps to put it more succinctly, who is still likely to be around?

Environmental regulation touches everyone. Whether it is as part of one's working life, or as consumers of the myriad products and services which the technological age has produced, everybody is, in some way, affected by controls on the environment. If the regulatory systems function correctly, the answer to the question "who benefits from high environmental standards?" must, surely, be *everyone*. If high environmental standards improve the quality of the physical world, this must also imply an improvement for its inhabitants. Better air quality, safer drinking and bathing water, and less contaminated land – the basic goals of environmental regulation – will improve health, increase life expectancy and add to the enjoyment of nature. Unfortunately, however, the level of conflict presently seen over environmental regulation shows that the benefits of regulating the environment are not evenly distributed.

There is no consensus on what should be included in the details of the environmental agenda. Whilst there is general agreement on broad outline goals, there still is great debate on the detailed programmes necessary to meet those goals. This is true even in an homogenous area such as the European Union. For some, the debate is anthropocentric. They would argue that all environmental regulation should seek to improve *human* health and well being, and that the environment per se is only a surrogate measure for that well being. For others, protecting flora and fauna provides sufficient legitimacy for strong environmental standards to be adopted. According to this world view, human beings have no particularly special place in the world but should enjoy the same benefits afforded to other species.

Of course, such viewpoints may represent the more extreme sides of the debate on environmental protection and pollution control. Nevertheless, there is a spectrum of attitudes and, depending upon where one is sitting along this continuum of opinion, views on environmental standards will differ greatly. For example, for those who believe that the legitimacy of environmental protection must be founded on a humanistic basis, the examination of any proposed environmental standards should include cost and benefit analysis. The question must be asked: will the positive benefit in terms of lower risk to human health be outweighed by the costs of implementing these standards, including increased unemployment and other impacts. At the other end of the spectrum, these human concerns are seen as largely irrelevant. Protection of habitat or species is sufficient justification for regulation. There need be no cost analysis of what are, in essence, uniquely human concerns. Until policy-making can reconcile these disparate views, identifying winners and losers will depend on one's own view of the real purpose of environmental regulation.

There is also a major geographical component to be borne in mind in identifying who gains or loses from strong standards. This becomes important in the context of enforcement of environmental regulations and the difference between what is on the statute book and what is actually enforced. It is quite clear that even within the European Union some States will accept legislation at the EU level but take an unduly long time in transposing those directives into national law. When these countries are finally forced or shamed into passing requisite national legislation, enforcement is frequently patchy and sometimes non-existent. Similar criticism can be made about disparate enforcement in the United States. There can be little doubt that enforcement of environmental regulation is tighter in some States than in others.

Outside the OECD countries the enforcement problem is even greater. Many foreign investors, even in the big emerging markets, find that the application of environmental laws is selective. Frequently, strict standards are applied to multinational companies and virtually no one else. A number of factors lead to this result. Much of the productive capacity of many countries is still in government hands, and regulators are loath to shut down those factories or even regulate them in a way which might mean extra cost. Local firms are often able to negotiate lower levels of enforcement in ways that international companies are not. Finally, many multinationals are operating with world-wide standards which require compliance with local law and local legislation, even if no other firms comply and local regulators have little interest in enforcement. Thus, any attempt to identify winners and losers must include an understanding of where they are located and the strength of enforcement in those areas.

All too frequently environmental goals and policies are distorted by government subsidies. In both Europe and the United States agricultural subsidies have especially pernicious effects, causing farmers to use very high levels of chemical fertilisers and pesticides with obvious localised impacts on environmental quality. In addition, the resulting surpluses create market imbalances which affect farmers in developing countries, forcing their produce out of markets even in the home country. The effects of subsidised fishing fleets are so dramatic that fish stocks are actually being eliminated. This has led to a number of well-publicised international disputes. Energy prices in many areas are kept artificially low to maintain the competitiveness of local businesses.

In the long term, these subsidies cannot be sustained from either an economic or an environmental perspective. Eliminating them will do a great deal for achieving environmental quality improvements without increasing regulatory burdens. For the purposes of this discussion, therefore, we must identify beneficiaries of subsidies, both direct and indirect, in order properly to identify winners and losers.

Since the Bruntland Report and the Rio Conference of 1992 the world has been committed to the concept of sustainable development. Whilst there is little point in giving here yet another recitation of the definition of sustainable development (because it is something that is constantly in change – there being no fixed definition), suffice it to say that the concept attempts to unite both environmental protection and sustainability with some measure of growth. Whether that is economic growth or growth in social well being, or some other measure of growth, is still a matter of great debate.

Also tied to the theme of sustainable development is the notion of intergenerational equity, and the need to think about the future, not just the present. Since sustainable development as an approach provides benchmarks by which policies can be measured, it becomes apparent that the better policies are those which promote sustainability and development (or, at the very least, promote one without limiting the other). When considering issues of intergenerational equity, it is clear that the current effect of such policies should enhance, or at least not diminish, the ability of future generations to meet their needs.

In the shorter term, one effect of the sustainable development approach will be to reduce some of the tensions mentioned above. Nevertheless, the regulatory process will become messier because it will be more inclusive and more open. Governments will no longer be the sole arbiters of the regulatory structure. Other stakeholders will have an equal status at the negotiating table. Environmental NGOs will compete with those NGOs devoted to public health or development, and NGOs or industry groups related to trade issues will also be competing for their voices to be heard at the negotiating table.

Regulation will be determined by consensus, in this case a real consensus of all the interested parties. There is already some evidence that this is occurring, examples being the European Consultative Forum on the Environment (established by the European Commission), the UK Round Table on Sustainable Development, and the recent G7 Meeting on Telecommunications where business sat at the table as equals with government.

Ultimately, the sustainable development approach will lead to a more coherent regulatory system. Environmental and social issues will be dealt with in their proper context, and pressure groups – whether industry or NGOs – will be less able to hijack the process because too many stake-holders will be involved.

Some trends are already identifiable and possibly consistent with the push towards sustainable development. Although these are being developed mostly in Europe and in the United States, the same issues are being raised in many other parts of the world. Most countries will eventually move in those same directions, albeit at vastly different rates and with different emphases, depending on local conditions.

The trends identified so far are:

- internalisation of environmental costs and prices;
- producer responsibility for their products throughout their life cycle;
- design for the environment;
- increasing polluter liability for damage to the environment;
- greater focus on integrated environmental management systems;
- more public disclosure of environmental performance data;
- use of fiscal and economic instruments;
- greater use of voluntary approaches;
- reduction of distorting subsidies;
- integrated cross-media permitting of industrial facilities;
- avoidance of technology standards in favour of risk assessment and cost-benefit analysis;
- privatisation of government services; and

- subsidiarity, *i.e.* an attempt to regulate at the lowest level at which it makes sense to do so.

Adapting environmental policies and standards consistent with these trends will help to shift the regulatory structure onto a sustainable development path. The trend towards more sustainable production and consumption patterns must be enhanced if the goal of sustainable development is to be reached.

For business – European business, American business, and businesses throughout the world – this means that continuing progress must be made to reduce the impact of products and services throughout their life cycle. This will affect virtually every stage, from design through to engineering, manufacturing, marketing, distribution, service of the product and eventually its treatment at the end of its life.

Importantly, business is already making significant progress in Europe. However, these improvements have not been seen by business in terms of sustainable production, but, instead, have been made for competitive reasons. Consumers have demanded the products, or competition has required lower costs. Business is about efficiency, as is sustainable production. Business needs to and will do more. However, it must always be remembered that business responds to market signals. Shifts in price signals will aid business in changing its production patterns. For example, a shift in taxation from labour to resource use will affect the mix of inputs which business will use. Ending or reducing distorting subsidies will also help to correct improper market signals.

However, what must be avoided is allowing sustainable production and consumption concerns to be used by governments or other interest groups merely as the excuse to regulate what products or services can be produced or consumed. Recent history has shown that central planning cannot correct market imperfections; only the market can do this.

It is now probably easier to identify winners than losers. This is partly due to the technology wild card. Any industry threatened with dislocation due to shifts in environmental regulation and enforcement may find technological fixes to ameliorate the situation. Even if a "technofix" is unavailable, the industry in question may have sufficient power and leverage to obtain a political solution to its problems. Such results will become less frequent as policy-making becomes more inclusive and consensual, although they will still exist for some time to come.

Who will benefit from these trends? The health care sector will thrive as a result of sustainable development, because good environmental regulation will reduce death rates and lead to longer life expectancy, especially in OECD countries. Longer life means greater need for medical and other health services, like nursing homes, medicine and so forth. Of course, in Europe the health sector is largely state controlled, but as the population becomes older it seems unlikely that the public purse will be able to bear all of the cost. Just as environmental services are being privatised, so medical services will have a greater private component. Private providers of health care services and products will be winners.

The telecommunications industry will also benefit from environmental regulation based on sustainability. In addition to investment in new technologies and updating of outmoded systems world-wide, the industry will benefit from the need and desire to curb work-related commuting and the attendant pollution. There will be a great increase in telecom-muting, with perhaps only one day in five or 10 being spent in the traditional office setting. As digital video communication becomes more common, even one day a week may disappear.

The leisure and tourism industry will also continue to grow, as will the industries which service it. Already the largest business sector in the world by some measures, there is no reason to believe that growth in tourism will not continue. As consumption of goods in wealthier countries is reduced (and it will be) the population will spend more and more on consuming leisure activities. A major leisure activity, especially among the older population which has left the workforce, will be travel. Tourism which is environmentally friendly – ecotourism – will benefit the most.

The relative scarcity of energy resources *vis-à-vis* demand will become an increasing problem. Thus, providers of alternative sources will benefit. The holy grail of solar energy has been pursued for years. At some point it will become a reality, although of limited application. Whilst it is doubtful that in the future whole cities will be powered from solar cells, nevertheless solar power will provide important capacity in many areas. In poorer nations, rural development may well be powered by the sun since this will avoid the heavy costs involved in building generation and distribution capacity. This will also avoid global warming problems which may be associated with fossil fuel power. In many developing countries solving the problems underlying system losses will go a long way to meeting energy needs well into the future. Energy utilities in OECD countries have this expertise and will see a growth in joint implemen-tation projects where this expertise is shared, with emissions credits being given to the technology provider.

Providing clean water to more than a billion people in the developing world will create significant opportunities for purveyors of low-cost water delivery and treatment systems. This is not rocket science technology requiring great leaps forward; however, there is a real need to discover ways of packaging the existing systems to incorporate lower installation and operating costs and improved durability. Companies which can do this will thrive.

The need to preserve energy and clean water will also benefit those companies providing products which conserve either or both, while providing high levels of performance. For example, the use of enzymes in washing powders has greatly improved their cleaning capacity. What is not widely known is that the widespread use of such products has also lowered the average wash temperature in Europe from more than 60 degrees centigrade to less than 40 degrees. This has meant energy savings equivalent to several large power plants. The public will demand more of such products in the future, although business may have to educate consumers that these products might carry a price premium relative to other products.

As environmental management is integrated more completely into general management systems, there will be numerous opportunities for consultants to aid business and government in bringing such practices in-house. Support will be needed in all aspects of designing, implementing and auditing environmental management systems, measuring environmental impacts and reporting to stakeholders.

Tighter limits on emissions to air, ground and water will also create numerous opportunities for companies supplying emission control equipment and measuring devices. Firms marketing new, cleaner production processes will also reap benefits. As an example, one major chemical company is currently building two large chemical facilities, one in Europe and one in Asia. The company describes them as "third generation facilities". It is intended that they will produce their products in virtually closed-loop waste-free environments.

Companies which can assist manufacturers in meeting their cradle-to-cradle obligations will also thrive. These can range from companies involved in recycling of paper materials, metals and other materials, to firms which provide contract disassembly for automobiles, electronic devices and electrical appliances when they are discarded.

Of course, some firms in the waste management sector will survive and thrive. Although the volume of waste will continue to shrink through cleaner processes, waste minimisation, and reuse and recycling, nevertheless a significant residue will remain. More stringent standards will demand that those residues are managed safely. This will require more technically sophisticated incinerators and landfills. That level of sophistication means higher costs of construction and operation, benefiting large, well-capitalised, technically sophisticated firms.

Successful waste management firms which have the capacity to provide clients with the required waste reduction services together with the ability to handle the residues in an environmentally sound manner, will survive.

It is more difficult to identify probable losers. Doubtless, companies which do not take heed of the trends mentioned above will not survive in the long term, but beyond that it is very difficult to forecast who will lose. Indeed, what has been said so far should give some indication as to why it is difficult to draw conclusions about winners and losers in view of the current regulatory structure. Nevertheless, the trend towards incorporating principles of sustainable development in policy-making will add a consistency of approach that will make spotting winners and losers somewhat easier in future. Moreover, if sustainability principles are truly incorporated into our lifestyles, the real winners will, surely, be everybody.

Chapter 4
New Economic Instruments for a New Development Model

Mikael Skou Andersen

Centre for Social Science Research on the Environment (CESAM), Aarhus University, Denmark

In the late 1980s it became clear to many environmental policy-makers that a great deal of the effort to curb pollution in the years since the UN Stockholm Conference in 1972 had been inefficient, because regulators had relied too much on inflexible command-and-control-type regulations. At the same time new and more complex environmental problems appeared. As a result, interest in using economic instruments has increased remarkably over the last few years.

The European Council, in its now famous Dublin Declaration of 1991, emphasised the advantages of a more market-oriented environmental policy, using environmental policy also to gain a technological and innovative lead. The European Commission's White Paper on Growth, Competitiveness and Employment 1994 most importantly develops this approach. It underlines how existing tax structures can lead to an underuse of labour resources and an overuse of environmental resources. It also emphasises the role of clean technology.

Recently the European Commission, in the Christoffersen Report, outlined the opportunities for using economic instruments, and concluded that in creating *sustainable development* economic instruments have a key role to play. In particular, economic instruments are seen as efficient because they leave it to the individual economic agents to find the most promising solutions. Economic instruments contribute towards deregulation and reduce bureaucratic interference by promoting self-regulation and, more generally, make it possible to achieve synergies by shifting the tax burden from distortive taxes on income and social security schemes towards taxes and charges on energy and pollution.

However, it also became apparent that important uncertainties remain among certain Member States with regard to the advantages of a more

27

market-based approach. Whilst a great deal of the ambiguity is tied in with national concerns about the taxes to be collected by Brussels and national capitals respectively, nevertheless concerns are also being voiced about whether the expected benefits from economic instruments are likely to appear in practice. Economic instruments have, in particular, been advocated by professional economists who often seem to ignore that public policy-making is a more complex process than the neo-classical analysis would like us to believe.

What now follows is a focus upon three case studies of economic instruments and their practical impacts so that the empirical evidence of the benefits of economic instruments can be considered.[1]

One of the first countries in the world to introduce economic instruments was Japan which, in 1974, introduced a system of charges on emissions of sulphur dioxide – a system which was actually introduced to finance pensions for all those pollution victims whose plight had been recognised in the big pollution trials of the 1960s. Subsequently, emissions of SO_2 in Japan declined much more rapidly than in comparable European countries. There are several Japanese and other studies which show this. It was a result of this system of charges which helped promote the development of cleaner technology.

This achievement in Japan can be calculated in many ways, and may give rise to a number of questions; but, even if it is measured in *per capita* terms or per unit of gross domestic product, the Japanese today have the world record in low SO_2 emissions. Japan became a leader in air pollution control and in scrubber technologies because of this charging system.

When Germany, in the mid-1980s, following the *Waldsterben* (Forest die-Back), took interest in reducing SO_2 emissions, it had to look to other countries – and in particular to Japan, which had the technological lead in this field. This charging system was only a "mosquito bite" on the economic elephant which Japan developed into in this period (there are also OECD studies which show this). The extent to which it had an impact on Japanese competitiveness is not measurable.

The second case study concerns water quality policies in Europe. Water quality policy has been the most costly part of pollution control during the last two decades, amounting to approximately two-thirds of total pollution control investments in the 1970s and 1980s. There were four comparable countries – all within the European Union – which had similarities in instrument choice. Nevertheless, they had one important differ-

---

[1] Further reading: Mikael Skou Andersen, 1994, *Governance by green taxes: making pollution prevention pay*, Manchester and New York: Manchester University Press. Mikael Skou Andersen og Ulrik Jørgensen, 1995, *Evaluering af indsatsen for renere teknologi 1987–92* (Evaluation of the cleaner technology programme 1987–92), Copenhagen: Miljøstyrelsen (National Agency of Environmental Protection).

ence. Three of the countries – France, Germany and the Netherlands – employed effluent charges, but the fourth, Denmark, did not subscribe to economic instruments during this period. The important question to be addressed therefore was, "what were the impacts of these differences in policy design?".

The Dutch charge was in this period the highest of the three charges. The German charge was phased-in only around 1980, and the French charge remained low throughout the period due to President Mitterrand's restrictive financial policies. During this period Denmark did not subscribe to economic instruments, operating instead a command and control policy, with decentralisation of competences, and a lot of public involvement and public planning. The result of this policy was that in the late 1980s gross emissions in Denmark were almost at the same levels as in 1972 (it should be remembered, however, that there was also increased industrial production during this period).

In Germany the situation was not much better. There, a charge existed, but was only a weak supplement which was actually impaired by an abundance of command and control regulations. Therefore, the decrease in emissions was rather modest, only about 20%. A further reason for this was that all the income from the charge went back into the Lander treasuries. It was not being used to aid pollution control in industry.

The Dutch had the most successful scheme during this period, with an impressive reduction in discharges from Dutch industry – about 80%. This was tied in with a long tradition of user payments in the Dutch water sector. The Netherlands, being a country with many canals and dykes etc, has a strong infrastructure for water management, which was an important factor, in some respects, in the decision not to bring subsidies into this sector.

However, another important aspect was "earmarking". Although the charge was the highest of the three countries, it was still relatively modest. There was an earmarking of revenue from this charge for those industries which were the most polluting and where pollution control could be undertaken most effectively and efficiently. Also, there existed very good co-ordination between public authorities, water boards and industry as to how to target these investments for water pollution control. This also made the scheme very effective.

Interestingly, the French system, although not as effective as the Dutch system, nevertheless utilised the same mechanism of concerted action between public agencies and industry in targeting funds for pollution control. Consequently, the French managed to reduce organic discharges by about 40%.

The Danish approach was costly because without a charge system industry does not reduce pollution at source. In the early 1970s there was a strong belief in public control and public responsibility for treating discharges, but they remained at a high level. A surplus capacity of public treatment plants was created which was quite expensive. Denmark made costly investments in public sector treatment plants, which then had to accept discharges from many industries.

By contrast, the Dutch kept public costs low throughout the period of the 1970s and 1980s. Industrial investments in the Netherlands were not much higher during this period than in Denmark. The reason for the high level of investment in Danish industry was because many industries were forced by command and control regulations into paying money for being connected to public sewage treatment plants – a costly solution.

An examination of the technological responses over this 20-year period makes an interesting study, since there is a long time-period from which to judge this. When the discharges at source are measured, it can be seen that Dutch industry in the late 1980s was comparatively much less polluting than Danish industry. This is also apparent for different industrial sectors. For example, food processing industry in Denmark, which is relatively of the same size as that in the Netherlands, has a much higher level of pollution compared with the Netherlands. Even the French were, at this time, more successful than Denmark.

However, Denmark has done a lot to improve the situation since the late 1980s and has now caught up with the other countries. A cleaner technology programme was initiated in 1987 (in Denmark the concept of cleaner technology refers to integrated pollution prevention, as opposed merely to end-of-pipe solutions). This cleaner technology programme funded pilot projects mostly in small and medium-sized companies (SMEs). The idea was to produce know-how and to demonstrate opportunities for pollution control. There was, of course, on the part of the authorities, an expectation about subsequent diffusion of these cleaner technologies into other companies, and, since 1992, it has even become a formal requirement, when new permits are being issued, that cleaner technologies should be incorporated when available.

The third case study illustrates the issue (or rather, the question) of how truly green companies are in reality. When cleaner technologies are available, to what extent do companies implement them?

The Centre for Social Science Research on the Environment carried out a study in 1994 on behalf of the Danish environment agency, interviewing around 600 SMEs about their knowledge and use of cleaner technology. On the basis of this report, it can be said that as far as companies are concerned the use of cleaner technology has, until now, been more or less a voluntary matter, with no regulations strictly enforcing the use of cleaner technologies. Therefore, in the course of this study a number of factors of importance for the use of cleaner technologies were investigated.

It was found that larger companies implement cleaner technologies to a greater degree than smaller companies. More interesting perhaps was the fact that the educational background of the production manager has no impact on the use of cleaner technologies. However, attitudes were found to be important, especially attitudes among production managers. Each production manager was given a series of questions concerning corporate environmental strategy, and an index of attitudes drawn up based upon this.

The graph set out at p 33 shows the relationship between these attitudes and the use of cleaner technologies. Participating companies were arranged into four groups – the first two being those with "very conventional" and those with "conventional" views about pollution control in general; the last two groups being those which were "modernisation oriented", and those which were "very modernisation oriented".

As can be seen, attitudes apparently had an impact only in some industrial sectors. Most importantly, in the wood and furniture industry and also among farmers, attitudes were significant for the use of cleaner technologies (however, it should be borne in mind that 50% of Danish farmers still deny that there is a problem with nitrate leaching). But there were also sectors in which attitudes did not mean as much.

The fish processing industry presented an interesting picture. A very high proportion of those industries which had "very conventional" views about environmental matters and pollution control are in fact using these cleaner technologies. When investigating these figures closely it was found that in the fish processing industry, economic instruments are important. If this is scrutinised for the impact of local economic instruments and local water charges and how they work, only those with conventional views – and who in addition were subject to economic instruments – actually implemented the available cleaner technologies.

A different approach to the analysis of the role of attitudes was by investigating whether SMEs had an environmental strategy. Environmental strategy was defined as follows. If a company has an environmental strategy, this means that it has someone in charge of environmental questions and some kind of deliberate environmental policy. This policy does not have to be written, but it must contain an obvious strategy. It was discovered that companies which have an environmental strategy were using cleaner technologies to a much higher degree than those which did not have such a strategy. One example is slaughterhouses, all of which have a strategy and use cleaner technologies. However, the interesting question is, how does such a strategy come about? It does not come about only as a result of attitude, but also as a result of regulatory requirements and various demands emanating from the public authorities.

By looking at this issue from a different perspective – the use of economic instruments to achieve pollution control – it would seem that if one is seeking to control pollution at source by utilising cleaner technologies, one must get inside the company, its operations, systems and practices. However, once inside it becomes clear that it is necessary to focus upon those outside the company – such as suppliers of machines, raw materials and services – in order to achieve effective pollution control. These outsiders to the company are often not resident in the same country. In many of the industrial sectors covered by the Danish study – for example, the fish processing industry and the wood and furniture industry – the basic suppliers of raw materials or machines were located in other countries. For example, in the fish processing industry German Bader is the dominating world supplier of fish processing machines, and in the wood and furniture business Italian CEFLA is the main supplier of machines.

Therefore, in order to pursue the strategy of cleaner technologies effectively, there is a need to go outside the national context. Consequently, more European cooperation on the development of cleaner technologies is needed. That was an important finding of the Danish study on cleaner technologies. Industrial networks are transnational, and as such cleaner technologies and the efforts towards greater pollution control must likewise become transnational.

The conclusion from the water quality study is that end-of-pipe solutions are potentially very costly. They were costly to Denmark, whose public is still paying those costs. In the future, with all the environmental issues that have now come onto the agenda, the water pollution sector will stand as just one sector amongst all those where new environmental improvements are being considered. In order to reduce these costs, or improve the environment, more cost-effective solutions will have to be considered.

The advantage of integrated solutions is not only that they are cheaper, but also that they are innovative and improve competitiveness. This is an added reason why there should be support for the approach being advocated in the Christoffersen paper and in the European Commission's White Paper on Growth, Competitiveness and Employment 1994.

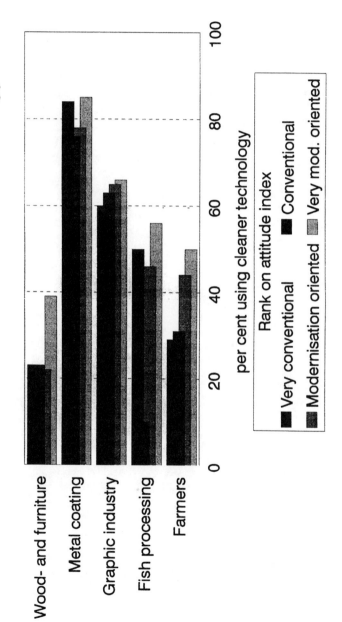

Ecological Modernisation
attitudes and use of cleaner technology

per cent using cleaner technology

Rank on attitude index

- Very conventional
- Conventional
- Modernisation oriented
- Very mod. oriented

Wood- and furniture
Metal coating
Graphic industry
Fish processing
Farmers

Chapter 5
Sharpening a Blunt Instrument? Environmental Regulation and Enforcement; Learning Lessons from the United States' Experience

Dean Calland
Founding Partner, Babst, Calland, Clements & Zomnir, Pittsburgh, Pennsylvania, USA

There is currently a substantial debate in Europe amongst the relevant stakeholders as to what the appropriate role is for the new European Environment Agency. In other words, what should its true function be (a summary of the powers and duties of the European Environment Agency by David Stanners, one of the Agency's senior officials, appears in Appendix II of this book)? The aim of this chapter is to explore some of the issues and to address some of the problems to which the United States' environmental programme has given rise. Not only might this prove useful for the purposes of discussing the future role of the European Environment Agency but, in addition, the conclusions drawn here might perhaps have a broader application to European environmental law and policy in general. Finally, the comments in this chapter may be equally applicable to any national environmental agency in the EU Member States.

First, the current position in the United States with regard to the environmental programme will be explained. Thereafter, the discussion will move on to several specific issues which merit more detailed consideration, including:

- the command and control approach;
- the need for a more holistic approach to regulation;
- cost;
- science and risk;

- pollution prevention; and
- environmental liability.

Contrary to the opinion of many outsiders (from Europe and elsewhere), the situation in the United States, so far as its environmental programme is concerned, is not all "doom and gloom", and this chapter is not intended solely as a criticism of US environmental policy, where very substantial progress has been made.

A fine example of such improvement is Pittsburgh in Pennsylvania. Forty years ago Pittsburgh was described by one writer as "hell with the lid off", due to the intolerable condition of the air and water resources of the area. Today, Pittsburgh enjoys one of the highest clean air indexes of any major US city, and its three major rivers have undergone a dramatic improvement, which, in turn, has generated new recreational and sports activities.

Most reputable gauges of environmental progress, including the United States' Environmental Protection Agency's (the EPA) own analyses, indicate that very substantial progress has been made in dealing with the major sources of pollutants in the United States, although there is general agreement that much more needs to be done.

The US programme is also marked by a complicated but nevertheless piecemeal regulatory regime. In its structure, the US system comprises an extremely complex group of individual regulatory schemes which have been developed, either on the basis of the particular environmental medium impacted – *i.e.* air, water or soil – or on a pollutant-specific basis. For example, there is a complete programme dealing specifically with just polychlorinated biphenyls (PCBs). Consequently, in order to operate a US facility of any sophistication at all, one must have command of literally thousands of regulations governing thousands of specific pollutants.

Companies in the United States have to build a very costly infrastructure in order to meet the compliance and remediation requirements imposed by the EPA. In general, a US company cannot make modifications to an existing process or introduce a new product in to the market without substantial EPA approvals. Worryingly (or perhaps encouragingly, depending upon the perspective one takes) more regulations are on the horizon. The biannual regulatory agenda published by the EPA in May 1995 has an index spanning over 100 pages, listing regulations which are either proposed or are due to be finalised during the next few years.

At the same time, a deeper understanding of the scientific, risk-related and technical elements involved is developing. During the past few years both the EPA and the regulated community have recognised the need for a better understanding of science and risk when attempting to establish workable regulations. Far too often, the regulatory scheme has been aimed at a reduction in risk that is either non-quantifiable or simply far too ambitious, the result being that sound reasoning inevitably takes second place to the confrontational style of litigation for which the US is well-known. Recognising this, most parties to the environmental debate in the United States are now showing some willingness to look at different approaches to regulation in this complex arena. All stakeholders in the US system clearly recognise that there is still much progress and, furthermore, many improvements to be made.

The EPA's regulatory style has historically been considered as a *command and control approach*. The rules are promulgated, after which any act of non-compliance with the rules is subject to stringent enforcement action. However, the command and control approach is no longer as effective as it was previously. In the past this approach did yield actual results. Command and control eradicated substantial amounts of pollution during the early stages of the US system. It is far less effective now that the focus has moved on to reducing pollution from more diffuse sources. Ultimately this command and control approach has failed because it results in mainly negative options for both the regulators and the regulated community.

In defence of the EPA, however, one might say that the US Congress has caused much of the difficulty with the Agency. For example, an agency twice the size of the EPA – which is already a very substantial organisation – could not possibly have policed all of the statutory requirements for which Congress has legislated. Moreover, Congress itself has exhibited a mistrust of the EPA's personnel and their ability to get the job done. As a result, Congress has drafted legislation which is, in reality, tantamount to direct regulation.

The following is an example. The US hazardous waste statutes specify the thickness and permeability requirements for liners of landfills. The statutes specify that incinerators must meet 99.99% destruction removal efficiencies. This is not what legislators ought to be dealing with. This is what regulators are supposed to do.

The command and control regulations require absolute compliance with few exceptions. The EPA has an almost irrational fear of setting a precedent for relaxation or waiver of the rules in an individual case, which may be used against the EPA later by other entities. An example of this occurred in Anchorage, Alaska, where the municipal waste treatment plant was required under the EPA pre-treatment regulations to reduce its organic loading by 30%. The treatment plant was strictly obliged to meet that efficiency standard; however, the standard was not being achieved because the influent (*i.e.* coming into the plant) was already so clean in Anchorage (based on the snow melt and on rainwater infiltration) that the plant found it impossible to produce the required 30% reduction. The EPA requested that they put $350,000 into renovating their system. The good burghers of Anchorage found another solution to the problem. They asked several fish processing companies to dump fish waste into the front end of the system, and the fish waste was then removed at the back end of the system. In this way the plant meets its 30% organic loading removal requirement.

In addition, the command and control regulations do not distinguish between historic or remedial waste, and ongoing-process waste. Many remediation projects are being held up in the United States, or have been abandoned altogether, because of the strict application of process waste regulatory requirements to remedial activities.

Furthermore, the command and control regulatory approach does not promote feedback, input or cooperation from the regulated community. If it is to function properly, the EPA needs to receive quality feedback from those operatives at the company's plant who understand how the plant operates and can produce the technical solutions. Presently, several EPA initiatives appear to have recognised this. For example, there is a process called regulatory negotiation in which the various stakeholders who have an interest in the particular rule being proposed negotiate the provisions of the proposal before it is issued for public comment. The effect of this is to encourage open discussion of the issues before the stage is reached where regulatory action needs to be taken.

The result of the use of this command and control approach in the United States is that change is now desperately needed. What is now required is a more integrated, *holistic approach*. This would have three benefits.

First, it would help to minimise the incompatible and overlapping demands of the various programmes. For example, it is not uncommon to have remediation programmes dictated by two different federal programmes *and* two different state programmes at the same time.

Secondly, the current piecemeal regulatory approach is simply too complicated for the regulated community to understand. The US hazardous waste statute is a good example of this. A record of hazardous waste regulatory requirements and developments under that statute, if collected since 1980, would now take up some 13 binders, each about one foot thick and containing double-sided text. Monitoring these developments is a difficult task for major multinational corporations, for the average small-to-medium-sized company it is simply a nightmare. An holistic approach would certainly help to simplify this particular programme.

Thirdly, risk-reduction goals may be better achieved through the use of alternative programmes. An example is the Amoco oil refinery in Virginia. Amoco carried out a joint study with the EPA in which it was asked to deduce ways of reducing benzene emissions. After a lengthy study Amoco concluded that it could reduce benzene emissions satisfactorily by spending $6 million to control the procedures for the loading of gasoline into barges, instead of spending $30 million upgrading the waste water treatment plant as demanded by the EPA.

The EPA is therefore beginning to recognise that more flexibility is required, and this new attitude is being reflected in some of the new programmes which the EPA is bringing forward. For example, under a new initiative called the Common Sense Initiative, the EPA works with key representatives of an entire industry, such as the petroleum, steel, or printing industries, to discuss an holistic approach and cross-media application of regulations to the entire industry.

In addition, the EPA has "recognised" certain initiatives by the chemical industry which aim to minimise the impact of overreaching regulations. So, in the context of waste management (as an example), the industry – if it handles certain waste in a particular way – could enter into a separate agreement with the EPA (an "enforceable agreement") which would then be implemented on an industry-wide basis. The requirements for an enforceable agreement in this context would be:

- all the companies which generate the particular waste stream must be parties to the agreement;
- the agreement must be enforceable and must contain sufficient penalty provisions;
- the agreement should eliminate practices which pose an unacceptable risk;
- it should allow for new entrants; and
- it must promote waste minimisation (which is the general direction in which the EPA's programme is heading).

It is ideas such as these which deserve serious consideration in future.

In addition to a more holistic approach, a more realistic and thoughtful attitude towards *cost* must be adopted. It is true that some US laws do not permit any consideration of cost in making regulatory determinations. This is certainly true under parts of the Clean Air Act, the Comprehensive Environmental Response Compensation and Liability Act (Superfund), and parts of the hazardous waste statute. However, this is in reality attributable to a failure of the legislators, and not necessarily to the EPA.

The polarisation of views in this area, something which is seen increasingly in the West at the present time, creates a very interesting dynamic. If an environmental group concedes that cost should be considered as a relevant issue in the debate, this is seen by other environmentalists not merely as a concession, but rather as a "moral failure". Clearly, society cannot continue to think in this way as the environmental debate moves on. The issue of cost must be taken into consideration.

Recent figures show that environmental costs in the United States in 1994 reached $140 billion, which was the equivalent of 2.2% of the gross domestic product (GDP). Future costs are estimated to reach 2.8% of GDP by the year 2000, and that is assuming that no new programmes are put forward (which is clearly unrealistic). Despite claims from some quarters to the contrary – with particular focus on certain parts of the growing environmental technology and services sector – no industry supports unnecessary regulation in order to create jobs. The cost of achieving environmental goals must continue to be assessed. Likewise, the question of how to allocate resources to achieve those goals must continually be evaluated by society. This requires real dialogue; in other words, communication in both directions, not just from government to industry, but also from industry to government, with all the relevant stakeholders in the debate taking their share of the collective responsibility for achieving those environmental goals.

There is also a need for a better understanding of *science and risk*, together with improved communication of risk to the public. Unfortunately, available resources are not currently dedicated to controlling the greatest risks. The EPA – as is probably the case with many enforcement agencies in other countries – often responds to public pressures and political agendas, rather than to sensible science. An example of this can be seen in the story of a large electroplating facility situated on the shores of Lake Michigan. Immediately adjacent to the facility is the Indiana Dunes National Lakeshore Park – a beautiful area, with many large blowing sand dunes, amongst which are located thousands of lupin plants. The lupin plants attract a small blue butterfly called the Carter-Blue butterfly. It is a very important resource to the area. The manufacturing plant, however, has existed since 1960. The manufacturer needed a permit for the expansion of an existing landfill on plant property, which is about 500 yards away from a blocked-off " buffer" zone, providing a buffer area separating the manufacturing facility from the actual park area. During a site inspection visit for the purpose of re-permitting the landfill, an EPA representative caught sight of a Carter-Blue butterfly which flew across the buffer zone and landed on a lupin plant growing on land within the steel plant's territory. As a result of this, the EPA ordered the manufacturer to physically remove every lupin plant growing on the plant property, and to translocate them some 500 yards over into the sand dunes in the park area where, in fact, there were already thousands of lupin plants growing and many butterflies. The latest tally of costs for this exercise, which the manufacturer itself had to bear, has reached $1.3 million. Of course, the EPA's concern was that the expanded landfill would harm the ecosystem and the environment. On many occasions, action of this sort might be appropriate. But in this situation it made no sense whatsoever and, worse still, the EPA was unwilling to discuss it with the manufacturer in any meaningful way.

Another example concerns alar, the chemical used by farmers to regulate the growth of apples or apple trees. In 1989, the EPA's Science Advisory Board deemed alar to be a probable human carcinogen, based upon the results of studies in which mice were force-fed very high dosages of alar. *Sixty Minutes*, a networked US television programme, took up this issue, and the resultant negative publicity caused a serious problem for farmers. It was subsequently estimated that about $100 million was lost by the apple growing industry as a result of this incident. Five years later, the American Medical Association, the US Office of Technology Assessment and the World Health Organisation concurred that the levels of alar found on apples presented little risk to human health. Officials of the National Cancer Institute indicated that it was more harmful to eat peanut butter sandwiches.

Once more, the conclusion is that a greater understanding of science and risk must be employed, which will allow for more informed regulations to be introduced. The focus must now be on creating standardised and reasonable risk analysis procedures, for use in cost-benefit analysis exercises. In fact, at the time of writing there are Bills currently before Congress which discuss these issues.

Of equal importance is the need for the EPA to persist in moving towards a *pollution prevention* model. In fact, public pressure has been utilised effectively to push forward this goal. For example, increased availability of information regarding waste types and generation rates has triggered a very interesting reaction from industry with regard to the US toxic release inventory (TRI) programme under the Superfund amendments. Under the TRI, industrial operators were required to publish lists of all toxic substances released from their facilities. These lists were subsequently picked up by the media, and the reaction from industry was dramatic. Unsurprisingly, nobody wanted to be known as the biggest polluter in the area.

Economic incentives to minimise pollution are also necessary, and these must be expanded. A carrot can be used here, as well as a stick. Fortunately, the EPA has now begun this process.

There are several programmes which are excellent in their scope, and are now taking on significance. One, the "33–50 programme", involved a voluntary 33% reduction in 17 specified harmful contaminants by 1992, rising to 50% by 1995. Approximately 1,200 major corporations have ascribed to this programme. "Climate-wise" is a programme which helps to reduce greenhouse gases. The "Green Lights programme" makes lighting more energy efficient. Another very interesting programme is the "Energy Star Computer Initiative" in which IBM and a number of other computer manufacturers have agreed to make computers which go into power "standby" mode automatically when not used for a certain period of time.

Industry has also produced programmes. The Chemical Manufacturers Association's (CMA) "Responsible Care" programme has been widely adopted. It is now a requirement for membership of the CMA that member companies comply with the Responsible Care provisions. Furthermore, many US companies are beginning to utilise the life-cycle analysis approach to product manufacture, which considers the product and its constituent materials from cradle-to-grave or cradle-to-cradle perspective.

Any analysis of the US system cannot conclude without some comment on the issue of *environmental liability*. Any scheme for remedying historic contamination must reflect a true understanding of the scope of such contamination and a real consensus on how to pay for it. There has been much talk about Superfund and its ills. It is becoming apparent around the world, particularly as the developing countries begin to operate their own programmes, that an environmental programme cannot be applied to a culture that fundamentally rejects the premise upon which that programme is built. The greatest problem with Superfund has been its retroactive, joint and several liability, which makes businesses liable for the entire damage even if they only created part of it, and liable for perhaps 100 years' worth of damage even though they played no part in causing it. Put simply, this has not been at all well received, not just by industry but by everyone concerned. It is one of the major reasons why Superfund is presently being examined for major reauthorisation. The main issue in the perceived failure of Superfund was a gross under-estimation both of the amount of money needed to bring about effective clean-up and of the number of sites involved. The level of funding for the Superfund programme has risen from $1.6 billion in 1980 to $11 billion in 1986, whilst the number of sites being assessed for possible inclusion in the programme has risen from an original 400, first to 700, subsequently to 1300, and most recently to 35,000. It is truly a programme which is out of control. In addition, unreasonable clean-up goals were set in this programme, which demanded a return to pristine conditions in all circumstances. This meant that no activity could be permitted unless pristine clean-up levels were achieved. Such an approach is simply unworkable and unreasonable.

Many in Europe have looked on in horror at the way the environmental programme has developed in the United States, particularly in relation to contaminated land clean-up and environmental liability. The prevailing sentiment appears to be that the US experience must be avoided at all costs. This is understandable. In particular, there is concern over the future role of the recently created European Environment Agency, especially in relation to its current lack of enforcement powers and the widely acknowledged shortcomings in enforcement of environmental regulations within the European Union. Nevertheless, there is much to be learned from the successes and failures of the US programme. Drawing, therefore, upon that US experience, the following recommendations are the main issues which this author believes should be properly addressed in considering the future direction of the EU environment programme and also possible future roles for the European Environment Agency (and even for national environment agencies in Europe):

- Legislation must not set unachievable goals which the agency cannot meet without creating a huge bureaucracy.
- Command and control regulation cannot be the sole approach to regulation and enforcement.
- The agencies should begin at the outset to distinguish between historic contamination and ongoing-process pollution; these are two very different issues, which must be treated in two very different ways.
- A greater effort at achieving an holistic approach to regulation would avoid the duplication, inconsistency and grossly exaggerated costs of many of the US regulatory programmes.
- Cost must be recognised as a real factor in any regulatory analysis.
- Defensible risk assessment must be the cornerstone of the agency's priority-setting standards.
- Incentives must be provided for entities which engage in pollution-prevention and waste-minimisation initiatives.
- Agency and industry source-reduction programmes should receive greater government recognition.
- Any clean-up scheme must not use retroactive, joint and several liability as its cornerstone.
- Reasonable future-use assumptions must be included in any agency decision-making criteria concerning the setting of clean-up standards and goals for contaminated land.

Chapter 6
Finding a Role for Economic Analysis in Environmental Law-making and Law Enforcement

Richard D. Morgenstern
Visiting Scholar, Resources for the Future, Washington, DC, USA

A number of new trends has emerged regarding the role that economic analysis is expected to play with respect to the US approach to developing environmental standards.

The US standard setting process starts with the United States Congress, which lays out goals such as protecting human health and the environment with an adequate margin of safety (Clean Air Act), or making all water bodies fishable and swimmable (Clean Water Act). In some cases, particularly in the waste area, Congress has called for specific technology approaches. Congressional authority generally establishes lofty policy targets, and grants broad discretionary authority to the regulatory agency, in most cases the US Environmental Protection Agency (the EPA), to develop and implement standards which carry out the intent of the statutes. Economic criteria, including benefit-cost analysis, are not generally required and, in at least one part of the Clean Air Act, such criteria are precluded.

Currently, there is a wide-ranging discussion about reforming the environmental management system. Concerns are widespread – not just in the business sector but among state and local officials, academics, and others – that the system is unnecessarily expensive and inflexible and, in general, is not working well. Environmental expenditures in the United States are more than 2% of GDP – higher than any other OECD country – and projected by the EPA to reach almost 3% by the year 2000. As the United States moves to expand controls on small businesses, whose emissions are a growing fraction of the remaining problems, the "one size fits all" approach clearly will not work. This chapter reviews the push to reform the system, and discusses three analytic tools which are receiving wide attention: *risk assessment, comparative risk assessment* and *benefit-cost analysis.*

Risk assessment

Risk assessment is a scientific, or quasi-scientific approach for developing quantitative relationships between emissions and human harm or risk. It is used to develop baseline estimates, as well as estimates of the reductions in risk associated with different policy options. Conclusions can be expressed in terms of risk to the most exposed individuals, or risk to population groups.

Generally, different approaches are used for cancer (as opposed to non-cancer) risk assessments. Despite the considerable history of work in this area, many technical questions remain; for example, methods for extrapolating from animals to humans, accounting for sex and species differences, body area versus body weight, routes of exposure, the use of linear versus non-linear models, and the treatment of uncertainty. One of the key issues in the whole process is how to characterise the risk for the general public. The EPA has been criticised for placing too much emphasis on worst-case assumptions, and for failing to communicate to the public the real likelihood that any actual person would ever experience those risks. This has led to the suggestion that regulatory agencies should be required to report so-called "most likely" or "best" estimates along with "worst-case" estimates.

Comparative risk assessment

Comparative risk assessment is designed to make comparisons between the risks associated with one pollutant versus another pollutant. It can be helpful in deciding which environmental problems to focus on: hazardous wastes, air pollution, drinking water, toxics, etc. Of course, many people think that society should focus on all of these problems – and in fact, in many ways, this does happen. Nonetheless, there is continuing competition for resources. Priorities need to be established. The comparative risk approach, which is based on currently available information, can be useful in the priority-setting process.

In the late 1980s the EPA carried out a study entitled *Unfinished Business.* The Agency gathered together a group of 75 experts from within the Agency. These were not political appointees; all were technical experts and career EPA employees. They studied the full range of EPA activities, and then ranked the residual risks facing Americans. There are many technical issues involved in conducting a study of this type, and the limitations of such an approach should never be underestimated. Nonetheless, one of the interesting conclusions of the study was that the environmental problems which were ranked as "high risk" by the expert group did not correspond well to the issues receiving priority attention by the EPA. The experts generally placed a lower priority on waste issues – both hazardous and non-hazardous waste – and much greater emphasis on traditional air and water pollution problems. It should be remembered that the mid-1980s was a period when federal involvement in waste management activities – under the rubric of the Resource Conservation and Recovery Act (RCRA) and the Comprehensive Environmental Response Compensation and Liability Act (Superfund) – was expanding rapidly.

As a corollary to the comparative risk study, the EPA looked at various public opinion polls which had been conducted on the relative importance of different environmental problems. Unsurprisingly, perhaps, the problems which ordinary people felt were most important were closely related to those to which the EPA was giving priority attention, and correlated much less with the problems which the experts had identified as "high risk".

The set of findings – from the comparative risk study and from the opinion polls – posed a dilemma for policy-makers. In a democratic society, the views of the populace carry great weight. At the same time, society has a respected group of experts whose conclusions differ markedly from those of the general public. What should one do? In the eight years since the publication of *Unfinished Business*, environmental policy-makers have endeavoured to integrate the public's and the experts' views more closely. While some progress has been made, it would be incorrect to conclude that a full integration has occurred. Some of the reform proposals currently circulating in Washington – but not yet enacted into law – would advance this process by creating a legislative mandate to justify environmental programmes on a comparative risk basis.

Benefit-cost analysis

Benefit-cost analysis attempts to put monetary estimates on both sides of the equation: how much does it cost to achieve particular objectives, and is it worth it? In order to determine whether the benefits exceed the costs, it is generally necessary to go beyond the risk assessment paradigm and put dollar values on the lives saved, illnesses prevented and material damages avoided by particular policies. Some critics demonise economics as an immoral means of setting public policy, while advocates presume that economics can solve all environmental dilemmas. The truth lies somewhere in between.

Many people think that benefit-cost analysis was invented quite recently. In fact, these techniques have been applied to environmental issues since the early 1970s. Presidents Ford and Carter issued presidential executive orders requiring regulatory agencies to consider benefits and costs of proposed major regulations – defined as rules with annual costs in excess of $100 million – prior to their issuance. President Reagan strengthened those requirements by including the explicit weighing of benefits and costs in the context of alternative policy options. President Clinton has reaffirmed the Reagan approach and has expanded consideration of distributional issues and non-quantifiable benefits.

Benefit-cost analysis has been used in a number of major regulations. The rapid phase-down of lead in gasoline that was mandated in the mid-1980s, was based on a ground-breaking benefit-cost analysis. Similarly, the decision to control lead levels at the drinking water tap was based on a benefit-cost analysis. Very recently, this technique has been used to look at the value of reducing toxic pollution in the US Great Lakes. In fact, over the past 15 years, benefit-cost analyses have been performed on more than 75 major regulations. However, critics have noted that these studies have not been considered consistently in the decision-making process.

Reforming the environmental management system

This discussion serves as background to the reform proposals under discussion in the United States. These reform proposals have been raised as part of the *Contract With America*, introduced into Congress by the new Republican majority in January 1995. The various proposals are best understood in the context of three distinct definitions of what ails US environmental policy: excessive regulation, too little flexibility, or inadequate science.

Those who believe that the US economy is plagued by excessive federal regulation generally advocate strong measures to curtail such regulation. The most extreme proposal is to develop a *regulatory budget* to cap the total level of expenditures devoted to environmental protection, including both government and private sector expenditures, at some predetermined percentage of GDP. Once the cap was reached, new regulations could be imposed only if some existing regulations were first removed. In fact, some advocates of this approach would set the cap below the current level of expenditures, thereby mandating immediate cut-backs. Clearly, the regulatory budget approach is inconsistent with a true economic framework which tries to balance benefits and costs. It seems inconceivable that any arbitrary expenditure level could possibly yield sensible social decisions. It is not surprising that some analysts have labelled this approach "chainsaw surgery", since it looks only at the costs of regulation and ignores the benefits completely.

Those who believe that the principal problem with US environmental policy is inadequate flexibility have developed an approach called "beyond compliance". Although concerns about too-rigid rules have been around for some time, the origins of the current beyond-compliance strategy lie in a study jointly funded by the EPA and the Amoco Oil Company in 1990. This study assessed the opportunities for achieving emission reductions at least cost, and compared them to the reductions mandated by regulation. The results, based on a detailed analysis of an operating refinery, indicated that regulatory costs could be reduced by as much as 30–40% if the least-cost methods of emission reduction were adopted.

This finding has spawned a number of reform proposals aimed at introducing more flexibility into the system and simultaneously achieving both cost savings and environmental gains. Some of these proposals involve administrative reforms, and some also involve legislative reforms. They apply generally to complex facilities which are subject to multiple regulatory requirements. Whilst these reform approaches are promising, serious questions remain about how much streamlining can actually be accomplished within the current system. Critics note that the Amoco study itself was originally intended to be a basis for action. Instead, it has led to a whole new set of very interesting discussions but, so far at least, very little in terms of real reform.

The third approach involves legislative changes regarding so-called "good science", "good economics" and what are referred to as "super-mandates". Proponents of this approach would mandate specific risk-assessment methodologies – including the use of "best estimates" as opposed to sole reliance on worst-case analyses – and would mandate the conduct of benefit-cost analyses for major rules. While many of these new requirements are not, at least in principle, different from existing approaches, the enforcement mechanism here would involve a new set of peer review procedures which would complicate the rule-making process enormously. Similarly, some of the proposals would revise the definition of major rules from those with an annual cost of $100 million to those with an annual cost of $25 million – thereby greatly expanding the EPA workload and increasing the complexity of the rule-making process even further. The super-mandate provision would require that benefits exceed costs or, in a slightly softer version, that benefits justify costs, before a rule could be adopted, notwithstanding any other provision of law. If this provision was enacted, it would effectively rewrite 25 years of environmental laws in the United States which contain a whole series of decision criteria which are generally quite different from the economic (*i.e.* the benefit-cost) approach.

A related, and equally controversial, proposal involves the so-called "reach-back" provisions, whereby petitioners could force the EPA to reopen already promulgated rules and impose, *ex post facto*, the benefit-cost/super-mandate approach. A further proposal – which is generally viewed as a "full-employment Act" for lawyers and economists – would make these new risk-assessment and benefit-cost provisions judicially reviewable. As much as an estimated 80% of all EPA rules already end up in the courts; this provision, if enacted, would greatly increase the legal challenges to regulations and further complicate and lengthen what is already viewed by many as an unwieldy process.

Where is all this leading? It is clear that many members of Congress are dissatisfied with the environmental management system that previous Congresses have authorised and that the EPA has implemented. Undoubtedly some of their dissatisfaction derives from imperfections in the system. At the same time, it is clear that some of the proposed solutions are overly simplistic, while other proposed changes – even if meritorious on other grounds – would increase the complexity and expense of the regulatory system to an unacceptable level. Still other ostensible remedies are blatantly anti-environmental and punitive.

Notwithstanding these Congressional proposals, poll after poll has shown that while Americans may be fed up with bureaucratic solutions, they consistently demand strong environmental protection. The new Congress would be well-advised to take a lesson from the early 1980s when an anti-environmental mood in the first Reagan Administration was quickly overwhelmed by a public concerned that "the fox was guarding the chicken coop". The US legislative process – which is just beginning to address these reform issues – is notoriously complicated and contentious. Whilst there probably will be some legislative changes, that is by no means certain. Even without legislative alterations, however, some of the reforms discussed here, including the move to stronger scientific and economic foundations for regulations, will probably be adopted. The swing of the democratic pendulum appears quite wide at this time, but is likely to find a broader centre in the near future.

Chapter 7
Deregulation, Subsidiarity and the Future for Environmental Regulation in Europe

Robert Hull*

Head of Unit for Policy Co-ordination, Integration of Environment in Other Policies, Environment Action Programmes; European Commission DG XI

When current developments across the world are considered in relation to policies designed to protect the environment, a number of common threads emerge which have developed over the last few years. What has been surprising until now has been the similarities between the approaches which have developed, influenced by the outcome of the Rio Earth Summit in 1992. There is evidence now, however, of one major economy starting down a road which is different. In the United States there are moves to deregulate environment policy in order to reduce the burden of such legislation on industry. The question is whether this is a trend that is going to be followed in Europe and what kind of effect it will have on the future of environment policy.

Already, the report prepared by the Anglo-German Deregulation Group entitled *Deregulation Now* – while not focusing on environment policy as such – does call for changes in legislative structure on chemicals, and for a revision of the pesticides parameter in the Drinking Water Directive. Also, the Molitor Group, set up by the European Commission to look at administrative simplification, reported to the Cannes Summit in June 1995, with one element of its findings focused on environment policy. Non-governmental organisations and others tend to see this as a threat to the environment and certainly, if what is happening in the United States is followed in Europe, then there may be a danger. However, European environment policy is already evolving in such a way

* This contribution reflects the personal opinion of the author and should in no way be taken as the opinion of the European Commission.

51

that the role of legislation and regulation, in the mix of actions designed to achieve environmental protection, is already changing.

Subsidiarity is an earlier example of a concept that was seen as posing a major threat to the future of European environment policy. Two or three years ago, during the debate of the ratification of the Maastricht Treaty, there were fears that environment policy would be sacrificed on the altar of subsidiarity. The concern was that far too much was being done at the European level, and that the Community was interfering in the "nooks and crannies" of national life. In fact, environment policy as it had developed over the period since its inception at the European level in 1972, had always focused on doing only what was necessary at Community level in order to protect the environment wherever results could not be achieved at national level. This was institutionalised in the Single European Act in 1986, when the foundations of environment policy were firmly laid in the Treaty, and where environment policy was the only area where a subsidiarity approach was spelt out. Subsequently, the approach set out for the environment was generalised in Article 3b of the Treaty on European Union.

In the debate on the ratification of that Treaty there was a tendency to question whether there needed to be any action at all on the environment. On the basis of an "internal political audit" over the issue of subsidiarity and other aspects of the Maastricht Treaty, several ghosts have been laid to rest. Important conclusions have been drawn as to the basic principles which underlie Community environment policy:

- it is a shared responsibility between the Community and the Member States given that environment policy frequently involves trans-boundary problems;
- the internal market requires homogenous environmental standards throughout the Community to avoid barriers to trade and distortions to competition;
- the Treaty of Rome sets out as one of the tasks of the European Community the improvement in the quality of life of its citizens, thus implying a minimum but high level of Community-wide environmental protection;
- proposals for environmental action need to be fully justified and proportionate to what is needed to achieve the aim;
- whilst a common approach may be necessary and may need to be defined at Community level, Member States are fully responsible for the effective implementation of the approach;
- above all, environment policy has to pass the acceptability test. It has to be seen as common sense.

As far as "deregulation" is concerned – although it may be more appropriate to talk about "re-regulation" – there is a similar kind of development, with considerable fears being expressed about the impact of environmental regulation on the ability of European industry to develop and compete in global markets. To consider this argument, there is a need to look back at what has happened in the past.

Experience in regulation to protect the environment goes back to the early 1970s, when there was no reference whatever to the environment in the Treaty. Some of the initial environment legislation had the twin objectives of environmental protection and assuring the free circulation of products. The body of directives regulating gaseous emissions from motor vehicles is a case in point.

A second group of directives date from the late 1970s and 1980s, and were targeted at the emissions and wastes from agriculture and from industrial plants. These are specific limitation directives setting limit values or targets to reduce emissions into the air and into water.

While the early directives were very much vertical directives, targeted at precise individual point of source emissions, a new approach to regulation started to develop in the early 1990s. This new generation of directives differs substantially in approach from previous directives and, since the adoption of the Maastricht Treaty, is now based on a set of clear and coherent principles. The focus of the new directives is more horizontal in nature, and many provide greater flexibility for Member States to implement in a manner which suits local conditions.

This new approach is typified in the directives on eco-management and auditing (EMAS), eco-labelling, biotechnology and on the waste management strategy. It is also typified by the Directive on packaging waste (recently adopted) and current proposals on industrial pollution and control (IPC) and ecological quality of water. In short, the development in environmental regulation has been from:

- specific rules on point emissions, towards general permitting and management requirements;
- highly prescriptive texts, towards greater flexibility for Member States to prescribe means of implementation within clearly determined quality targets;
- specific pollution targets, towards directives dealing with behaviour and prevention.

The principles on which regulation is based are very clearly spelt out in the Treaty. The Maastricht Treaty builds on the principles first brought into the Treaty by the Single European Act, and in Article 2 places the protection of the environment and the sustainable use of resources at the very heart of the Union's *raison d'être* when it states: "The Community shall have as its task ... to promote ... a harmonious and balanced development of economic activities, sustainable and non-inflationary growth respecting the environment ...".

There will continue to be a need for European legislation, but over the last few years and in line with experience in other developed countries, it has become apparent in the EU that a regulatory approach alone is subject to significant limitations in achieving effective environmental protection. The environment should properly be regarded as an interdependent system. Controls on pollutants within a single medium cannot adequately protect the environment, unless these are considered alongside other media and are set within an overall framework which co-ordinates regulatory and other instruments – such as the use of economic incentives, development of technologies, research, training, voluntary approaches, etc.

The use of a variety of policy instruments does not mean that regulation is no longer necessary. The Community will need to continue to legislate in the environmental field. Indeed, Community legislation has created the framework for national policies where these did not exist in some Member States, and has helped to ensure that progress towards environmental protection develops on broadly similar lines in a Community of 15 Member States. However, of growing significance is the development of a new economic approach, which will increasingly integrate economic instruments in the regulatory framework of the future. There is a wide variety of possible instruments which can be used, including charges, taxes, compensation payments, subsidies and tradeable permits.

Already in 1992, with the publication of *Towards Sustainability*, the European Commission's Fifth Action Programme on the Environment (1993) (COM (92) 23 Final) – the broad strategy and approach of which were agreed by the Council – the path was set for a different approach. That Programme focused on how to move towards sustainable development, respecting the environment in Europe by focusing on a number of key targets and themes, by calling for a shared responsibility and partnership between the various actors in society, and, above all, by identifying the need to broaden the range of instruments required to achieve environmental and sustainable development objectives.

The Fifth Action Programme does not deal only with short-term problems in the environment but presents a challenging perspective and ambitious goals for the long term. *Sustainable development* is the keyword for the transition from the current economic system with its large imbalances in terms of environmental, economic and social conditions, to a more balanced economic system which should be more in equilibrium with the carrying capacity of the environment and the availability of resources for present and future generations.

In the Fifth Action Programme, the Commission identified many advantages in using market-based instruments. For example, the setting of a charge on polluting activities (or the provision of an incentive for environmentally friendly behaviour) has the following advantages:

- in response to market signals, operators have the flexibility to choose the technical means they will adopt, thus providing a basis for the assumption that the least cost approach will be adopted, and reducing the cost of environmental improvement;
- in response to market signals, polluters will seek constantly to improve performance as opposed to regulation where, once standards have been achieved, there is no incentive to do better;
- a stimulus to innovation and the development of clear technologies is provided.

There are now numerous instances in which economic instruments are used for environmental purposes within the Community. For example:

- apart from fuel taxes, tax differentiation is one obvious way of rewarding investment in cleaner cars which are more energy-efficient or are fitted with catalytic converters. For instance, tax advantages of up to 40% have been introduced in Greece. In the Netherlands, a tax is charged in relation to the quality of a car's exhaust gases. Tax differentiation may be used increasingly to encourage investment in cleaner technologies;
- charges on waste water discharges, which have been a success in several Member States;
- charges for recycled raw material, which will include charges in waste streams and in the production process itself;
- deposit refund systems for beverage containers.

There is no doubt that incentives or charges applied to industry will in many instances be more effective if applied Community-wide, as firms plan their strategies and develop new (cleaner) technologies to serve a single Community market. One of the Commission's aims is to identify best practices and to determine how these might be applied in a Community-wide context.

It is clear there are many situations in which market-based approaches are impossible or inappropriate, and where regulation is the most appropriate course. But such regulation needs to be adapted to changing circumstances, and so the regular review, improvement and streamlining of regulations is necessary if they are to operate effectively and efficiently.

The Commission has therefore embarked on a process of reviewing the main body of EU environmental legislation with a view to:

- consolidation and streamlining;
- improving ease of implementation;
- removing unnecessary and costly bureaucratic procedures;
- determining more cost-effective techniques;
- increasing the use of market-based instruments.

This review process is continuing in a number of key sectors. An example is the water sector:

- the Commission has made proposals for an extensive revision of the 1980 Directive on Drinking Water to make it easier to implement, reducing the number of parameters from 68 to 44 and to provide greater flexibility in respect of monitoring procedures;
- the Commission has made a proposal to revise the Bathing Water Directive;
- a new Commission proposal dealing with the ecological quality of water could, if adopted in the form proposed, replace three existing specific directives;
- a groundwater management proposal is in preparation;
- similar processes are under way in the waste, air quality and biotechnology sectors – processes which have or will give rise to revision and improvement of regulation. In these review processes the role of new instruments, *e.g.* charges, trading permits and voluntary agreements are being actively considered alongside regulation, with the aim of achieving the most appropriate mix consistent both with the objectives to be achieved and the costs of achieving them.

The Commission is equally concerned that environmental regulations should be properly implemented and enforced in an even way throughout the Community. There are delays and even failures to transpose Community directives properly into national law, and in some cases failure to enforce compliance to the transposed law. This can cause resentment and distortion of competition. President Santer stated in this regard, in his first major address to the European Parliament on 17 January 1995:

> "… the Commission will assume its responsibilities and, if necessary, ask the Court of Justice under Article 171 of the Treaty to impose financial penalties on Member States who do not comply with a judgement … I wonder if the idea of inserting penalty clauses in Directives is not worth promoting."

The Commission is currently considering this area, which is important both for the environment and for fair trade.

The Review of the Fifth Programme, which is currently underway, will focus on how to take all of this forward in the context of the overall objectives already agreed. The aim of the Review will be to look at experience to date in implementing the programme and seek to identify best practices and ideas which will allow the approaches set out in the Programme to be implemented more efficiently and effectively. In relation to regulation, the process of changing the philosophy underlying earlier regulations (whereby specific and prescriptive rules were elaborated for very many individual contaminants) into a more horizontal and locally sensitive approach of permits based on a mixture of environmental quality standards and best available technology, is likely to continue.

The pillars of environmental action for the future, on which European Union intervention will be based, are as follows:

- an adequate scientific base which, taking into account the "precautionary principle" will ensure proper justification for intervention;
- increasingly precise appreciation of the impact of intervention not simply on the target sectors, but also on allied sectors;
- increasingly precise targeting of measures so as to facilitate choice of the optimum, most cost-effective instrument;
- leaving the maximum flexibility to Member States and individual firms to achieve objectives at least cost;
- an "acceptability test" to ensure that proposed actions are necessary and relevant.

There is a growing awareness that European environmental regulation is by no means a burden across the board. Options do exist for simplification of current legislation, and the Commission is pursuing these. The evidence is that in the short term, however, the private sector is more concerned about consistent enforcement of legislation than about missed opportunities for simplification. There is awareness growing that in the longer term, selective re-regulation could help improve the environment and lead to cost savings. What will be important therefore, in developing policy, will be to take account of the constraints within which industry operates, and to harness industry's potential for innovation and efficient management of environmental resources. This is likely to imply a greater emphasis on fixing harmonised quality objectives at a high level, which can then be implemented locally. Major improvements in the efficiency of achieving environmental objectives may also be realised by allowing industry a greater degree of flexibility in choosing how to implement specified environmental targets. There may also be increased scope for the use of voluntary agreements.

Chapter 8
Environmental Regulation and its Effects upon the Competitiveness of European Industry

Genevieve De Bauw

Director, European Union Government Affairs, Dow Europe formerly Environmental Affairs Adviser, Union of Industrial & Employers' Confederations of Europe

Responding to the question of how and to what extent environmental regulation affects the competitiveness of industry – European industry in particular – is a very difficult task. Consequently, the aim of this chapter is not to attempt a comprehensive review of the issue or provide a complete answer to the problem, but merely to raise some important issues which must be borne in mind whenever one is dealing with this subject.

In this chapter three issues will be discussed. First, how does one properly define the notion of *competitiveness*? It is important to know what is meant by this word, since it is a word which is often employed for many different reasons. Secondly, how does environmental regulation affect the competitiveness of European industry? Finally, what might European firms do to improve their competitiveness by harnessing the negative effects of environmental regulations, recognising that there is no merit in simply focusing upon the problems – it is far better to concentrate upon the solutions?

What is discussed below comes from the perspective of the author's work at the Union of Industrial & Employers' Confederations of Europe (UNICE) as adviser on environmental affairs. UNICE is the voice of European business and industry. Based in Brussels, it has 35 member federations in 25 European countries. The federations are the national industry and employers' organisations. UNICE's mission is to ensure that the European legislator takes business views into account. One of its objectives is the achievement of sound environmental protection based on sustainable development.

Much time has been spent on defining what competitiveness is. The following definition has been used by UNICE for some time, most notably in the framework of a major study carried out in 1994 on the competitiveness of European industry. The definition reads as follows: "the competitiveness of a firm is its ability on a sustainable basis to satisfy the needs of its customers more effectively than its competitors by supplying goods and services more efficiently in terms of price and non-price factors". This definition incorporates a distinction between the competitive advantages which a firm might have (*i.e.* its differentiation with competitors in terms of assets, which then enables delivery of services at superior levels) and the competitive capabilities of a firm.

This is subdivided into what UNICE calls the "three pillars of competitiveness". These three pillars are very simple concepts. The first is the *innovation pillar*, the ability of a firm to develop new products and services, and to exploit them effectively. The second is the *operating efficiency pillar*, *i.e.* the ability to produce goods and services at world class levels of cost, quality and flexibility simultaneously. The third is the *adaptability pillar*, that is, the ability to adapt to and exploit major and unexpected changes in the competitive environment. These three pillars – the three competitive capabilities of companies – are all influenced by regulation, because regulations in general, be they environmental or otherwise, either increase or decrease the ability of firms to achieve these capabilities.

Regulations can have an impact on firms in three ways. First, there might be a direct impact in areas such as costs, operational flexibility, capital expenditure, the speed of key processes and the use of management time within firms. Secondly, there might be an indirect impact via the value chain of individual firms. This value chain relates to suppliers and customers; for example, the way a supplier is influenced by regulation can have repercussions for its customer and others with whom it comes into contact. Thirdly, there might be a further indirect impact stemming from the effect regulation has on the overall business climate within which firms compete.

What then is the impact of environmental regulation on competitiveness? There is no clear-cut view on this. It differs among the various industrial sectors, depending upon the competitive position and prospects for the industry in question, the particular strategy of individual firms, and even the quality of the regulations themselves. It is clear that European companies need to integrate, and increasingly are integrating, the environmental dimension into their business strategies. What is also clear however is that in order to do this companies need a stable, coherent and predictable regulatory framework. This is an essential requirement.

One of UNICE's members, the Confederation of British Industry (CBI), recently published a report on environment costs. The CBI found that there is little evidence of direct short-term competitive gain for non-specialist businesses arising from the introduction of new environmental regulations. Of course, opportunities can occur for providers of clean technologies, pollution-abatement equipment and environmental consultancy services. Furthermore, opportunities can arise where businesses are able to plan strategically for change and, as a result, gain the advantage of being "first off the starting line" within European and global markets.

UNICE has been carrying out a major study to evaluate the impact of regulation in general on the competitiveness of European firms[1]. Part of this study deals with environmental regulation. A large number of companies have answered a questionnaire (sent out as part of the study) aimed at delineating the impact of environmental regulation on competitiveness more clearly and identifying possible solutions to any negative effects of environmental regulation. The preliminary findings of this questionnaire are highlighted below in brief. It is an interesting but far from complete view of the situation.

The three main areas where it was felt that individual items of EU legislation were impacting most on competitiveness were first, increased operating costs; secondly, increase in or diversion of capital expenditure; and thirdly, diversion of management time. The top three explanations given by the companies surveyed of why such negative impacts occur rank as follows. First, the regulation is not proportionate to hazard and risk; secondly, the regulation is too complex or too prescriptive; and thirdly, enforcement is inconsistent between countries.

This then is just one aspect of the impact that environmental regulations can have on the competitiveness of firms. Of course, this is a very important point. The impact also varies very much according to the ability of the firm in question to manage the regulation itself. Particular attention must be paid to small and medium-sized companies which do not always have the same capabilities as large businesses to deal with that type of regulation.

These are some of the problems. What then are the solutions?

Clearly, there are no simple solutions to the problems created by the complex impact of government regulation in general on business. In the framework of the study previously mentioned, a mix of possible solutions was identified. These were: deregulation; greater transparency in the decision-making process; a greater awareness of the effect of government intervention on competitiveness; a greater use of alternative forms of government intervention; and an improvement in the quality of the

---

[1] Now published as *Releasing Europe's Potential Through Targeted Regulatory Reform – The UNICE Regulatory Report, 1995.*

regulations. These general solutions are to a large extent also applicable for environmental regulation purposes.

The first three of these issues are generally discussed elsewhere in this book. Consequently, the remainder of this chapter will concentrate briefly on the last two proposals – the greater use of alternative forms of government intervention, and improvement in the quality of environmental regulations.

There are many possibilities for alternative forms of government intervention in the environmental policy field. Economic and fiscal instruments are one form of intervention and are now being used increasingly at the national level, although in UNICE's opinion they must conform to certain criteria in order to be really effective. Another form of alternative instrument is the use of negotiated agreements or covenants between industry and government. These may offer, in certain cases, greater flexibility and efficiency for achieving well-defined objectives, and have yielded very positive results in some Member States.

UNICE members perhaps favour an increased use of this type of instrument in very well-defined conditions as a possible means, for example, of implementing new directives.

However, negotiated agreements are not a panacea for all woes. What is important for business, for government and for citizens, is the right choice by government (in consultation with all interested parties) of the most appropriate instrument or mix of instruments for achieving a given environmental objective, whilst preserving industry's competitiveness. Environmental policy-making in Europe is set within a dynamic process, where policy-makers have to adapt constantly to new scientific evidence, technical progress, institutional development, and changing market conditions. Therefore, improvements will have to be made to the environmental policy-making process in Europe, which seek to combine enhanced environmental protection (which is absolutely essential for the future) with sound economic and social development. To quote the CBI in its report referred to above:

> "Government and business strategies must work to the mutual advantage of society and of business. Whatever we do to the environment costs, but together we can make sure those costs are those we and our children can afford."

Setting high environmental standards is not an end in itself. Standards are only a means of achieving a set of clear and balanced environment policy objectives. They also play a certain role in ensuring a level playing-field for companies throughout the European Union. But to achieve these goals, standards must respect the proportionality principle – in other words the requirements set out in the standards must be proportionate to the objective pursued – and be based on risk assessment.

President Jacques Santer, near the start of his presidency of the European Commission, made a plea for "better Europe" rather than "more Europe", and this also should sound a strong echo in EU environmental policy-making. Very clear signs of this are beginning to be seen within the Commission and within the European Parliament, and there is now a tendency to rethink some of the regulations in a more strategic way. That is a very welcome development indeed.

Chapter 9

Can We Create a Level Playing-field in the Implementation and Enforcement of Environmental Legislation within the European Union?

Olivier Kaiser
Counsel, Exxon Chemical Europe

In literal terms the phrase "level playing-field" conveys the impression of an even surface, free of obstacles and hurdles; no mounds, no hills and no holes. To employ a sporting metaphor, the phrase "level playing-field" can also mean that all players, whatever their background, are subject to the same rules. For the game to progress properly, it is clearly essential both that the pitch is flat and that the rules are applied equally to all participants.

When discussing environmental regulation the level playing-field metaphor is interpreted somewhat differently. Here the players are citizens, public authorities and companies. Their concerns, interests, cultures, activities, and political and legal systems are all different. Therefore, in the context of EU environmental regulation the playing-field comes to represent the array of environmental legislation and enforcement rules applicable to these economic actors, whilst the concept of a level playing-field merely becomes another way to describe the harmonisation of these rules throughout the European Union. However, the change of setting from sport to regulatory concerns makes it both less obvious that a level playing-field is necessary or desirable, and at the same time more obvious that a true, level playing-field in environmental regulation is much more complex than in sporting theory and also much harder to achieve.

A number of questions arise. For example: is there currently a level playing-field in the area of environmental regulation within the European

Union? Does it exist within the context of the EU's relationship with the rest of the world? If the playing-field is not currently level, is it possible, even desirable, to attempt to level it? If so, what is the best way to achieve that result?

To answer these questions it will be necessary to attempt to demonstrate that there are several different but complementary ways to achieve a level playing-field. Harmonisation of legislation is one way, but only as long as it avoids certain pitfalls which threaten to render this approach counterproductive or, at best, useless. However, this is not the only way. Voluntary initiatives, voluntary agreements, and commitments from industry also need to play a growing role. Furthermore, it is important to ensure that European competitiveness is not jeopardised in the process.

First, therefore, is there an EU environmental playing-field that needs to be levelled? It has been said in the past that the main arguments for EU intervention in matters of environmental liability are first, competitive disadvantage and secondly, the fact that pollution does not stop at borders. This is also used as an argument for intervention in areas other than environmental liability. Nevertheless, these two assertions are debatable.

Turning to the first assertion, it is quite clear that the standards and instruments of environmental regulation and enforcement within the various Member States are different, and that they create a very complex background and entail very high costs for companies. Whether that, in turn, creates a competitive disadvantage is not absolutely clear. Various studies are still underway to try to determine that. But the most important point is to ensure that this competitive disadvantage, if it does exist, is not merely an excuse for justifying the intervention of the European Union in all areas, even when there is no real need for intervention. It is clear that in some areas intervention is needed, but in others it is not.

The second assertion, that pollution does not stop at borders, is usually justified by citing examples such as Chernobyl and the pollution of the Rhine, and these transboundary pollution incidents can be very serious and very harmful. Thankfully, however, such examples are rare. Admittedly, in such cases harmonisation may be important, especially to deal with the legal aftermath so as to pinpoint exactly who is competent to solve issues such as what laws should be applicable and which tribunals should be competent. However, if pollution does not stop at the internal borders of the European Union, neither does it stop at the EU's external borders.

Chernobyl is a good example. Chernobyl is not even within EU territory, even though it is often used as an example of serious pollution. It is necessary to look at the wider international context rather than merely the EU context. In seeking to take the wider international context into account it is necessary to examine the different systems existing in other countries, although where useful examples of systems are found, care must certainly be taken not merely to incorporate their components wholesale into the EU system. The pros and cons of every piece of legislation available must be evaluated. To give one example, much has been said about the excesses of US environmental legislation, in particular the Comprehensive Environmental Response Compensation and Liability Act (Superfund). Questions have arisen when considering ways of adapting or adopting similar rules into the European Union for environmental liability. Clearly, in taking this approach the Union should be very careful to ensure that only good ideas are translated into EU law, not the whole US system.

The EU playing-field must be seen in a global context. Furthermore, consideration must be given as to the level (in terms of regulatory standards) at which this playing-field should be set. In other words, how high should the minimum standards be? If the European Union has a level playing-field that is pitched much higher than the other playing-fields in the world, then there will clearly be a competitive disadvantage for European business. Even if the playing-fields are more or less on the same level but, nevertheless, are distinguished by large areas of regulatory incompatibility, then the players will be unable to compete fairly on each other's playing-fields. That will also hurt international trade and international competitiveness.

How then can the EU playing-field be levelled? Simply increasing the sum total of applicable regulations is not the solution. The European Union must avoid creating a "level playing-maze", a virtual labyrinth of legislation. Admittedly, there is a definite need in some areas for well-targeted, science-based and risk-assessment-based legislation. Such laws should indeed be harmonised at the European level.

An example concerns electric cars, which are one instance of what many people believe is environmentally successful progress, replacing petroleum and diesel fuel cars. However, an article published in April 1995 in the *New York Times* noted:

> "Electric cars, long promoted as a way to reduce smog, could create other significant environmental problems because of the lead based batteries that power them. A study by three researchers at Carnegie Mellon University in Pittsburgh concludes that emissions from mining, smelting and recycling the lead needed to make batteries for a large fleet of electric vehicles would pose serious threats to public health. Even an electric car made with advanced technology, not yet available, would push six times as much lead into the environment as a tiny automobile burning gasoline with the lead additives that were eliminated in the 1980s."

This is a good example of the need for risk assessment to precede policy and legislative initiatives in the environmental arena. In other words, before imposing legislation it is first necessary to look at the whole picture and make sure that one is in possession of as much data as possible to assist in making informed decisions.

Furthermore, harmonised, EU-wide legislation must not merely be added on top of the already existing, abundant and growing body of national legislation – otherwise, enforcement will become both very difficult and probably also uneven and unfair.

Enforcement is really the crux of the matter in many cases. However, enforcement within EU countries is still based on local traditions and legal systems. Even when there are harmonised rules at EU level their enforcement is always left to national and even local authorities. These authorities will inevitably implement, apply and enforce these rules in different ways, because of their different cultures and backgrounds.

Consequently, even if a level playing-field for the European Union can be attained it might become "unlevelled" at the enforcement stage. This is clearly a significant risk. It is evident that many EU directives are not even implemented, or only very partially implemented, in the different EU Member States. Although the European Commission has attempted to deal firmly with this failure in the system and force the Member States properly to implement directives, there is still a long way to go before all directives are fully and similarly implemented.

The baseline is that legislation which is not implemented, or which is improperly implemented or improperly enforced, damages the effectiveness of the whole body of EU environmental legislation. The applicable maxim here should be: "not more legislation, but instead better legislation and better enforced legislation".

Furthermore, better legislation is not the only solution. Some alternatives exist, not necessarily to replace legislation but at least to be used side-by-side with legislation. Some of these are industry initiatives. One such initiative is the chemical industry's international Responsible Care programme. Such programmes need to be given due consideration because they create homogenous codes of conduct which an industry commits itself to following, and which it can and will understand and apply. These rules have been created by the industry itself, and they are still very strict. Industry would not risk losing credibility by imposing on itself very loose and lenient rules. The rules are strict, but they are also realistic; they are tough but they are also comprehensible.

Of course, these industry initiatives should be complemented by individual corporate actions. Exxon Chemical, for example, has put in place a world-wide management system designed to ensure the integrity of all its operations in terms of safety, health and the environment.

However, if the debate is to move beyond mere words, then it is really the responsibility of each company and each industry to put in place environmental action programmes. In fact, for several years most of the responsible industries have "thought green" and have realised that "business as usual" is not a sustainable option. The important aspect of company policies, and especially industry programmes, is that they have a world-wide impact. When Exxon Chemical puts in place a world-wide environmental programme it applies that programme not only in the countries where there is strict legislation already in existence, but also wherever the company has operations, including in countries where high environmental standards do not yet exist.

What is important is that in any event individual industry initiatives and even some standardisation initiatives also need to be supported by clear and efficient legislation and enforcement. Legal instruments should be tailored to address specific issues. Truly global instruments may not be effective for local problems any more than national laws can effectively address world problems. Furthermore, there is a need to make sure that legislation is well-targeted. Consequently, cooperation and understanding between all the players involved is essential to achieve a truly level playing-field.

Chapter 10
Trends and Developments in Corporate Environmental Liability and Responsibility: A United States/European Union Comparison*

Dean Calland
Partner, Babst, Calland, Clements & Zomnir, Pittsburgh, Pennsylvania, USA
Ursula Schliessner
Partner, Oppenheimer, Wolff & Donnelly, Brussels

The purpose of this chapter is to comment upon some of the current trends and developments in the field of environmental law and regulation both in the United States and in the European Union, and, furthermore, to highlight various differences between the treatment of environmental issues in the United States and European Union. This discussion will be conducted under the following headings:

- trends and goals of legislators and regulators;
- enforcement;
- permitting;
- acquisition and disposal of corporate assets;
- abandoned site clean-up; and
- public participation and interaction.

---

* Another version of this article was previously published: *International Environment Reporter*, Vol. 18, No. 15, pp. 589 *et seq* (July 26, 1995). Copyright 1995 by The Bureau of National Affairs, Inc. (800-372-1033).

Trends and goals of legislators and regulators

United States

The history of this issue began in the early to mid-1970s, when a variety of the now famous "command and control" regulations were passed in the United States. The breadth and complexity of the US regulatory scheme is almost legendary. In addition, in the United States non-compliance is punished quickly and severely, in a large measure due to the very extensive enforcement operation there.

What has evolved most recently is a very serious examination of the concepts of *pollution prevention, source reduction and waste minimisation*. In practical terms, this has come about as a result of a number of different groups within the US economy – not just industry, but also environmental groups and the enforcement agencies – working together to try to develop a specific policy. It is very interesting to note that there are currently no targets imposed on US industry by statute or regulation for any of these things (*i.e.* pollution prevention, source reduction and waste minimisation). It is purely voluntary. What US industry is required to do, however, is to certify that it has a programme in place to deal with waste minimisation and pollution prevention.

Secondly, *reuse and recycling* is a very contentious issue in the United States at present. Industry honestly believes that many materials and secondary products are so similar to basic products used in commerce and manufacturing that they ought not to be regarded as waste materials. This highlights the difficulty in defining exactly what is waste and what is a product. Under US law, it is extremely important jurisdictionally to decide whether items fall within the broad category of "waste" or whether they can be defined as products or by-products. In practice, the debate centres on whether one can reuse and recycle the materials without the need for regulation; or, if regulation is required, how stringent it should be.

All sides involved in the debate are encouraging reuse and recycling. However, the environmental groups, and also some officials of the United States Environmental Protection Agency (the EPA), honestly believe that industry conceals many toxic substances in its recycled materials (colloquially labelled "toxics along for the ride" or "TAR"). Despite the fact that industry claims that these materials are not harmful by virtue of the fact that they are being recycled and reused, objectors believe that there may be a transfer of pollution merely by virtue of the recycling activity itself. The EPA has now set up a high level task force to examine various ways in which secondary materials are recycled, and will propose a system of continuing control relevant to the type of recycling activity involved.

With regard to the use of *risk assessment*, both the Republican Congress' "Contract with America" legislative programme and President Clinton's regulatory reform programme emphasise that risk assessment should be a primary tool in considering future regulatory activity in the United States. In fact, a Bill recently introduced in Congress will require both risk assessment and cost-benefit analysis, not only of every existing major Rule (defined as any Rule having a cost implication exceeding a certain figure), but also of every other Rule issued by the EPA in future.

Europe

In relation to *resource reduction, pollution prevention and waste minimisation*, the European Union is working on research projects which may result in regulations being introduced with regard to so-called "priority waste streams". These are: car recycling, electronic waste recovery and health care waste. Later, there may be more streams added, such as paper, batteries and solvents.

With the aim of making products better for the environment, the Union passed a regulation on eco-labelling, whereby products are rated for their environmental impact. The regulation aims to ensure that about 20% of products should receive an environmental label or "eco-label" as it is commonly described. Unfortunately, this system is moving forward very slowly.

Also relevant here is the proposed directive on integrated pollution prevention and control, which is aimed at creating an integrated permitting process. Any application for permits for industrial installations will have to contain documentation by the companies about waste minimisation and about environmental impact assessment of the installation itself. Consequently, even at the permitting stage the European Union is attempting to include regulations which will help to minimise waste.

With regard to *recycling and reuse* obligations for industry, a Directive on Packaging and Packaging Waste has been adopted by the Council of Ministers and the European Parliament (in December 1994). This Directive sets recycling goals and recovery goals similar to those set in the United States; however, in Europe these goals are being set for the Member States themselves to achieve, rather than placing the obligation directly upon industry. By the year 2001, the Member States must achieve recovery rates of between 50–65% and recycling rates of between 25–45%.

The use of *risk assessment* for regulation is at an infancy stage; whilst there is much talk about it, there is little understanding of what it actually is, and strenuous efforts are presently being made to define it and establish a set of criteria.

Enforcement

United States

Enforcement is perhaps one of the characteristics of the US system that sets it apart from many other countries. Certainly, the enforcement system is swift and severe.

Most US environmental statutes provide for penalties of $25,000 per day for each violation, where any provision of the statute in question or the implementing regulations have been violated. These penalty provisions make no distinction between a substantive violation and a procedural violation, such as failure to file a form or document.

The following is an example of how these penalties are calculated in a typical enforcement action brought by the EPA.

A US petroleum company was using a concrete unit for holding and treating waste waters from a refining process. In 1980, the EPA passed regulations under the Resource Conservation and Recovery Act (the hazardous waste statute in the United States which required owners or operators of any treatment, storage or disposal unit to install groundwater monitoring systems in order to determine the impact of the unit on the underlying groundwater). The company's unit was a minimum four-well system – one up-gradient, three down-gradient. The company sincerely believed that this unit fell within an exception in US law which provides that materials handled in tanks under a permitted national pollutant discharge elimination system (NPDES) or surface discharge system, are exempt from the groundwater monitoring requirements. Consequently, no further action was taken by the company.

Presently, the company is engaged in litigation with the EPA in the federal courts over whether the company's decision – which was made in 1980 – was correct. If the court were to rule against the company, then the violation penalty would be calculated at $25,000 x 365 days x 15 years; a very large sum of money indeed! In practice, the EPA does not usually ask the federal court for the entire penalty sum. Nevertheless, recoveries in the range of $6 million to $10 million are not uncommon in this type of scenario.

In 1994, the EPA brought 2,249 federal enforcement actions, collected a record $165.2 million in civil and criminal fines, obtained injunctive relief that exceeded $777.5 million, referred 430 cases to the Justice Department, and filed 1,597 administrative penalty actions. This will give the reader some idea of the amounts of money and the numbers of actions involved. It also sheds some light on why the United States is such a litigious society. There are many signs that Europe is also moving in this direction, but the present situation reached in the United States is clearly something which Europe needs to avoid.

Another important aspect of the enforcement debate concerns criminal liability. The United States has taken an aggressive stance in the area of criminal enforcement action. It is fair to say that corporate America is very concerned about criminal liability. In effect, there is no requirement for *mens rea* or a criminal intent to be demonstrated on the part of the company or its officers before they may be found criminally liable in the US environmental system. As such, the United States is moving towards a strict liability system for environmental crimes.

In this context it is worth mentioning the "Responsible Corporate Officer" doctrine, which was first developed under the Clean Air Act Amendments of 1990. Its effect is to require that each corporation designates a specific upper management person by name who is to sign all permit applications and submissions to the Government. Thereafter, this person is always held responsible if anything goes wrong in the system. Some companies jokingly refer to this person as the "designated jail bird".

A further point here is that directors in the United States are extremely sensitive about their roles. Even with regard to very large public companies, directors are very concerned about the decisions being made by their boards and about whether they can be held liable personally under the Superfund statute.

Another issue related to the enforcement question is shareholder liability. Under traditional US common law, it was necessary to demonstrate that any entity related to the company – such as a shareholder or a parent – had had direct control over the proscribed activity, before that party could be held liable. US environmental statutes made it much easier for the EPA, or even ordinary citizens, to sue and bring these types of entities back into the fold as potentially liable parties. Consequently, lawyers are often asked to analyse a parent company's actions with regard to the effect upon a subsidiary, so as to ensure that in relation to environmental problems, such action would not cause a "piercing of the corporate veil" with consequences leading up to the parent company level.

Europe

In Europe, whilst administrative penalties and criminal fines feature as part of the systems within the Member States, in reality punitive damages of the sort which occur in US law are not seen.

With regard to criminal sanctions, the situation is very diverse because at European Union level EU directives do not contain any criminal sanctions. Nevertheless, a general clause appears in all EU legislation which permits the Member States to introduce measures to apply criminal sanctions. Some Member States have criminal sanctions in their various environmental statutes. Almost all of them have general provisions in their penal code which may be used so as to hold polluters criminally liable. For example, if somebody becomes sick as a result of drinking contaminated ground water, then whoever put that contamination into the ground, whether negligently or with intent, may be held liable for any personal injury which results.

In addition, some of the Member States' penal codes contain special criminal provisions for environmental pollution. However, this occurs only in very advanced jurisdictions, which may be one of the reasons why the Council of Europe has now started work on a Convention on criminal liability for environmental damage.

The issue of shareholder or parent company liability for environmental damage is not an issue which is under discussion in Europe at the moment, and there has been very little litigation on that subject.

Permitting

United States

In the United States, comprehensive permits remain the veritable backbone of the system. Companies are required to obtain very detailed and specific permits with regard to every pollutant that is emitted or discharged. However, there are certain notable developments here.

First, there is a definite trend towards self-reporting. The EPA recognises that federal inspectors and state inspectors cannot be at every plant all the time. As a consequence, many permits require a substantial amount of continuous monitoring by the company, followed by the self-reporting of results. This initially started in the water discharge pro-grammes under the NPDES permit programme, where site operators had to carry out a weekly or monthly analysis, and each month submit a report to the EPA specifying whether any violations occurred during that month. If a violation did occur, the company was required to highlight it in the report and then describe exactly what the company had done or was intending to do in order to remedy the situation.

This self-reporting concept is now also governed by the new Clean Air Act, under the Consolidated Title V permits programme, which requires many industrial facilities to obtain comprehensive operating permits for all air emissions at the facility. As a result of this, US site operators will be carrying out more self-reporting in future.

Secondly, there is the issue of what is termed the "clean-up price of permitting". Starting in 1984, under the US hazardous waste statute, Congress decided that if operators were to be given the right to treat, store or dispose of hazardous waste and other types of toxic materials on their sites, they should pay a price for it. That price was not merely limited to obtaining a very comprehensive permit, putting in the necessary controls and doing whatever was required by the permit, but also to carry out a complete site-wide investigation of every impact of any waste whatsoever on the existing industrial plant, whether that be hazardous waste, all types of solid waste, all types of material, and any pit, pond, lagoon or other place where materials could be disposed of. This obligation was imposed as a permit condition. Both obligations have been implemented via a programme which is much less celebrated, but nevertheless equally expensive as the Superfund programme.

Europe

Whilst the various Member States have always issued permits for different operations and discharges, a directive implementing a scheme for integrated pollution prevention and control (IPPC) permitting at the European level is about to be introduced, following experiences with the concept in Ireland and in the United Kingdom. This proposed directive has been passing through the EU legislative machinery during 1995 and, once adopted by the EU, will introduce a new permitting framework to be implemented by the Member States.

This should achieve several goals. One of these is that full and proper consideration of the effects of industrial discharges and emissions on all environmental media should be integrated into the permitting process. In other words, not only must there be an assessment of air emissions from an industrial installation, but also water discharges and waste products. When this proposal first entered the legislative process, industry was quite happy with the proposed system of having a comprehensive permit and a comprehensive permitting procedure, since industry was led to believe that one authority would be responsible and would co-ordinate the process and, furthermore, that there were time limits for the permits to be issued. Now, however, both the co-ordinating authority and the permit-issuing deadline concepts have been deleted from the proposed directive during negotiations in the Council of Ministers, and consequently some of the advantages of this directive have been taken away. In addition, the framework to be established by the directive is very loose, which may lead to different interpretations of the directive's provisions in the various Member States.

Nevertheless, it is a new approach, and means that a limited environmental impact assessment must be carried out prior to the issue of a permit. It also means that in making an application for a permit, comprehensive documentation must be provided, demonstrating that the applicant has taken waste minimisation measures and has assessed the impact on the environment of the applicant's facility. It also means that a renewal procedure for each permit granted will be introduced, and that IPPC permits will apply not only to new installations but also, after a transitional period, to existing installations. This will impose a completely new permitting procedure in the majority of the Member States of the European Union.

The directive also stipulates that the installations must adhere to certain emission limits and quality standards. Of these emission limits and quality standards, very few have been set at the European level. Consequently, the task of setting emission limits and quality standards will in the main be referred back to the Member States, which clearly may lead to different requirements being imposed in different EU countries.

Acquisition and disposal issues

United States

There are two issues of note here. The first is the issue of "*brown-fields*" *development* (*i.e.* industrial site redevelopment initiatives). This is an extremely important topic in the United States at present, because in many of the old manufacturing areas, particularly the area called the "rust-belt" (so called because it was home to numerous iron and steel factories), there are a substantial number of property sites in very advantageous locations alongside riverbanks.

For example, in Pittsburgh, Pennsylvania there are three major rivers which meet exactly at the point where the Ohio river begins in Pittsburgh. Here properties are sited which have been used as industrial sites in Pittsburgh for decades. However, they cannot be redeveloped. The reason for this has in part to do with the lender liability issue (discussed below) which naturally affects the availability of finance for acquiring such sites. However, the primary reason is that any investor who buys such a site places himself in jeopardy of having to pay for all of the contamination which occurred at that site throughout its history. This could go back 100 years and perhaps through four different industries, each of which manufactured on that location. When faced with such a potential risk, which obviously no reasonable person would take, an investor is more likely than not to go to a green-field site and build the new factory there.

Environmental groups are very sensitive to the idea of companies taking up new green-field areas. They want to leave green fields green. Furthermore, they would like to see the brown fields recycled. Industry itself would like to use the existing infrastructure and location of these "new" brown-fields sites, but this has not been possible in the United States, for all of the reasons discussed above. Recently, the EPA, recognising this problem, has started funding certain environmental studies of identified brown-field locations so that a potential buyer of the site would not have to foot the bill for such a study in order to understand the condition of the property before being willing to purchase the new land. Some $50,000 per site is being made available, and sites are being selected in each of the EPA regions.

This alone will not solve the problem. However, the real solutions are now being found at state level in the United States, where legislation is being passed by many of the state legislatures to protect new buyers or developers who take over old industrial sites. Usually, the essence of the protection is that the buyer will avoid responsibility for historic contamination which occurred prior to his ownership and which did not result from his own activities. A further bone of contention has always been the issue of whether a distinction should be drawn between what is clean (*i.e.* that which is pristine, and restored to prehistoric cleanliness) and what is safe and fit for use. It is now recognised by many of the legislatures that absolute clean-up goals do not need to be set in order to reuse and recycle industrial sites. Of course, sites must be safe, but they do not have to be pristine clean. Clearly, however, this gives no licence whatsoever to the new operator of the site to avoid any compliance responsibilities, which must all still be met.

The second issue is *lender liability*. A few years ago a regulation was passed by the EPA which sought to define when a lender would or would not be considered to be exerting enough control over a site such as to be held to be a potentially liable party under the Superfund statute. That regulation unfortunately was struck down by the Court of Appeals, on the basis that the wording of the statute in question did not give the EPA the authority to promulgate that rule. The EPA is now attempting to introduce another "lender liability" type rule, as well as promoting draft wording which would address this issue, for inclusion in the Superfund reauthorisation bill. Lenders are not completely satisfied with the changes which are being promoted. Nevertheless, this approach would dissipate much of the force in the argument that lenders should be considered as liable "owners" under the language of the statute.

Europe

There are developments in Europe where the Member State, or some sort of semi-private, semi-public company, redevelops old contaminated brown-field sites, but this is usually only on a pilot-project basis, and even then only in those countries which suffer from a lack of development space. Otherwise, there is still a tendency to use green-field sites wherever they are available.

In fact, generally speaking there is still a lack of awareness about environmental liability issues in Europe. There are large numbers of commercial transactions being completed without environmental due diligence exercises being carried out. Although the parties to these transaction are often aware of some environmental problems existing, they simply push these aside because nobody wants to discuss them properly. Furthermore, banks and insurance companies in Europe have often failed to consider potential environmental liabilities, although this situation has now changed considerably in some countries, even to the extent that in certain instances insurance companies have become a sort of environmental watchdog. Nevertheless, lender liability is a non-issue in certain countries.

That lender liability is not perceived as a major issue in continental Europe is probably due also to the nature of the legal systems in operation there. For example, lender liabilities relating to contaminated land may not arise where foreclosure procedures do not exist under the national legal system.

Furthermore, there is still a more communicative climate in Europe than in the United States. It remains possible to negotiate remediation plans with the authorities. In addition, except for certain jurisdictions, there are no established clean-up levels. Consequently, if the investor establishes good communications with the relevant authority, he can agree remediation plans with the authority which require clean-up only to a standard appropriate for the intended use of the site, rather than to the pristine state of the environment.

Abandoned site clean-ups

United States

It is generally acknowledged that the Superfund programme has not been a success. Superfund has become the national, and perhaps even international, metaphor for the type of environmental clean-up programme which should never be implemented. Certainly it has created an immense amount of litigation. Various studies carried out in the United States have indicated that approximately 90% of all costs under the Superfund programme have gone to lawyers and consultants. Approximately 1,300 sites have been put on the national priorities list (which is the listing of the most contaminated sites in the US), and, in addition, there are around 30,000 sites which are being assessed for potential placement on the list.

In short, there is common agreement that Superfund must be revamped. Superfund was due for reauthorisation in 1995, as it was during the previous year when a coalition of four or five different media groups – who were each opposed to a different aspect of the Superfund reauthorisation proposal – concerted their opposition to it. On that occasion the reauthorisation proposal failed to make it through the legislature largely because other Clinton administration proposals (such as health care) pushed it out of the way. In 1996 fresh hearings have taken place in both the House of Representatives and the Senate. The new reauthorisation Bill, if passed, will deal with clean-up standards, lender liability, and the institutional and engineering controls which are to be used in place of the very stringent groundwater clean-up standards which have so far been in place. These proposals will constitute a complete overhaul of Superfund if the Bill passes through Congress.

It is true to say that the key to the unfairness of many of the US environmental programmes has been the concept of *strict joint and several liability*, so that regardless of a person's own contribution to the problem, he can be forced to pay for the entire clean-up. Opinions differ widely as to how this particular aspect of Superfund is going to be changed and, in fact, whether it will be changed at all. It is very possible that the programme will remain ineffective and inefficient.

An important aspect of abandoned site clean-up is *corrective action*. Reference was made earlier to the hazardous waste statute, under which many properties in the United States were cleaned up (which was the "clean-up price" to be paid in order to get a permit). The EPA also has unilateral authority to enter onto a site and force the owner/operator to carry out site-wide remediation and investigation. This power can be exercised simply on the grounds that the owner/operator had on some occasion treated, stored or disposed of hazardous waste during the history of the operations carried on at the site in question, since 1980. This means that an industrial facility does not in fact have to be "abandoned" in order to suffer a site-wide investigation at any time.

Europe

As a result of the European Commission's 1993 Green Paper on Remedying Environmental Damage, there is a very lively debate going on in Europe at present on the topic of environmental liability. What will be the outcome of this discussion? First, it is very likely that, contrary to the US experience, a distinction will be made between past damage (*i.e.* environmental damage which was caused prior to any EU system entering in effect) and future damage. Secondly, it is also very likely that any directive proposed by the European Commission will cover only future environmental damage. Thirdly, liability will most probably be strict and both joint and several.

It is very likely that the Commission will leave the question of how to deal with historic environmental damage to the Member States to decide upon, on the basis of *subsidiarity* (meaning that action should be taken at the most appropriate level). The only action which the Commission itself may take is to issue guidelines as to how the Member States should deal with the problem.

In fact, the Commission met together with delegates from the relevant authorities of the Member States in 1994 and it was decided that a programme would be established whereby clean-up standards would be developed. Consequently, although there are initiatives presently being undertaken in this area, these are at intergovernmental level (rather than via the EU institutions) and have passed largely unrecognised by the public. No overall solution to the issue of remedying historic damage has yet emerged, although schemes based upon voluntary incentives and/or the availability of some sectoral or regional funds for remedying historic damages may emerge in future.

Public participation and interaction

United States

In the United States, the public is both very active and very interested in almost every environmental determination. Every regulatory programme which has been put together has retained a vital function for the public within it. Permitting procedures under almost every statute provide for mandatory public notice, which includes meetings, hearings, public comment periods, etc. Furthermore, citizens groups are empowered under US statutes to bring law suits against companies which are not in compliance with the law. Alternatively, such groups can bring actions against the EPA for failure to comply with its responsibilities under a statute which requires it to regulate in a certain way. In fact, the EPA is often caught between competing groups, which sue the agency constantly.

With regard to corrective action or clean-up decisions, there is a requirement that before any clean-up decision is entered as final, it must go out for public notice and comment. This is a procedure which has developed over the past five or six years, and in which the public has now become very involved.

Another issue relates to the concept of *environmental justice*. The EPA is carefully considering the impact that its decisions have on poor communities, the reasoning being that controls on industrial operations in poor districts appear to be less stringent than in other districts. As a result, the EPA is now taking this factor into consideration when regulatory decisions are made.

Over the past 15 years there appears to have been a dramatic change in the way in which companies deal with the public. Corporate attitudes have changed from the "my plant is my castle" mentality, to a willingness to give more information to the public, and perhaps deal with some of its fears, so that industry can move on with the business in hand. Certainly, time and experience has demonstrated that this is an excellent business practice.

Europe

It would seem that Europe and the United States are probably moving side-by-side in relation to public participation and interaction, although perhaps the United States is still a few years ahead of Europe.

There is already an EU Directive on public access to information on the environment (Directive 90/313/EEC), which means that all information which is available and contained in public records – and which is not a business secret – must be made available on request to any interested persons.

Another scheme which allows for information to be given to the public concerning corporate behaviour and activities in industrial installations is the Eco-Management and Audit Scheme (EMAS), a site accreditation scheme. In order to register, a company must make available to the public, on a periodic basis, a non-technical statement detailing the company's environmental programme and the environmental improvements planned for the site.

One issue – which is largely unresolved and still in the course of development – is the issue of environmental reporting. There are no statutory guidelines on environmental reporting yet, and it remains to be seen whether the European Union will take action on this issue.

A further issue concerns the concept of Pollution Emissions Register (PER), which in the United States is known as the Toxic Release Inventory (TRI). This is also largely an unresolved issue. Emissions reporting to the public on a list of substances is expected to be introduced by the European Union at some stage. The European list of substances will probably be shorter than the US list because initially perhaps only 60 or 70 substances will be involved, whereas in the US there are about 600 substances. It is not clear whether this proposal will be included in the IPPC Directive, whether it will take the form of a separate directive, or whether it may even be introduced as a regulation (*i.e.* EU legislation directly binding upon and effective within the Member States). However, it is certain that the European Commission would like to develop such an instrument, which would lead to companies having to disclose information about their emissions to the public.

Conclusions

Clearly, therefore, there are many issues involved. In a number of areas the United States is obviously ahead of Europe, but there are perhaps one or two areas where Europe is ahead of the US.

- On the issue of recycling and reuse, Europe is probably ahead of the US because it has mandatory rules, and not just recycling goals. Europe has targets which have to be implemented by the Member States. The use of environmental taxation for encouraging the recycling of products is being seen increasingly in Europe.
- On the issue of environmental liability, regulations exist in the individual EU Member States, but not at EU level itself. However, Europe is moving closer to a proper liability system, although there is a strong desire not to make the same mistakes in Europe as have been made in the United States.
- On the issue of environmental reporting and communication with the public, Europe is probably behind the United States, although there are developments in this area in Europe – one might say that the European Union is starting out on its learning curve. In doing this, EU

legislators are attempting to avoid the same problems that have been encountered in the United States. For example, the European Union is likely to arrive at a much shorter list of substances for PER than appears in the United States.

In conclusion, therefore, there is still some hope for industry in Europe that a suitable regulatory framework will develop over time. Europe certainly has many lessons to learn from the situation in the United States. Hopefully these lessons will be learnt. In some areas, however, it is true to say that the United States is almost certainly looking very closely across the waters at what is happening in Europe. Clearly, there are many lessons to be learnt in both directions.

Chapter 11
Trends and Developments in Environmental Regulation and Policy in Central and Eastern Europe; The Effect on Industry

Elizabeth Smith
European Bank for Reconstruction and Development, London

The European Bank for Reconstruction and Development (EBRD) is an international financial institution which has a specific mandate for environmental issues and sustainable development. Much of this book has already been given over to discussing issues of liability, harmonisation of standards and enforcement in the European Union and the United States. These are also the primary issues seen in Central and Eastern Europe and the former Soviet Union. With this in mind, what follows is a discussion of the problems which the Bank typically encounters in Central and Eastern Europe and the former Soviet Union, and suggestions of what therefore could be the risks or challenges for industry investing in that region.

The EBRD was established in 1991 with ECU 10 billion capitalisation to assist the transition of the former Soviet Bloc to market economies[1]. The EBRD currently has as its shareholder-members 58 countries, together with the European Commission and the European Investment Bank. It finances both public and private sector operations, although 60% or more has to go to the private sector. Public sector investment is only financed where it would assist the private sector, for example areas such as utilities and transport.

---

[1] A further ECU 10 billion was voted by the shareholders at the Annual Meeting in Sophia in April 1996.

Approximately 38% of the EBRD's funding currently goes to financial institutions or funds in the region, which in turn lend monies to small and medium-sized enterprises (SMEs). Therefore, there is the additional challenge of making sure that the banks using this money to lend to SMEs are also taking environmental issues into consideration.

The EBRD has a unique environmental mandate in its foundation charter that directs the Bank "to promote in the full range of its activities environmentally sound and sustainable development". The environmental mandate does not mean that the EBRD avoids environmentally risky projects; indeed, the Bank does tend to take on projects with significant environmental risk, and attempts to improve the environmental standard within a reasonable period of time.

The EBRD's Environmental Appraisal Unit looks at all the projects which come into the Bank, sets requirements for environmental due diligence, reviews the information and the operation team environmental results presents to the Board of Directors along with the financial and economic review of the project. The Unit reviews about 200 investment projects and 250 technical cooperation projects each year. From this experience certain conclusions can be drawn.

Typical projects are not "green field" projects. Most of the EBRD projects in Central and Eastern Europe are existing operations, sometimes called "brown field" projects. Many started in the 1970s and 1980s but funding ran out. The EBRD becomes involved in both privatisation projects and direct lending to companies in the region. The Bank also takes equity shares in companies.

The first challenge to investors comes in the area of legislation. In Central and Eastern Europe legislation is complex, and in transition. Most of the Central and Eastern European countries have some sort of framework environmental law in place and most have environmental impact assessment legislation. In some cases (for example, health legislation) there are tens of thousands of standards and regulations. There is great confusion in identifying which regulations are in place and which ones have been replaced by new legislation.

Consequently, the situation is very complex. In fact the most difficult requirement the EBRD many impose upon companies is to outline their regulatory requirements and to compare those to an international industry standard.

Sometimes foreign companies plan to bring their own Western programmes, such as worker health and safety programmes, into their Central and Eastern European operations. However, companies need to remember that there is already a regulatory regime in the country in which they intend to operate. Companies need to find out what the regulatory requirements are in that country and then make sure that that operation will meet those requirements.

Some laws which have been adopted in Central and Eastern Europe and in the former Soviet Union are based on foreign legislation. This can lead to difficulties if the authorities have not had training in the new methodology. Moreover, the methodology used to measure emissions may differ (for example, ambient versus point source measurement) which can present problems with implementing new legislation. For example, in the Komi Republic in the Russian Federation the environmental impact assessment legislation contains requirements for life-cycle analysis and detailed public participation.

Another major problem for investors is that when governments decentralise power, with the consequent realignment in the division of authority between central and local or regional government, the question of who has authority over the environment may become very confused. Local and regional authorities will often tell a company that they are the appropriate regulatory authorities for the company, but the federal authorities may still want to become involved. If a company talks to the wrong authorities in the wrong order it can delay a project. Furthermore, it becomes an increasing problem if the company does not get all the authorities who have a claim to regulating its operations to agree on the parameters of the environmental studies which need to be carried out. Failure to do this may result in companies having to go through very long delays when yet another authority with a jurisdictional right appears and demands that a further analysis or study is undertaken.

The number of stringent regulatory standards encountered also presents a problem This was something which surprised some of us when we first started working in the region back in 1991, because we assumed that there would be significant gaps in legislation. There are definitely some gaps, but these countries also have very stringent environmental regulations which technically cannot be met by almost anybody or any technology that is available today.

Some standards are much more stringent than those in OECD countries. Poland's air emission requirements, for example, are twice as strict in some places as TA Luft in Germany. These requirements are also measured by reference to ambient quality, and the quality of air in some areas in Poland is so bad that it already exceeds the limit prior to the start-up of an operation. Another example of very stringent regulatory standards is shown by a consumer products company in Russia that had waste water discharge requirements imposed on it that were six times more stringent than drinking water requirements in EU countries.

As indicated above, there are also gaps in legislation. Many countries in Central and Eastern Europe do not have legislation in areas such as PCBs and asbestos, and some lack legislation in relation to hazardous waste. In this context, it is also important to examine whether the country in which a potential project is located has signed international conventions or protocols. Countries such as Russia (as an example) may not have all the hazardous waste regulations in place but have signed and ratified the Basle Convention, and in the annex to that Convention there is a definition and list of hazardous wastes. These commitments should be taken into consideration by the investor.

Companies should take into account the fact that most of the countries in Central and Eastern Europe, have formal association agreements with the European Union. During the term of EBRD loans (which may be eight to ten years for the private sector) some of the requirements under the association agreements will be coming into force. Financial institutions will need to know how improvements to meet predicted regulatory changes will be funded and how that is likely to affect the company's cash flow.

Many industrial facilities seen by the EBRD are out of compliance in many areas of environmental regulation, and pay fines routinely. These fines can even be built into production costs in budgets. This is something which is certainly a problem for international financial institutions (and would probably also be so for most domestic financial institutions) who are constrained to fund only those companies which are operating legally. As mentioned earlier the standards can be very stringent, and it is a basic way of conducting business in that part of the world to pay fines merely as part of the company's routine operating costs. This presents a considerable problem to investors. When the EBRD reviews a company's environmental problems and its action plans for those areas which are out of compliance, agreement has to be reached with the authorities to confirm that they are satisfied with the company's plans for coming into compliance.

Environmental liabilities are an obvious problem. Not many of the privatisation laws cover environmental liability or (if they do) cover it adequately. Virtually none of these laws cover third-party liability. Consequently, in addition to environmental laws, companies and their advisers need to work with their lawyers to examine civil codes, privatisation laws and a variety of legal instruments on the statute books to identify responsibility for environmental damages.

To deal with the environmental liability issue, companies may receive an indemnity, in relation to responsibility for past contamination, from the parent company of the acquired subsidiary or from the former owner of the site. However, the parties have often failed to carry out an environmental audit or set a baseline for measuring changes in the level of contamination at the site, and no agreement has been reached on the condition of that site. An indemnification agreement is rarely adequate if it does not refer to quantitative data that is accepted by all parties as the condition of the site on the date of the agreement.

Finally, in order to help investors in Central and Eastern Europe who have told the EBRD what problems they are experiencing, the Bank has started to develop a series of tools to assist investors.

The Bank has produced an "investors' environmental guidelines" handbook. It covers nine countries in Central and Eastern Europe and was financed by the European Union PHARE programme. The handbook covers liability, regulatory requirements and other issues of concern to investors, and is now being enhanced to cover additionally occupational health and safety in the Russian Federation. A similar handbook for the rest of the former Soviet Union is also being produced.

The EBRD has developed a programme on the harmonisation of standards, and has completed a review of soil and groundwater contamination standards for the Polish Government. Furthermore, the Bank is trying to encourage ministries of privatisation to work with ministries of environment and make decisions in cooperation with each other, so that much of the mass privatisation goes through with environmental issues being taken into consideration. In addition, the Bank is running training programmes for bankers on these issues, starting with the Hungarian Bankers Association, and subsequently taking the programmes into other countries.

For companies and investors, therefore, there are considerable opportunities in Central and Eastern Europe, which suffers a lack of environmental technology, environmental services and waste management problems. The West now has technologies which can take what has up until now been disposed of as waste, and recover a great deal more raw materials from that waste than the region might previously have thought was possible. There are enormous energy efficiency opportunities and opportunities for recycling systems. There are also significant environmental management opportunities, for consultants to significantly increase profitability in these companies by increasing environmental efficiency. Consequently, investment opportunities in Central and Eastern Europe should not all be seen simply in terms of risk.

Chapter 12
Opportunities for Business in the Greening of Central and Eastern Europe

Dieter Rompel

Chairman of the Executive Board, Hölter Industrie Beteiligungs AG, Germany

The dramatic political and economic changes that have occurred in Eastern and Central Europe in the last five years are far more sweeping than the more developed and industrialised democracies of the world could possibly have foreseen. The pace of that change will accelerate – it must accelerate – if Eastern Europe is to achieve any kind of parity with the European Union and the rest of the free world within a reasonable time-scale of, say 10 to 20 years.

It has now become clear that caring for the environment has to be a shared responsibility – it is not a task that can be left to others to deal with. It is a question of *interdependence* as well as *change*, calling for cooperation within countries, between countries and between continents. Pollution does not respect national boundaries. It is wasteful and harmful, and it diminishes the resources of the one planet shared by all mankind.

Countries vary dramatically in the ways in which they care for their environment. Scandinavia, Switzerland and Germany, for instance, have long had strict and enforced legislation against various forms of industrial pollution, and there is no reason to suppose that these high standards will not be demanded by the other Central European nations as well as the newly democratised nations of Eastern Europe. However, they have a long way to go to set up acceptable standards and even longer to enforce them.

The European Union, likewise, has drawn up, and continues to impose, new directives for cleaning up the environment of its Member States. Higher standards force industry to design more and more sophisticated technologies for waste management, for "scrubbing" the smoke discharged from chimneys, and for cleaning the water and effluents discharged into rivers and seas. Although standards vary, no country can afford to be complacent. All are guilty to varying degrees and all have problems which clearly must be tackled.

Eastern Europe, in particular, has an enormous distance to make up. Those newly freed countries have many problems, and pollution is one of the greatest – a fact which they clearly recognise. Antiquated factories, coupled with decades of irresponsible management often in breach of existing national laws, have produced unprecedented levels of air, water and soil pollution, with damage to life and health expectancy. Although the exact scale of the problem is difficult to quantify with any precision, it has been unofficially estimated that it would cost some $400 billion to clean up Central and Eastern Europe. That, of course, does not include the cost of unemployment and retraining which would arise from the closure of major polluting factories, and furthermore does not include any cost figure for damages created by large environmental accidents.

Poland has suffered from discharges of fluorine gas from aluminium plants, the escape of organic solvents from a pharmaceutical factory, fallout of cadmium dust from smelting works, the release of lead from factory chimneys, and the pollution of rivers by the discharge of untreated sewage and industrial effluent.

The former German Democratic Republic has also suffered. For example, when one group of Soviet troops were set to return home from the former GDR, their barracks and training areas were found to be heavily polluted with waste oil, kerosene and other chemical compounds. The Bonn Government has had to set aside DM70 million simply to assess the damage to one area that it wants to turn into a nature reserve.

It would take far too long to recite in detail the many horror stories which have come to light about the nature and extent of the pollution of such countries. Nevertheless, thankfully there is light to shed upon the gloom because:

(i) these countries recognise that they must improve their environ-ments as part of their long, uphill road to recovery;
(ii) they are, in their various ways, taking steps to prevent further dam-age, as well as to eradicate the damage already done; and
(iii) they recognise that they will need assistance from the rest of the world.

Following reunification, Germany, of course, accepts its particular obliga-tions towards Eastern Europe, and furthermore recognises that the way in which the reunified Germany is dealt with will probably point the way for the rest of the Eastern bloc countries.

Aid is, therefore, necessary, but therein also lies an opportunity for business. The Hölter-ANI Group, whose achievements in the environmental protection technology field are considerable, are very active in Eastern Europe, where the company is able to put to dramatic use its technologies for gas cleaning, or water, waste and soil treatments, including waste coal treatments. There is no doubt that these countries need such technologies, and many others in addition.

However, any company wishing to make headway in Eastern Europe must bear in mind three very important criteria:

(i) they should consider joint ventures with local companies, rather than "going it alone";

(ii) when setting up a subsidiary, they must be prepared to finance the venture very generously; and

(iii) while offering first-class technology, it must be a practical technology which is affordable within the spending limits of these countries.

It is also wise to set up a reliable network of local contacts and associates, so as to chart a way through the local bureaucratic jungle. It must be remembered that the countries of Eastern Europe have been heavily regulated in the past and, although bureaucratic delays are expected to diminish, this will not happen overnight.

How is a venture in Eastern Europe financed? The best way, of course, would be with the help of subventions and aid from the governments of all industrialised countries. Unfortunately, however, this way is – with the exception of the increasing number of EU programmes – also the rarest!

Credit could be obtained from a private bank. The German Government, for instance, will pay or subsidise the interest rates incurred and/or will give credit insurance up to 85% via the HERMES scheme. This assistance is easier to obtain if the company in question can arrange to have its own equipment and technologies imported from the former East Germany, remembering, of course, that materials are still much cheaper there. European Commission grants and financing are now becoming increasingly important and it is an area worth considering.

It is completely unrealistic, however, to assume that one can offer expensive plant and technology to Eastern Europe, and then expect the orders to come rolling in. The assumption fails simply because these countries do not possess the money to buy the technologies at such prices.

The Hölter Group has been working on a strategy to overcome this problem. Hölter's approach has been to devise innovative structures to finance individual projects, and to provide technology which makes the impossible possible. A technological solution to financial problems is precisely Hölter's recipe for success in Eastern Europe. Hölter sells "economic environmental protection". The following is one example.

The Hölter Group has, historically, specialised in the mining of coal. Once coal has been extracted, it is washed and separated from other mineral matter. In Eastern Europe, however, the quality of this washing process is generally inferior. The result is a vast quantity of coal sludge, which litters and disfigures large areas of Eastern Europe, besides polluting the ground water. These ugly sludge ponds, however, can contain as much as 30% of high-quality coal. Hölter has the technology to process these residues and extract high-value coal which can then be sold on the world markets. In effect, this turns waste into a marketable asset, earning much-needed foreign exchange business.

Similarly, Hölter has devised a low-cost technology for de-sulphurising the flue gases spewing from the chimneys of many East European plants. Because this technology tackles the problem at source, by reducing the sulphurous content of the coal prior to burning, it can be employed at about one-sixth of the cost of a conventional gas de-sulphurisation facility. This is precisely the kind of initiative which the countries of Eastern Europe need. They recognise that they have seriously polluted environments and need solutions which they can manage and afford. Ideally, these solutions should improve their efficiency and productivity and help to earn the foreign exchange they so desperately need.

That is the challenge for Hölter, and also for others doing or considering doing business in Central and Eastern Europe. The following are some examples of the ways in which Hölter has taken up that challenge.

In Moscow, Hölter will construct a turnkey plant for the disposal of domestic waste, 300,000 tonnes a year of which will act as a fuel to generate steam for a district heating scheme. The advanced revolving fluidised-bed technology being installed at this plant will be supplied by Hölter-ABT, the group's waste to energy company. It will bring to Moscow clean, leading-edge technology that not only solves a serious environmental problem, but also gives a much needed benefit to the local community. The requirement for innovative financing schemes to be utilised, as was mentioned earlier, means that part of the cost will be covered by the exporting of mineral resources.

In the Czech Republic, Krüger-Hölter, the group's water treatment company – in a consortium with a French partner – expects to be awarded the contract to reconstruct a major sewage plant in Prague. At present the existing plant pumps its effluents into the Elbe and Moldau rivers, resulting in dreadful environmental pollution. In fact, except for a pre-wash, over one-third of the sewage discharged is completely untreated. Thanks to the planned Krüger-Hölter reconstruction of the plant, the entire amount of sewage, which is about 120 tonnes per day, will be treated. This particularly successful plan will incorporate the old, existing plant into the construction of the new one. New equipment and advanced technology will be introduced, including a patented biological water-purification technique, which removes contaminates from the effluent. In addition, local companies will be integrated into the project and existing staff kept on. This innovative project will give Prague a modern plant with the best technology available today. Of course, the horrendous environmental damage that has occurred will take time to repair, but progress will be made, albeit step by step.

However, big is not always beautiful. In the former East Germany, where populations are widely spread, Krüger-Hölter have waste water treatment plants on a community scale. Even if only 20,000 to 50,000 people are living in an isolated community (which is common in the north of the country, for example) they will still have a sewage problem. Krüger-Hölter can build a small to medium-sized, self-contained plant which deals with the problem, and for a relatively small investment good returns are projected. At present Krüger-Hölter has 11 such plants built, with five more under construction, and sees this as an important target area.

Of course, the historical heart of Hölter has always been coal. Mentioned earlier was the fact that Hölter has technology which can extract the residues from coal sludge. This technology is used in Siberia, Poland and the Czech Republic. It is cleaning the environments in those countries and earning much needed foreign currency. In harnessing its experience and expertise to this end, Hölter can help Eastern Europe to sell its products on the world market, whilst at the same time enlarging the scale of its own international business. The countries of Eastern Europe still produce little which can readily be sold on the international markets. They do, however, possess considerable mineral reserves which, in many cases, can readily be extracted. It follows then that the financing of (or payment for) the technologies and plant they need to buy must be backed by the export of oil, gas and coal.

Technologies which help those countries to exploit their natural reserves more efficiently and more cleanly will create foreign exchange business, as well as helping to solve their environmental problems. This is the kind of strategy which guides the work of the Hölter Group in Central and Eastern Europe. Hopefully, it may commend itself to others also.

Chapter 13
Lender Liability and Deep Pockets; Managing Environmental Risks in Financing Business in Europe

Peter Blackman

Formerly Assistant Director, British Bankers' Association

Although the subject-matter of this chapter will be discussed from a lender's perspective, the issues are exactly the same for other "investors" and also for insurers, namely the requirements to be able to identify and quantify, to monitor the management of, and to cost and price risk. Lenders or investors hope to get their money back one day in the future, and insurers will take premium income today in the hope that they will not have to pay out later.

For the financial sector the environment is becoming ever more important. This centres mainly around the concept of environmental liability, in particular the financial consequences which may flow from it, and in turn the risk which environmental liability poses to the investor's/insurer's "interest" in the company in question. Environmental liability is a growing concern for business in Europe and the financial sector is clearly also very concerned.

It is important at this point to appreciate briefly the effect which the US experience in the area of environmental liability has had on the business world. It is developments there – in particular the *Fleet Factors* case (*US* v *Fleet Factors* 819 Supp 1079 (SD Ga 1993)) – which have led to the current situation, where it is now much more difficult for businesses to be able to borrow money or to obtain investment where potentially damaging environmental factors are present. Certainly, the insurance companies' practice of "red-lining" of environmental factors also stems directly from the US experience. Because of this, the US factor is clearly very important.

Currently, there is little support in Europe for following the US experience. However Europe, both at the national level and internationally, is tending to drift towards it, and this is something which must be strongly resisted. In 1989 the European Commission published its draft directive on civil liability for damage caused by waste, which was the first inkling that banks in Europe had that they might be at risk from environmental liability. It appeared that the Commission had been inspired by legal developments in the United States. Naturally, in view of the serious problems which environmental liability had caused in the United States, the European banks went to great lengths to persuade the Commission that its proposals were misguided.

The debate has moved on since then, first to the Council of Europe's Lugano Convention (on remedying environmental damage), and latterly to the European Commission's 1993 Green Paper consultation exercise on remedying environmental damage (COM (93) 47) which appears to have subsumed the earlier proposals on civil liability for damage caused by waste. The issues now, of course, are much wider than "civil liability", although that still features as a central issue in current proposals for remedying environmental damage.

In considering environmental damage – past, present and future – it is important to start with some hard thinking on how to deal with the question of liability for the historic damage brought about by the industrial processes of the past 100 to 200 years. Finance is obviously a key component here. However, legal and regulatory uncertainty might prove to be the first and major stumbling block to the provision of this finance. Banks, investors and insurers will not and cannot pay for the mistakes of others. Indeed, there have already been a number of very large and important regeneration projects which the banks would have liked to have financed, but were unable to do so. This is simply because these are long-term projects involving money being lent out for up to 40 years, and the banks cannot be certain that the business environment is going to be sufficiently stable over such a period to enable them to take on this sort of lending without also taking on the risk of incurring any untoward liabilities.

However, it must not be thought that the financial sector is solely concerned about environmental liability risks. It is important that the issue of liability for past pollution is properly considered, but thereafter efforts must be turned towards delivering sustainable development and towards overcoming the global challenges of climate change which presently face mankind. There is increasing concern about the role which financial sector companies must play in putting the concept of sustainable development into practice. There is growing recognition that the solutions to the environmental problems now facing the world can only be delivered ultimately by the business community. In seeking to address these problems, the issue of funding is a very important consideration because for most of the environmental issues currently under discussion the availability of finance will be a key element in enabling business to deliver the right answers. As a consequence, banks will play a central role.

Essentially, bankers are in the business of investing in and supporting "good business". From a bank's perspective "good business" is business which is both environmentally beneficial and well managed. Consequently banks have a "bottom-line" interest in the environment. It makes commercial sense. Banks want to have good businesses as customers so that they can work successfully in partnership with them. Clearly, a company's response to environmental concerns will be a key measure of business success in the future, and this means that bankers have got to take these concerns into account as well.

Nevertheless, environmental liability remains a key point for banks, for obvious reasons, and the ability to assess these environmental risks correctly becomes paramount. Bankers will use a system of credit risk assessment, which should include proportionate and equitable attention being paid to the environmental factors involved. One such credit assessment system is summed up by the mnemonic CAMPARI, which summarises the basic cannons of lending which have stood for centuries.

The CAMPARI process represents consideration of the following issues: Customer – Ability – Means – Purpose – Amount – Repayment – Insurance (*i.e.* security/collateral). This leads to consideration of the appropriate level of interest. Lending is about common sense and prudence. Therefore, a banker looking at a proposition in which he is interested will want to make an assessment of the *customer*, his *ability* to perform his obligations, the customer's *means*, the *purpose* for which the loan is required, the *amount* required and finally, how the customer is going to *repay* it, which, for the bank, is the bottom line (the ability to repay is always the key to the banker's decision as to whether or not to lend). In the light of the results of this risk assessment the banker finally decides whether or not security/collateral is required. This security or collateral is the bank's *insurance*, which is there purely and simply as a safety net, in case things go wrong. Following this, the banker decides what level of *interest* and fees will be appropriate in the circumstances.

Environmental factors may be a major consideration here, because these factors are related to the nature of the customer's business, the customer's means and the customer's ability to perform. But these factors are only one element, important as they may be.

Fundamentally, banks have to protect their depositors and shareholders. Furthermore, banking regulators will not allow banks to leave themselves in a position where they may be taking on potentially unquantifiable liabilities, well beyond the scope of the business that is being entered into. In this context, the uncertainties surrounding environmental liabilities begin to cause major problems for the banking sector.

For example, average borrowing for a small to medium-sized business is £20,000; the average cost of cleaning up a contaminated site in the United States – that is, the few which have been cleaned up – is $30 million. This is such a wide discrepancy that banks could not possibly accept the risk of such potential liabilities. Therefore, if average interest rates were 10% per annum, a £20,000 loan would produce interest of £2,000 per annum. If just one such loan led to the bank becoming liable for compensation and clean-up costs, even limited to just £3 million, it would wipe out the interest earned from 1,500 loans. Experience has shown that the compensation and clean-up costs could amount to much more than £3 million. If that figure were £20 million for example – which is much nearer to the US average cost per site – it would take the interest from some 10,000 loans to cover it. A prudent lender would not expect more than two loans per hundred to become bad debts, and even so the loss would normally be limited to the amount of the loan itself. With environmental liability, not only do lenders risk losing the value of their security (and with it the amount of the loan itself), but they also risk incurring liability for paying the attendant compensation and clean-up costs.

Consequently, banks now build in environmental factors into their lending decisions. Over the past few years bankers have learned what are the right questions to ask; not necessarily all of the questions, but nevertheless a good many of them. The banks now know what are the good "environmental" questions which need to be asked. Unfortunately, what the banks do not yet know is what are "good answers" to these questions. This dilemma is an issue nationally, across Europe and internationally. Environmental studies are, relatively speaking, still in their infancy. Whatever the banks do, the measures which they put in place to find out about the environmental factors affecting their customers (remembering, of course, that the customer will also need this information for his own environmental assessment/environmental management purposes) must be cost effective. If a bank lends £20,000 to a small or medium-sized enterprise there is very little margin to allow for an environmental assessment to be carried out. There would only be a few hundred pounds available, which would not even cover a phase I desktop study, let alone a full site investigation.

There is then a need to develop a degree of certainty in the definitions used in this area; for example, what constitutes pollution or contamination? There is also a need for certainty of standards. But above all, banks need legal certainty. Banks need to know that businesses are not going to be penalised tomorrow for having met today's standards. They also need to know today that good commercial transactions will not be overturned retrospectively tomorrow by changes in liability regimes, as governments cast around to find someone who will save the public purse from having to pay for the legacy of contamination and pollution inherited from the past. The uncertainty created where commercial arrangements can be overturned retrospectively undermines confidence, which leads in turn to a contraction in business opportunities, and the consequent restrictions upon access to finance simply compound any recessionary trends already present.

Furthermore, banks believe that they should not be made liable for the mistakes of, or the damage caused by, their customers. In particular, banks should not become liable for compensation and clean-up costs resulting from the actions of their customers, simply because the banks have assessed the commercial proposition in question, decided to lend on it, held some collateral in the form of the customer's land, monitored the borrowing to make sure it remains safe and viable, or supported an ailing customer when it has fallen into difficulties.

In addition, the "safe harbour" protection which the limited liability status of customer companies brings to co-partners in the business process, such as banks and insurers, must not be breached. Unfortunately, extending environmental liability to lenders, investors and insurers does just that. Ultimately, the effect of this is to undermine fatally the business process, something which cannot be tolerated economically and socially, particularly in view of the consequences for small and medium-sized companies which normally form the backbone of any successful economy.

Furthermore, only a fault-based system would be commercially equitable, not one based upon strict or absolute liability whereby the company and its lenders and other commercial supporters may incur liability despite their best efforts to work in an environmentally responsible manner. In this last respect, a "state-of-the-art" defence (*i.e.* the company has used the most up-to-date technology and techniques for minimising and abating pollution) must be allowed.

In future, therefore, responsibility and liability will go hand-in-hand and there will be a need to ensure that banks lend to customers who are working in accordance with (rather than in contradiction to) sustainable development programmes. However, banks are not, and cannot become, some kind of "environmental policemen".

These then are the liabilities which banks need to be able to avoid if they are going to be able to lend to business. Certainly, lenders and investors want to be able to play their part in the drive towards a cleaner and safer environment. They recognise it as socially and economically desirable and, furthermore, that it makes good business sense. Half of all commercial banking customers are affected by environmental factors. The eight major retail banks in the United Kingdom alone are presently lending over £200 billion to just such customers. That sort of business is vital, both for lenders/investors and for the economy.

The financial sector does want to be able to play its part, but what it needs are clear definitions, better-defined standards and legal certainty, so that banks and others can identify, quantify, manage and cost the environmental risks involved. If this can be done – and if the liability challenge can be met and overcome – then good environmental progress will be made. The financial sector wants a liability regime which acts as a carrot and not as a stick, to encourage environmental progress. Inevitably, this is something which will have to be taken one step at a time. There are no magic wands, but it is clear that extremely significant progress can be made over a relatively short period of time if a sensible approach is adopted to what is clearly one of the major challenges that the business world has faced for some time.

Chapter 14

When Things Go Badly Wrong; Managing Environmental Risks in a Crisis

Lawrence Werner
*Executive Vice-President/Director, Ketchum Public
Relations Worldwide*

This chapter will first consider environmentalism as a public affairs issue, with particular regard to environmental accidents and disasters. Secondly, it will discuss how companies should manage their communications when crises occur. When an environmental crisis, or any other kind of crisis occurs, a company's reputation is at risk. Managing communications during a crisis is critical to maintaining a company's credibility, its reputation and, sometimes, its survival.

Turning first to environmentalism as a public affairs issue. In both the United States and Europe environmental activism has been fuelled by crises. In fact, Pittsburgh, where Ketchum Public Relations is headquartered, could be described as the birthplace of the modern environmental movement. It was the home of Rachel Carson, whose landmark book, *Silent Spring*, first appeared 33 years ago. *Silent Spring* dealt with the dangers of DDT, a pesticide which the United States banned largely because of her study. However, it spawned more than an attack on a pesticide; it also gave rise to a movement that has spread throughout every part of the world.

In the United States, the growth of the environmental movement has been tied to major catastrophes, such as the toxic pollution at Love Canal in New York, the radiation leakage at Three Mile Island in Pennsylvania, or the *Exxon Valdez* oil spill off the Alaskan coast. Europe has also suffered mishaps, one of the most notorious was at the Rhine River in 1986. In this case, the Sandoz chemical plant in Basle, Switzerland, accidentally spilled toxic herbicides into the Rhine. As the so-called "Red Rhine" flowed towards the sea, it left behind an international trail of protest, accusations and scandal.

In such cases, environmental accidents create a strong public backlash against the offending companies. They also generate distrust towards business in general. Corporations are perceived as the wrongdoers, and are accused of negligence and greed. Often this public distrust assumes a political form. The foremost example of this is seen in the rise of the Green Parties which emerged throughout Europe in the 1980s. Germany's Greens were particularly verbal and powerful as a political and cultural force. Another expression of public concern has been the growth of international organisations. The past two decades have generated more than 40 international organisations devoted to environmental protection. Greenpeace is perhaps the most famous. But there is a wide range of other organisations equally committed to their agendas, groups such as Earthwatch Europe, Friends of the Earth International, the Rain Forest Action Network and the Worldwatch Institute.

Yet another public response is government regulation. In the United States, the Federal Government has 16 major environmental statutes on the statute books, plus dozens of lesser ones, including the Clean Air Act, the Clean Water Act, the Endangered Species Act, the Marine Mammal Protection Act and the Oil Pollution Act. This does not include hundreds of state statutes concerning the environment. In addition to the US Environmental Protection Agency there are state environmental protection agencies to contend with, which often impose stricter air and water regulations than the Federal Government Agency itself.

Europe also has a staggering number of national, international and regional organisations devoted to the environment. Nearly every country has its own Ministry of the Environment. In addition, nearly 20 international government organisations exist which have environmental departments or environmental agencies. These include such bodies as the European Union, the Council of Europe and the United Nations Environmental Programme – organisations which are committed to monitoring the environmental performance of international businesses. Furthermore, there is now the European Environmental Agency.

With the arrival of the EU Single Market and GATT, transnational companies seek global markets and global economies of scale. Now that the borders are unguarded throughout much of the European continent, many companies will expand their sales and marketing throughout Europe. This, in turn, will mean that the nations with the strictest environmental regulations will set the standards for other nations in the region.

Clearly, environmentalism takes many forms, involving political action, international security and government regulation. We are now living in a very different world to that of the 1970s when the environmental movement first began to stir – a world that is suspicious of business and sometimes militant over environmental protection. One thing remains the same, however. The environmental movement is still a child of crisis. When accidents happen, public reaction is swift and strong, which is why companies must be prepared to manage crises and communicate effectively with the public when a crisis happens.

Because environmental concern is universal, any accident anywhere in the world can attract public interest. If a worker in France is killed in a crane accident, people in Australia may not care too much. But when medical waste washes up on the New Jersey shoreline, people in Italy – who will see it or hear of it via the media – are concerned. They can identify with the problem. Likewise, pictures of otters and seagulls covered with oil arouse sympathy throughout the world. Environmental crises attract intense public interest and media interest around the globe. Companies must be ready for this. They must have communications, plans and strategies for handling such contingencies.

One thing is certain; no matter how much care is taken there is no guarantee that a crisis will not occur. Royal Dutch Shell discovered this a few years ago. A French nuclear submarine, the *Rugas*, ran into one of the oil supertankers off the southern coast of France. The company could not have anticipated this kind of event. Of course, the French Navy accepted responsibility, but that did not make the oil spill any less severe.

Bad things do happen, and there are people just waiting to criticise. One cannot predict when or where the next crisis will occur. However, one can be prepared. This is the first critical part of crisis communications –*preparation*. The first step in the process is to build a reservoir of goodwill with the community and with government officials and the news media. Goodwill is the "intangible" that allows a company to call in favours and friends whenever they need them most.

Building goodwill takes many forms. Sometimes it involves supporting environmental causes. An example is Heinz's donation to the British Government of a cape in Cornwall a few years ago. The land is now set aside as a nature reserve. Another example is Chevron's annual awards recognising the achievements of leading environmentalists.

Goodwill also involves continual dialogue with the public and with the news media. A company that is reclusive or unfriendly should not expect sympathy when a crisis happens. It is vitally important to have a bank account of goodwill to draw upon during a crisis.

Building goodwill is an ongoing process. However, it is hard to define and quantify. That is why in order to construct a crisis management programme, effective planning must begin with thorough research. A company needs to conduct a comprehensive vulnerability assessment. Internal and external audiences need to be interviewed and a perspective evaluated. An effective assessment reviews the most likely areas where problems would arise, but it also takes a look within the company to evaluate management capabilities, communications and credibility. On some occasions it may become apparent during the course of such an assessment that there are serious gaps between what management believes it is communicating and what employees or outside audiences are actually hearing from the company. Such insight needs to be obtained well before an emergency starts. These assessments, like every other part of the planning process, must have the commitment of the entire company, from the chairman's office down to line officers. The assessment should be conducted by an impartial third party to ensure reliable responses and evaluation.

Armed with this research, a company is ready for the next step in the preparation process – the development of the crisis plan itself. Unfortunately, too many companies prepare elaborate preparations and operations plans which deal with every possible catastrophe, but neglect the communications process. The company must have a crisis management plan in place before a crisis occurs. It is nearly impossible to build a crisis communications plan once the crisis has begun.

An example of this occurred during the *Exxon Valdez* disaster. The 1989 *Exxon Valdez* oil spill off the coast of Alaska was the largest in US history. Shortly after that spill occurred, Ketchum was asked to be part of a team of Public Relations professionals assembled from around the nation to advise Alyeska, the Alaskan pipeline company which supplied the tanker fleets in the region. This team was not hired by Exxon however. Unfortunately, although Exxon was part of the consortium involved in the incident, it did not respond – as events have shown – with the same sense of urgency in communicating with the public as Alyeska did, and for whatever the reasons may be, during the first critical hours of the spill the correct information was not put out to the public. Consequently, the media created its own story and used whatever fact or rumour it had come across to interpret the incident. As a result, the reputation of Exxon was badly damaged and the company was portrayed as arrogant, insensitive and confused. In particular, it was criticised because neither the chairman nor the chief executive officer (CEO) went to the scene of the accident immediately. The public was outraged. Thereafter, 10,000 Exxon credit cards were destroyed. To this day, the Exxon accident remains a rallying cry for environmentalists.

To avoid such a disaster a company needs to have a plan in place before the alarm sounds. This process begins internally. Every level of the company's management must be involved, because each has a role to play. There are many different approaches for developing a crisis management and communications team. Usually, team formation is dictated by local conditions, the size and culture of a company and the internal capabilities of management. For the most part, every team has a crisis manager, the person who is in charge of implementing the crisis management plan.

The crisis team manager must assign other team managers to communications, operations, security, personnel, liaison with government officials and administrative support. It is also important that each member of the crisis team has a substitute, to accommodate vacations, illnesses and other regular or foreseeable absences. The size of the team will, of course, depend upon the seriousness of the crisis. However, it is a good rule to keep the team compact, so as to expedite decision-making. Once a crisis plan is in place and a team is prepared, the company should rehearse it periodically, which is vital. This will prepare top managers for actual crisis management itself.

Another critical element in the planning stage is media training. Because of the sophistication of the news media, the company must have managers and CEOs who can speak quickly and concisely about the situation. Communications in a crisis should follow the outline detailed in the company's crisis plan.

In the case of a serious environmental crisis, the crisis management process is the ultimate responsibility of the CEO. Every situation is unique in its details. However, in general there are seven major steps which crisis managers must follow. These steps are not necessarily carried out chronologically. Sometimes, however, depending upon the seriousness of the crisis, many of the following steps may have to be taken concurrently (although the company should ensure that all assignments required by the crisis plan are clearly understood by all the personnel involved, so as to avoid confusion):

(i) Control on-site damage, and keep the situation from getting worse. In the case of disasters such as the chemical explosion at the Union Carbide factory in Bhopal, India, the spread of toxic substances must be stopped and personnel evacuated before anything else is done. The potential problems must be defined beforehand, because in many instances the company's crisis policy will emanate from this exercise. At Bhopal, this element did not work well.

(ii) Begin fact-finding. Never trust rumours. Do not speculate, and do not assume anything until the company is able to confirm the facts itself. The company is probably better off assuming a worst-case scenario in any major crisis, so that it is prepared for the worst.

(iii) Assemble the crisis management team. Be sure that the crisis management team is informed and updated on a regular basis.

(iv) Establish centralised communications. Instruct employees to direct all questions to a supervisor, and have the supervisor report to the team's "fact-finder".

(v)   Establish a "crisis command centre" to handle communications and respond to media enquiries. The command centre should be equipped with multiple phone lines, word processors, printers, television and radio equipment, and monitoring equipment. The location of the command centre should be off-site in order to conduct media briefings. It should be equipped with a sufficient supply of power and telephone lines to accommodate reporters and cameramen. Maps and visual aids can be very important and very effective, particularly during oil and chemical spills, as was the case with the Allied Forces briefing room for Operation Desert Storm during the Iraqi occupation of Kuwait.

(vi)   Prepare information for release to key segments of the public. This should include the media, employees, customers, shareholders, families of injured employees, the board of directors, and government law enforcement officials. It is important during any crisis, when talking to these audiences, to show empathy – something which many companies forget when conveying all the technical details.

(vii)   Designate a company spokesperson. This is a very important step. The company will need a single point of contact for conveying its position and receiving media enquiries. That person should be trained to handle the media and should be able to express the company's views in a clear, credible and concise manner. The spokesperson is a personification of the company, which is why many companies use the CEO as spokesperson during times of crisis.

The important point to remember is that the company should control the communications process. It should issue official statements to the media as opposed to letting the media get the information from some other source. If the company fails to do this, the media will rely on less friendly sources, and what then comes out will not be very favourable to the company.

The Chernobyl disaster was a classic example of mishandling the world's media. At first, the Soviet Government tried to cover up the incident – which was impossible for such a large catastrophe. Information – like the radiation – leaked out. When the Soviet Government finally admitted to the disaster, it had lost its credibility. If a company had behaved that way it would be out of business.

The best approach is to be thorough and consistent with the media. First, the company should develop a "core message" as the foundation of all communications, no matter what the audience. Core messages will change as a crisis unfolds and moves towards a conclusion. Nevertheless, their development is essential, so that everyone speaking on behalf of the company delivers the same message, ensuring consistency.

As the crisis plan is being put into action, a major factor will be the constant pressure of the media. The one crisis communications question asked most often is, "how should one deal with the news media?". The response to this question will be dictated by the way the media functions in the country concerned. In most cases, however, the media's objectives are quite different from the company's objectives during a crisis. The reporter's story will be covered by his needs, and some of these will include reporting a story with emotional appeal, getting a story before someone else does, revealing a new angle on a crisis, and searching out newsworthy figures and experts. The questions which reporters will want answered are: what are the facts?; what is the significance of the story?; who is responsible?; how will the company resolve the problem?; and, when will the company resolve the problem?. A company's crisis team should bear in mind these likely questions when it is preparing itself for talking to reporters.

It is also necessary to consider the needs of each particular news medium. News is more visual now than ever before. When working with television reporters, the company must provide them with visual images. Even when a Chernobyl-type disaster occurs, where it is impossible to get close to the site, the company should have videotape as an available facility. The reporter will use what is called "B roll" as a visual backup for his report. Likewise, if dealing with radio reporters, the company spokesman needs to construct its message to concise soundbites of 15 or 20 seconds, because if the spokesman cannot express his point quickly he will not be heard.

New technology has added a novel dimension to the communications process. The computer Internet is now a major source of comment on stories around the world. It is revolutionising the activities of grass-roots organisations on both sides of the Atlantic. When the Oklahoma City bombing occurred on 19 April 1995, people around the world debated the issue directly via the Internet. People from the United States and Great Britain discussed international terrorism with each other, without reliance upon the media. Meanwhile, news reporters tapped into the Internet to get stories and public comment, which then appeared in the newspapers and on television. Certainly, the same thing will happen the next time a Rhine disaster occurs, or when the next oil spill occurs off the coast of Great Britain or the coast of France. Companies must understand this new technology and make sure that its views are included in the global village's new public forum.

Companies should never underestimate the media. In today's world, news organisations have access to a vast amount of background material. They have a cadre of experts to give a comment on just about any crisis imaginable. In short, they cannot be fooled; candour is the company's best defence.

When a crisis is over, nevertheless the planning process continues. Questions have to be asked concerning how well the crisis plan worked, what was learnt from the crisis, and how the company can better handle the next one. Some companies conduct exhaustive market research with a variety of audiences, in order to get feedback on how well the company performed during a particular crisis.

Many situations spell disaster for one company and opportunity for another. It would appear that a company's true character is often likely to come out during a crisis. Starkist, which is the world's largest tuna company, turned criticism into praise when it became the first company to announce a dolphin-safe tuna fishing policy. The company worked with leading environmental groups and obtained their endorsement. Starkist is now recognised as a leader in the movement for responsible use of harvesting the world's oceans. Through such initiatives, companies can overcome the public perception that industry is not trustworthy, compassionate or fair.

In times of crisis and afterwards, the company's communications goal should be:

- to build trust with important audiences;
- to project fairness on the part of the company;
- to convey a sense of community involvement and control;
- to humanise communications as much as, and whenever, possible;
- to localise issues; and
- to communicate on both the intellectual and emotional levels at all times.

In summary, therefore, the company should plan for a crisis before it occurs. It should develop a crisis team with clear responsibilities. It should become a primary information source during a crisis. It should understand the media and its requirements. Finally, it should institute follow-up after a crisis so as to restore goodwill and maintain the company's reputation.

Effective communications, particularly during environmental crises, are vital to a company's credibility and to its public relations. When one considers what is at stake – a company's reputation and perhaps the careers of its management – it is easy to see that the cost of developing and maintaining a crisis plan is a small investment to make for the future.

Chapter 15
Meeting the Challenge Head-on? The World Business Council for Sustainable Development

Margaret Flaherty
Projects Manager/Trade and Environment Specialist at the
World Business Council for Sustainable Development

1 January 1995 marked the inaugural day of the World Business Council for Sustainable Development (WBCSD), a merger of two well-known business organisations; the Business Council for Sustainable Development (which was set up to provide a voice for industry at the 1992 United Nations Conference on Environment and Development in Rio de Janeiro) and the World Industry Council for the Environment (which was a post-Rio initiative of the International Chamber of Commerce).

The organisation is a coalition of chief executive officers (CEOs) – to ensure top level commitment from member companies – and membership of the organisation is by invitation only. The WBCSD currently has 125 member companies from around the world; many of these companies are large concerns.

In terms of industry sectors, the membership includes manufacturing, producers of natural resources, the professional service sector, law firms and accounting firms, environmental consulting firms, and the banking and financial sector.

The organisation operates by locating experts within certain companies to work on particular issues. First, the CEO appoints a liaison delegate. That individual then works with the WBCSD on a daily interactive basis and, where specific projects are undertaken by the WBCSD, the liaison delegate will involve relevant specialists in his company – be it public relations, communications, acquisitions, etc specialists – which enables the WBCSD to have access to a broad spectrum of professional skills and expertise within a company.

Fundamentally, the WBCSD aims to "operationalise" sustainable development. There is a certain amount of frustration within the business community at the weight of expectation which has been placed upon its shoulders for delivering sustainable development. Of course, it is true that business has a crucial role to play here, and this needs to be explored fully. The real conundrum, however, is how to move beyond what policy-makers and decision-makers are saying and towards real sustainable development – not necessarily in regulatory or political terms, but in practical business terms.

The WBCSD has merged the work programmes of the two organisations, and the general topical areas which the WBCSD is working on run across a spectrum, from very policy-oriented research and report writing to "hands on" demonstration projects. The WBCSD is also involved in education and training, and the development of management tools.

In general, WBCSD projects are identified by preparing a set of scoping papers which lay out what the issues for business are, why the issue in question is relevant and important for business, and what the WBCSD can do about it. Thereafter, depending on where the member companies themselves place the priorities, the WBCSD determines whether a particular issue is ripe enough to be developed into an actual project.

In the *policy development area* the WBCSD has six projects:

- trade and environment;
- sustainable consumption and production;
- climate issues;
- sustainable forests;
- financial markets; and
- Central and Eastern Europe.

Trade and environment

Trade and environment is currently a major topic, given the degree of emphasis placed on this issue by the non-governmental organisation (NGO) community, and given the level of discussion on this topic that took place during the conclusion of the GATT Uruguay Round (which has significantly elevated the relevance of the whole trade and environment issue).

It is a very complicated issue, and one where the correct approach is difficult to determine. In discussing "generalities", the business community is normally all at a consensus. As soon as the boundaries of "generalities" are crossed and very specific issues are addressed (such as dealing with regulation of process methods, trade restrictive measures, international environmental agreements) attitudes within the business community become much more fractionalised. It is a challenge for the WBCSD to try to draw a broad-based global inter-sectoral business perspective on this issue.

The WBCSD aims to have a set of conclusions and recommendations developed in time for the ministerial meeting of the World Trade Organisation, which will be held in Singapore at the end of 1996. The aim is to move away from the generality of policy discussions, which have so far been dominated by trade negotiators and trade mission officials. It is business that makes the management, technology and investment decisions which will ultimately influence sustainable development and sustainable trade. Consequently, business must have something to say on this issue that contributes in a forward-looking manner.

Sustainable consumption and production

This is an issue that is increasingly relevant to business. The United Nations Commission on Sustainable Development has began work in this area, but dealing with this issue internationally and at an institutionalised level may present problems for business. For example, should international directives or multilateral negotiated agreements really dictate to consumers such mundane issues as how many tubes of toothpaste they can buy each year? Nevertheless, the business community wants to be fully involved in discussions in this area, and furthermore wants to work as a credible partner with the policy-makers in moving towards progressive solutions in this area.

In fact, for competitiveness reasons and also for good financial reasons, business has for some time been working towards producing and consuming in sustainable ways. An example is the concept of product steward-ship, which is one of the bye-lines of the chemical industry. It is clearly a well-developed programme, and one that has very sustainable consumption and production components to it. For the WBCSD, the main question is how to replicate these types of projects and, at the same time, work with the international rule-making bodies to ensure that a business perspective is taken into consideration in this area.

Climate issues

Climate is also a very politically sensitive issue, depending on which end of the energy spectrum one is on. The WBCSD is involved here in two ways: first, in bringing some business recommendations to the negotiating table of the conference parties to the UN Climate Change Convention; and secondly, by working on joint implementation programmes (which is where business can make an interesting contribution to the debate in a very progressive way).

Sustainable forests

Sustainable forests is an issue where the WBCSD felt that many industries were affected. Although it appears to have a very sector-specific focus – for example, the management of forests, the effect on the pulp and paper sector, the chlorine issue, the dioxin issue – there is a very substantial trickle-down effect from forest issues and forest management issues into other areas of industrial activity.

Consequently, although this issue is unique to one specific sector, it has some broad-based implications and the WBCSD is tackling this in its work programme.

Financial markets

This focuses on how to provide the kind of information that the financial community would find most relevant, and how to improve the types of environmental information that can be used in financial decision-making.

Central and Eastern Europe

The aim here is to define "environmental" barriers to investments by western companies, and to recommend measures which would assist in removing those barriers. Furthermore, on a practical level, the WBCSD is currently involved in a number of demonstration projects in Central and Eastern Europe.

In the *management tools* area, the WBCSD is involved in two projects, the first dealing with *environmental risk assessment* and the second dealing with the concept of *eco-efficiency*.

The *eco-efficiency* project looks at examples of where and how companies are currently producing and acting in an eco-efficient manner, and attempts to address the issue of how to maximise resources whilst at the same time making cost-effective decisions, without necessarily compromising either one.

The WBCSD is also focusing on developing an *environmental assessment* tool to be used in the context of risk assessment. Guidelines are currently being drafted. Approximately 50 WBCSD members are working on this environmental assessment project. The intention is to produce a set of guidelines to be used in this type of decision-making.

In the *demonstration projects* area, a number of projects are being undertaken, for example:

- projects involving actual industrial plants, which address issues of retrofitting and upgrading the manufacturing plants. This is called the Industrial Process Plant Reconstruction (IPPR) project and focuses on underperforming facilities (in the most part in developing countries) which are either underproducing for environmental reasons, underproducing for efficiency reasons or underproducing in terms of overconsumption of energy. The aim is that instead of closing down those facilities, public/private partnerships should be sought to finance the retrofitting and upgrading of those facilities;
- projects relating to "sustainable project management", dealing with infrastructure projects in developing countries, in the main targeted on waste treatment, wastewater treatment and solid and hazardous waste treatment facilities;
- the PEER project (Partnerships for Environmental Emergency Response), in collaboration with Green Cross International, an initiative started by former Soviet President Gorbachev, which works on a process of education and training for emergency response technicians, primarily in Central and Eastern Europe;
- the "environmental liabilities project", again in Central and Eastern Europe, which focuses on developing protocols for dealing with environmental liabilities, particularly as companies move from being publicly owned concerns to privately held operations. The WBCSD considers what exactly the liabilities are, what some of the appropriate protocols and models currently being developed are, and whether there is a way to enhance and replicate them. The WBCSD has already completed one detailed case study which looks at the Czech Republic and considers how to replicate, in other Central and Eastern European countries, some of the examples discovered there and to work with regulators within some of the other emerging economies;
- the "multiplying managerial skills" project, which has a similar objective to the environmental liabilities project. The WBCSD is now working on establishing an institute in St Petersburg to work on the education and training aspects of managerial skills.

Furthermore, the WBCSD has in the past worked on projects which, for example, dealt with environmental reporting, and guidelines for design for the environment.

Besides the current work programme, the WBCSD is constantly following and participating in the environmental debate to determine where business action and input are needed and, in particular, organising seminars and conferences to analyse emerging environmental trends and their consequences for business.

With members in 36 countries representing more than 20 major industrial sectors, the WBCSD is a powerful business voice on sustainable development issues. It plays an important role in developing closer cooperation between business, government and others, and in encouraging high standards of environmental management in business itself.

The projects described above are the practical out-working of the WBCSD's mission: to provide business leadership as a catalyst for change towards sustainable development, and to promote the attainment of eco-efficiency through high standards of environmental and resource management in business. Ultimately, putting the theory into practice is absolutely essential if the concept of sustainable development is to become reality over the coming years.

Chapter 16
Environmental Risks and Rewards for Business; New Challenges for the Twenty-first Century

Herbert Enmarch-Williams
Solicitor and Head of the Environment – Health – Safety Group at Lawrence Jones Solicitors, London

The preceding chapters of this book all stemmed from a conference entitled "Environmental Risks and Rewards for Business", which was staged in Copenhagen in May 1995 by EU-LEX International Practice Group together with the Centre for Environmental Law and Policy and Foreningen Af Registrerede Revisorer. The Conference was an attempt to examine a variety of the themes and issues in the environmental arena facing European business as it heads towards the twenty-first century.

Undoubtedly, there are many such issues and the conference covered only some of the main topics. Nevertheless, it was an opportunity – coinciding with the appointment of a new European Commission and a new Environment Commissioner (Ritt Bjerregaard who, being a Dane, was expected to bring a Nordic, pro-environment perspective to the job) – to speculate upon what the growing concern over environmental issues and the growing level of environmental regulation world-wide would mean for companies in terms of legal, financial and other risks. Conversely, what would this mean in terms of business opportunities?

The development of the debate in the environmental arena can perhaps be characterised in terms of waves of activity. The *First Wave* could be seen as the awakening of mass public environmental consciousness. This was sparked in particular by events such as the publication of Rachel Carson's *The Silent Spring*, the Love Canal incident (the major influence in the pressures which led to the US Superfund scheme), the nuclear incidents at Three Mile Island and Chernobyl, the chemical accidents at Bhopal and Seveso, and major shipping incidents such as the *Exxon Valdez*, the *Amoco Cadiz* and the *Braer*. This wave culminated, one might say, in the electoral popularity of the European Green parties which perhaps reached its zenith during the 1989 European Parliament elections, before subsiding somewhat (although some might say only temporarily; the Greens appear to be resurgent in Germany at present).

The *Second Wave* could be seen as the realisation by mainstream politicians (in particular) and policy-makers that public environmental concern, or environmentalism to put it in another way, not only was here to stay, but also was having a serious effect upon public priorities for the direction of government economic policies and (if one takes a more cynical view) voting preferences.

The culmination here can be seen in the 1992 United Nations Conference on Environment and Development, commonly known as the Earth Summit or the Rio Summit. In an unprecedented fashion, a coterie of the world's heads of government and state assembled to discuss the globe's environmental problems and to introduce laws to begin to address these problems. Several treaties were signed (and subsequently ratified), including a Convention on Climate Change, which would have major ramifications for economies and business world-wide.

Although there was some suspicion (to an extent justified) that this global eco-political jamboree might end in broken promises and endless delays in progress, to the surprise of many the Rio Summit appears to have produced genuine progress and momentum towards real change. The business community understandably has particularly been in the line of fire. Sensing the momentous occasion, big business got together before the event to form the Business Council for Sustainable Development which acted to ensure that business would have some kind of voice at the negotiating table at Rio.

The *Third Wave* – our current situation – has been characterised by the growing appreciation, by both business and the more enlightened of the environmental non-governmental organisation (NGO) community, that since industry historically has been the cause of many of the major environmental problems now facing the world, it is industry, to a large degree, that has the means and power to bring about change and improvement. However, this requires a *partnership* approach – particularly between industry, policy-makers and environmental NGOs – if this new approach is to gain the support necessary for implementing the measures which it will entail. Such an approach may prove especially difficult to achieve if it means bringing to the same table parties who have spent the last several decades heavily criticising each other's positions.

In particular, industry has become very sensitive towards some of the more cavalier activities of the environmental NGO community, designed to bring "corporate polluters" to heel. Usually such activities have been aimed at large multi-national companies. These companies, whilst undoubtedly having the capacity to cause major pollution incidents well beyond the scope of most smaller companies, often have in place corporate environmental policies and management systems which – when compared to the level of environmental awareness in industry in general – the environmentalists themselves would surely approve of, however loath to do so. Consequently, there appears to be a real sense of anger and frustration in some sections of industry that their efforts are going unrecognised, and that they remain sitting ducks for the sort of high-profile environmental direct action which is designed mainly to score political points with governments and raise funds for the environmental groups.

It could be added that possibly the failure of some highly activist environmental groups to recognise a genuine desire within certain sections of industry for change may in future be seen as a grievous error, a missed opportunity to garner such support as genuinely exists within industry for higher environmental standards. Already, whilst some groups are embarking upon genuine dialogue with industry (either willingly or, in some cases, seemingly grudgingly and strictly on their own terms), others are beginning to find themselves marginalised. Indeed, what started off as a fresh, challenging movement may become an ossified, luddite neo-institution, starved of funds and finding fewer and fewer friends amongst an increasingly consumerist and politically disillusioned public.

From the environmentalists' point of view however, whilst some companies undoubtedly are making genuine attempts to lead the way in raising environmental standards, many others are making only half-hearted attempts at exploring the real meaning of sustainability at the corporate level, and for some of these it may be a mere public relations exercise. It would be fair to say that industry faces a real conflict between actions and measures needed in these post-recessionary times to ensure survival and growth (particularly at the level of the small or medium-sized company) and the added expense and increased management time involved in raising or complying with higher environmental standards. It would also be fair to say that so far industry in the main has focused upon reducing the cost of, and burdens involved in, doing business even if this is to the detriment of environmental considerations in many instances.

Industry might argue that greater environmental protection will be welcomed only when it can be afforded, but such a stance hardly appears to accord with the principle of *sustainable development* which industry claims to support. Such an approach appears to countenance sacrificing the needs of future generations for the sake of meeting the requirements of the present. It could be concluded that there is a considerable degree of lip-service being paid to the issue.

Certainly, the rabid reaction of some sections of industry to the recent EU-wide discussion on civil liability for environmental damage would suggest that constructive criticism is in short supply in some quarters, probably because at the fundamental level there is a deep distrust of change. It is very interesting that just as Chernobyl has become the "bogey-man" for advocates of opposition to nuclear power – a stance seen as unreasonable by the nuclear industry (which holds the view, with some justification, that "it could never happen here") – likewise the US experience with the Superfund clean-up system has become the universal bogey-man for all who wish to oppose any movement towards a harmonised system of liability for environmental damage within the European Union. It could be argued that since Europe can now act with the benefit of hindsight of the US experience (something denied to the Americans themselves), the retort "it could never happen over here" might be equally applicable.

It is no coincidence that this *Third Wave* comes at the same time that the environmental debate is being seen less in terms of political protest and activism, or even legislative action at the national and supranational levels, than in terms of sustainable development. Attempts have been made elsewhere in this book to define that concept. However, in the context discussed here it can be said that sustainable development also includes the notion of balancing economic growth with environmental protection, albeit not in a crude and simplistic "set-off" fashion. Industry is clearly in the business of creating wealth and producing economic growth, and most certainly a discussion of its aims and activities must be at the heart of the sustainable development debate.

Apposite to the idea that the involvement and cooperation of industry is central to the drive to achieve sustainable development, is the notion that the inevitable arrival of sustainable development as a macro-economic and political philosophy presents both opportunities and threats to business. For example, consumer expectations for "green" products may give environmentally aware and proactive companies the edge in terms of marketing and increased market share. However, for those companies which fail to appreciate the "new dawn" of eco-friendly consumerism, declining and heavily regulated markets may be a real prospect and problem. Of course, this is a black and white way of looking at the issue, but it does at least give pointers to the challenges which some companies inevitably will face in the not-too-distant future. Other threats and opportunities have already been examined in detail in other chapters.

Like this book, the Conference was an attempt to bring proponents from both sides of the fence to the same forum, so as to encourage an exchange of views. It is becoming clear that the way forward in the environmental debate is that of partnership between the different "actors" in this arena – governments, industry, NGOs and others. An exchange of views can only therefore be a good thing, provided it leads to more than simply debate. A talking shop was not the intended purpose of the Conference, nor this book.

Whilst it is clear that business and environmentalists are beginning to talk to (rather than at) each other, and even to use the same language, nevertheless there are many areas of disagreement which lie ahead in the path towards creating a sustainable economy. Furthermore, it is clear that policy-makers have much work to do in understanding what both business and environmentalists are saying, and translating this into credible policy initiatives and good legislation. Reconciling the myriad standpoints taken in this debate is perhaps the major task facing political and business leaders, if apparently overwhelming problems such as global warming are to be tackled successfully at the same time as retaining public support for the initiatives taken. This is because clearly, whatever measures are decided upon, the problems faced are so serious that a substantial change in attitudes and practices will be required almost everywhere. This is implicit in the notion of sustainable development. As has been said by several of the contributors to this book, "business as usual is not a sustainable option".

However, given the pressing need to stimulate growth, eradicate poverty (particularly in developing countries, where anticipated population growth is likely to exacerbate the poverty problem greatly) and increase employment opportunities, whilst at the same time meeting increasing consumer expectations (particularly, but certainly not exclusively, in Western countries) of increased living standards, it is uncertain whether the task has now become almost impossible. "No gain without pain" is the expression which first comes to mind. However, there are serious doubts as to whether Western politicians in particular are prepared to sacrifice the short-term electoral gain that comes from making promises of near-immediate increased prosperity, for the long-term economic and environmental stability which surely carries the greater moral imperative.

What is clear from this book, and the Conference, is that there are a number of areas where major disagreement as to the way forward persists. One of these is the purpose and nature of environmental regulation at EU level.

Many commentators have perceived an unhealthy penchant for harmonising legislation at EU level, apparently for the sake of it. In fairness to the European Commission, there is often a hidden economic justification for harmonising legislation which escapes some critics. For example, EU legislation on nature conservation is often criticised as being so remote from the fundamental purpose of the European Union – the

Single Market (seen by some as the sole justification for the existence of the Union) – that it should be repealed wholesale and dealt with purely at the national level. Nevertheless, the legislation on protecting wild birds and their habitats – often the focus of such criticism (*e.g.* "why should we not treat our birds in the way we want to in our own country?") – is a prime example of the narrower justification for EU environmental legislation (espoused by certain "eurosceptic" politicians during the Maastricht debate) *viz*, the European Union should only deal with transboundary matters; why? Because the wild birds so beloved (perhaps even for culinary purposes) by the citizens of certain EU countries very often spend time, as part of their migratory patterns, resting in or flying through other EU Member States. Similarly, a Single Market justification can be put forward for the much-criticised EU Bathing Water Directive, on account of the possible effects of different levels of safety and cleanliness of Member State bathing waters upon competition within the EU tourism industry (a major source of income for many States), and perhaps also the effects on the growing private-sector water services industries.

However, whilst there may indeed be a real justification for EU harmonising legislation, the policy-makers must always weigh-up the competing interests and considerations involved. What may, on its own, appear to be a perfectly justified priority, might, when balanced against other priorities, be seen unfortunately as non-essential. Furthermore, it might always be possible to achieve the stated aim via non-legislative means.

One might ask the following question then, wherever nature conservation concerns, for example, need to be set against economic development considerations (*e.g.* where the construction of a business park, retail units, new housing and attendant major infrastructure, by a developer in partnership with a central or local authority, necessitates an environmental assessment, the conclusions of which become a major point of contention): has the EU truly ensured that a mechanism exists in the relevant legislation for reaching a balanced solution which takes into account not only the wider concerns which led policy-makers to legislate at EU level in the first place, but also the more intimate local economic or other concerns to or from which policy-makers at EU level may be less sensitive and much further removed or even totally insulated?

It is indeed paradoxical that EU environmental legislation, whilst supposedly based upon the subsidiarity principle at least since the Single European Act 1986, has so often led opponents of development projects to appeal to a central authority at EU level in order to protect what is often primarily a domestic conservation concern, and thereby defeat what appear to be opposing domestic or local economic concerns. The effect is that local citizens may have less control over their environment and economic circumstances than the central authority. One wonders whether sometimes the EU machinery is in effect hijacked by those who feel that the national, regional or local authority has let them down. "Brussels" then becomes a convenient court of last appeal. The declaration in Article A of the Maastricht Treaty, that decisions should be taken "as closely as possible to the citizen", becomes somewhat of a mockery, and the opportunity to consider environmental requirements in the context of economic needs, and vice versa, is lost. It is understandable therefore if business feels aggrieved where EU initiatives appear to treat as absolute, considerations which – according to sustainable development – are relative and need to be skilfully weighed and balanced.

Subsidiarity has also been discussed in this book as the way forward for EU environmental regulation. Despite official protestations to the contrary, environmentalists are probably justified in still being wary of how the principle is being used in practice. As a principle for allocating competences between central and national/local authorities, it cannot really be argued against. Whilst recognising, of course, that in many instances its political use has been deliberately ambiguous (and occasionally somewhat less than honest), it has an obvious democratic pedigree. Certainly, it has a key role to play in the future development of EU environmental legislation, particularly if the "absolutist" tendency in some areas of EU environmental legislation is to be balanced against other concerns. However, suspicions are aroused by the fact that proponents on all sides of the debate far too easily look to subsidiarity as supporting their particular standpoint, despite the fact that when taken together the viewpoints of these proponents remain contradictory. The same subsidiarity which industry believes will lead to less environmental regulation at EU level (and perhaps less regulation altogether) at the same time seems to bolster the environmentalists' arguments for greater environmental protection both at the lower national and regional levels and at EU level.

In addition, it is easy to be suspicious of the fact that this principle appeared to surface into the public debate exactly at the same time as the debate on unemployment, competitiveness and deregulation began to occupy the minds of Europe's leaders following the severe recession at the beginning of the 1990s. Without doubting its historical antecedents, there is a definite smack of political expediency here. Industry may do well, if it wishes to enhance its credibility in the sustainable development debate, to be a little more discerning and judicious in its support for subsidiarity and the reliance upon promises of deregulation which it implies.

This subsidiarity debate has also been about the question of the appropriate degree of harmonisation of legislation within the European Union (harmonisation, of course, being a major part of the rationale behind EU legislation). In this respect, industry's main complaint, it would appear, is not against the harmonisation process per se, but against the practice of harmonising upwards, or, in other words, introducing legislation which takes a very high (and unreasonably high, industry says) baseline for setting standards, and thereby increases the regulatory burden on industry, with consequent cost and employment implications. Harmonisation may bring benefits in terms of creating an EU-wide level playing-field, and this is very important to industry, particularly the larger players and those companies active outside their own purely domestic markets. However, industry does not see the level playing-field concept as an excuse for raising the lowest standards within the EU up to the level of the highest, although clearly some policy-makers do see it this way.

For some, however – and this includes several advocates within certain sectors of industry itself – this process of setting higher levels of compliance across the European Union actually raises environmental standards and increases the competitiveness of industry, especially in growing markets such as the environmental technologies and services sector. That is a view taken, for example, by the Environmental Industries Commission (whose Director, Adrian Wilkes, took part in the conference debate), set up in 1995 in the United Kingdom to lobby for higher standards and better enforcement in environmental legislation. Certainly there is a commonly held view in some quarters – even amongst some pro-business NGOs – that without high environmental standards industry would not in the past have (and will not in the future) improve its environmental performance. It is perhaps unfortunate that advocates of a freer regulatory regime tend to come from those companies which in practice are more environmentally aware and responsible than the average company, and are therefore less in need of the regulatory "stick" but more responsive to the economic "carrot".

This "carrot and stick" approach is becoming much favoured by policy-makers within the European Union. It is believed that companies will respond better to market-oriented solutions to environmental problems than to crude regulations. Unlike the latter, market-oriented solutions can provide economic incentives for environmentally responsible companies and, conversely, penalties or disincentives for recalcitrants. There is then the question of the balance needed between the use of regulations on the one hand and the use of other tools or instruments (economic instruments such as charges and fiscal incentives, and shifting the burden of taxation away from labour towards resources) on the other. Regulation is a relatively easy tool for policy-makers to grasp at, but often it can be a blunt instrument to use, like taking a sledgehammer to crack a nut, to use a colloquial phrase. Furthermore, there are clearly problems with the regulatory "command-and-control" approach such that even policy-makers and regulators are beginning to appreciate – not least, failures in implementation and enforcement of legislation which effectively render some initiatives near-useless.

It is, perhaps, more so the small and medium-sized companies (SMEs), less in the public eye and less responsive to the message of sustainable development, which require legislative "encouragement" before any real progress will be made. Doubtless, many environmentalists would dis-agree. Also, industry representative bodies would no doubt argue that the typical SME is less in a position to bear the added costs of compliance than even a major company would be. Given predictions that the majority of employment and wealth creation opportunities in Europe are likely to be created by SMEs, it is argued – and understandably so – that what SMEs need is not more burdens but rather greater incentives if they are to improve environmental performance and create jobs and wealth at the same time.

The argument that it is only by creating more wealth and economic success that the added resources needed for increased environmental protection can be found, has some weight, if not at the micro-economic level of the individual company's performance then certainly at the macro-economic level of enabling both developed and developing coun-tries to find the resources necessary for implementing sustainable develop-ment at the global level. However, this in no way justifies the view that greater environmental protection cannot presently be afforded. The problems currently faced are too pressing and too enormous to counte-nance delay, and the consequences of delay and further neglect may now be too terrible to contemplate.

Furthermore, there is the question of *intergenerational equity*, as has been mentioned by several of the contributors to this book. "Cheating on our children", to use the words of UK environment minister John Gummer (uttered at the launch in 1994 of the UK Government's own programme for implementing sustainable development) is not a morally justifiable option in terms of the present use of the world's natural resources. Hard-pressed as they might be, it is for business leaders – together with politicians – to begin now to make the undeniably hard choices about the use and allocation of resources, choices which must be made in order to secure a future of equal, wealth-creating opportunities for the next generations to come.

The issues of harmonisation, subsidiarity, market mechanisms and resource allocation all figure in the debate about *competitiveness*. The com-petitiveness issue goes much wider than concerns about regulation, although the role of legislation remains at the core of arguments in this area.

In relation to competitiveness, regulation can be seen as possibly imposing an unfair burden on one's own team, so to speak, which prevents fair
competition with the other team. Given the global nature of the market-
place, this debate focuses on two levels. The first concerns competition
intra the European Union. The second concerns the competitiveness of
EU companies *vis à vis* non-EU companies. This is not only in export
markets but also in terms of competition in home markets with
companies based outside the EU, whose operational costs at home are
significantly less than those of the EU company, perhaps as a result of
lower levels of environmental regulation there. This has already led to the
concern that EU companies will re-site their operations into regimes
where environmental and other standards, and therefore operating costs,
are lower; in effect, exporting pollution – a sort of "environmental
racism".

In relation to competition within EU borders, the key issue for
industry appears to be enforcement, or, to be more specific, the lack or
unevenness of enforcement in certain EU countries. Clearly, proper
implementation and enforcement of EU legislation is a serious problem.
The European Commission has recognised this and is making efforts to
address the problem. However, it is a sensitive area, touching upon
national sensibilities, where criticism of national efforts to implement and
enforce EU rules can easily be seen as a criticism of the nation itself.

Furthermore, although it is said to be common knowledge that certain
EU countries have a laxer attitude towards enforcing EU legislation than
others (and, it is said, are therefore prepared to agree to almost anything
in the Council of Ministers, since they know it will never be enforced in
their own country), the situation is surely more complex than this. Other
issues are the constitutional structure in the relevant country, the
structure of the legal system and access to justice, and even the budgetary
resources available to enforcement agencies, let alone cultural and political traditions in the way the relationship between business and state
authorities is conducted. Unfortunately, however, enforcement will
remain a bone of contention, particularly for the larger industrial concerns in Europe, until the enforcement issue is sorted out.

Hopes have been expressed that the new European Environment
Agency will, at some stage, be given enforcement powers ("real teeth" as
some say) rather than the data-collection powers and duties it presently
has. It must be said that these suggestions are not emanating from the
Agency itself. Despite the obvious shortcomings in the enforcement of
EU environmental legislation, this may be a vain hope, particularly in the
light of the subsidiarity debate. The likelihood of creating another

supranational body with the power to poke its nose into the "nooks and crannies" of national life is not something which current sentiment amongst EU politicians, or indeed their publics, is likely to favour.

Dean Calland, in Chapter 5, dealt with the US experience of enforcement and the role of the US Environmental Protection Agency. It is clear from what was said there that the US experience will colour – to a largely negative effect – any European aspirations for an all-powerful environmental agency. Paradoxically, however, notwithstanding the US experience, one of the repeated calls from delegates and some of the speakers at the Conference was for more (presumably, better and more even-handed) enforcement in Europe, and the response of one of the US speakers was that of amazement!

If competitiveness within the European Union is a thorny issue, then in relation to the EU's relationship with other global trading partners it could be described as a near nightmare. In the absence of an economic and legal framework at the international level involving all the relevant political economies (and, given the difficulties which even EU Member States find in working together, implementing a global Treaty-based framework with sufficient legal guarantees and enforcement powers between the parties is, at very best, mere wishful thinking), realistically the only direction in which the European Union could, in the short term, take its environmental standards unilaterally is surely downwards. To compete on the same level with the so-called tiger economies of the Far East – where the rapid drive towards economic growth hardly leaves time or occasion for raising environmental protection to Western standards – the European Union would probably have to drop its standard of environmental protection to levels which are unlikely to garner the widespread public support necessary for such a drastic course of action. Of course, this is only part of a much wider debate within Europe and in the United States over levels of taxation, and social and employment protection.

If there is an answer to this conundrum, then once again it appears to lie in the concept of sustainable development. Sustainable development poses both opportunities and threats, and risks and rewards for business, as it does for society as a whole. Both this book and the Conference have attempted to explore some of the issues, but there is still much to be done. This comes across never more clearly than in the debate over the need for a new economic model – or rather, a new development model – for Europe.

One of the launch pads for this debate, incidentally, was a meeting co-organised by this author under the auspices of the Centre for Environmental Law and Policy at the London School of Economics in February 1994, where the then Environment Commissioner, Ioannis

Paleokrassas, gave a paper entitled *Crime and Punishment; a New Development Model for Europe*. The ideas then expounded also found their way into the European Commission's White Paper on Growth, Competitiveness and Employment 1994, which perhaps provided the *major* examination of the future development of the European Union this decade, prior to the 1996 Intergovernmental Conference.

It would be grossly unfair for anyone to describe the section in the White Paper on the new development model as merely the environmental "tag-on". Far from being an *ad hoc* addition to Jacques Delors' final grand attempt to put Europe back on the right track, it clearly contained the seeds – approved by the whole Commission – for a fundamental realignment of the EU economic system in a way that moves towards, rather than away from, sustainable development.

The White Paper and the new development model have both been discussed in this book, and whilst they deal with issues very much at the macro-economic level, nevertheless the message is clear for industry. There is likely, at some stage in the future, to be a fundamental change in the way economies are run, with an obvious consequential effect upon how business is conducted. It may be that it is currently impracticable, even near-suicidal, for the European Union to chart such a course alone in the global economy. However, there are some stark realities facing the world, centred around the fact that humankind cannot continue with impunity to use and abuse the environment in the way in which it has done for so many years. The realisation must come, that change is inevitable and, ultimately, only global economic solutions will suffice.

This, it is submitted, is the greatest risk and reward facing business today and in the future. Those in industry who perceive the coming fundamental shift in economic and social patterns and can adjust and adapt to them in good time, will be well-placed to exploit the opportunities which the twenty-first century will present.

However, for those companies unable or unwilling to consider this adjustment, sadly the environmental risks – such as increased liabilities and regulatory penalties, greater restrictions on the availability of finance, added expense and inefficiency of resource use, and poor public profile and public distrust of marketing efforts – may outweigh any other possible rewards of conducting business, right down to the bottom line.

Appendix I
Speech* to the Conference
Environmental Risks and Rewards for Business; the Challenge Facing Industry in Europe (Copenhagen, 11 May 1995)

Ritt Bjerregaard

Member of the European Commission, responsible for the Environment

I am very pleased to have the opportunity to speak at this conference where so many distinguished speakers have been invited. The theme and the issues announced during these two days give the impression of a very balanced approach. I think we are mainly to thank the efficient organisers for this.

I will first make some general remarks about EU environmental policy. I will point out various environmental issues which I think are of importance to industry. These issues will be structured in such a way that I (first) mention some areas where I think that the environmental authorities, in this case the Commission, ought to improve their performance. Finally, I will discuss issues which may seem difficult and burdensome for industry and those which may seem profitable. The common denominator is that they are presently being dealt with or considered by the Commission, so I think industry may as well start to prepare itself in these areas.

First, some general remarks concerning the reality for industry within the Union today. The situation for industry is very complex in relation to environmental protection. I am not denying that. Nevertheless, my message to industry is a very simple one: THINK GREEN! This implies that industry has to learn to include environmental concerns into the running of its day-to-day operations and its long-term planning. It also

* This is the edited text of a speech given by Ritt Bjerregaard at the conference *Environmental Risks and Rewards for Business* in Copenhagen on 11 May 1995.

implies that industry has to realise that taking account of environmental protection is in the self-interest of industry and can be rewarding. In other words, it is in the self-interest of industry to take its share of the responsibility for the protection of our environment.

I realise that often a dark picture of the EU economy has been painted and thereby a dark picture for industry. This picture is painted by colours such as: heavy taxes, huge budget deficits, an unflexible labour market, expensive and insufficient welfare reforms. These factors are severe burdens on the economy, which have resulted in a weak private sector, loss of competitiveness, stagnation and state interventions. Traditionally environmental objectives have been considered a further impediment for industry, on top of this.

Keeping in mind this traditional view of environment being an impediment for industry, I think that this is an old-fashioned and outdated way of thinking which needs to be changed. I will explain why.

A relevant starting point may be to recall the environmental objectives of the Treaty. As you know it is among the tasks of the Commission to achieve these objectives during the coming years. Looking at the Treaty as it was amended in 1992 by the Maastricht Treaty, it is clear that the Member States in 1992 did think green. Article 130, rule of the Treaty deals with objectives such as:

- preserving, protecting and improving the quality of the environment;
- protecting human health;
- prudent and rational utilisation of natural resources.

Summarising these points one can say that the Member States committed themselves to moving towards sustainable development and strengthened the importance of environmental protection by making provision for a specific Community policy on environment. Further, they introduced new principles, such as the principle of integrating environmental aspects into other Community policies. This, of course, includes the policies which affect industry the most.

In *Towards Sustainability*, the European Commission's Fifth Action Programme on the Environment, this new approach is reflected. It lays down the approach whereby everybody – including industry – have their share of the responsibility for the protection of our environment. And as it is stated in the Programme: "industry is not only part of the problem, but also part of the solution".

This approach is taken a step further by the White Paper on Growth, Competitiveness and Employment which was produced in December 1993. Its purpose was to examine how to tackle the problem of unemployment and economic growth in the European Union. In the final chapter, thoughts on a new development model for Europe were included. For the first time in a major policy document from developed countries, it was recognised that short- and long-term policy recommendations to overcome recession and unemployment should also work towards correcting inefficient use of resources in the European economy, namely in relation to labour and nature. The White Paper showed that the current European economic model was characterised by an insufficient use of labour and an excessive use of natural resources resulting in a deterioration of the quality of life. It concluded that there was a need to analyse how economic growth could be promoted in a sustainable way leading to higher intensity of employment and lower intensity of energy and natural resources.

This goes to the very heart of the debate about sustainable patterns of production and consumption set out in the conclusions of the 1992 Rio Earth Summit. The Commission is currently working on this by developing ideas and by identifying key ingredients which will make economic growth and environment more compatible. The conclusion is that the Member States have already started to think green. And the Commission has started the ball rolling. I see no movement against this approach in the present preparation for the 1996 Inter-Governmental Conference on the adjustment of the Treaty. Consequently, in my opinion industry will gain influence in this green process if it thinks green itself and enters into a productive dialogue with the environmental authorities, at all levels.

What then do I see as the most urgent issues for the environmental authorities to deal with and where can we improve our performance? Let me concentrate on a few current issues. Right now we are working with implementing the new Treaty provisions which came into force with the Maastricht Treaty. An important part of this implementation is to get the political message through to decision-makers in business. For industry the keyword is integration. Integration for me neccessitates cooperation and implies shared responsibility. I think that the environmental authorities at all levels will have to become more used to interacting with industry and to increase dialogue. Otherwise the integration of environmental issues into business-related policies for the good of everyone cannot be achieved.

Green tax reform is likely to be considered a long-term integration approach. Currently a CO_2 layer tax is being discussed and a broader discussion on the possibility of using fiscal instruments in general, is on its way.

Greening of taxation means two things. First, the Commission – in line with the ideas set out in the White Paper – recognises the possibility for Member States to undertake broader reforms within their national tax systems. One aspect would be to reduce the indirect cost of labour. Another aspect would be to reduce taxation, which is environmentally unfriendly. (One example is that the possibility of deducting the cost of owning a private car from the tax bill motivates people to have private cars rather than using public and more environmentally friendly forms of transport.)

Secondly, greening of taxation is about the possibility of applying fiscal instruments directly to environmental policy. So far the test case has been the current CO_2 tax discussion. The Union has been unable to reach agreement on a Community tax and the Council has not been able to adopt the Commission's proposal from 1992. The Commission has now decided to amend the 1992 proposal in order to make the directive more flexible to Member States. Until now the CO_2 proposal has been stalled due to the requirement for unanimous decision, which is required in the Treaty, when fiscal instruments are to be adopted by the Council. We will now be preparing guidelines which will allow more flexibility of approach.

Looking to the future, I would like to develop further the possibility for using fiscal instruments in environmental policy. We know that taxation can change behaviour, which is what environmental policy basically is all about. It is a difficult ambition to handle. Member States are not likely to give up the principle of unanimity. Initiatives setting a framework based on the principle of subsidiarity seem to be the solution. The basic point is that there should be a common recognition of the need to reform our fiscal systems so as to make them at least neutral in their environmental impact and to allow for a systematic reaping of the benefits which arise from potential synergies in this field.

Turning to the question of how to improve competitiveness, we cannot ignore that environmental legislation in some respects has the potential to create competitiveness problems. Already, environmental authorities have to start to think green on behalf of Central and Eastern Europe. The environmental aspects of programmes like in PHARE and TACIS have to be strengthened, and environmental protection has to be an absolute precondition for financial support in accordance with those programmes. I am doing my best in that respect and have so far managed to obtain an enhanced status for the environment at the recent revision of TACIS. But a whole lot more has to be done. All these ideas and environmentally progressive policy-making are worthless if the implementation and enforcement of the environmental rules fail. We are at present investigating how to improve this.

We have chosen a broad approach and are looking at the overall chain of legislation. This involves the development, implementation and enforcement of environmental legislation. We are focusing on which measures at which stage induce a positive effect on the enforcement. Improved enforcement is an absolute necessity if we are to reach our environmental objectives. Why is this discussion relevant for industry? It is a highly relevant discussion for simple reasons. Irregular enforcement of Community legislation in general and of environmental legislation in particular, creates distortion of competition.

What will industry then have to be aware of? Many things I am afraid. Again, I will only mention a few major issues. Part of the issues may be grouped under the heading: "unsustainable companies" are out!

It should be realised that for some industries there are immediate gains to be obtained by reducing their emissions and the amount of waste they produce. Emissions and wastes represent raw materials and energy loss, the value of which is often not adequately taken into account by the producers.

I think that we have only seen the start of the waste problems. Lately the Commission adopted a proposal to ban the export of hazardous waste for recycling to non-OECD countries effective as from 1998. The Commission has proposed a total ban on export of hazardous waste. The idea is that it is immoral to dump our dangerous waste in poor countries. But one could easily ask whether the same argument is not equally valid concerning waste in general. As already mentioned the ball has started rolling and industry should join the game by taking on responsibility for the waste it produces.

The ongoing discussion concerning environmental liability I see as another aspect of sustainability. The question of environmental liability has gained importance by the Maastricht Treaty. Article 130, rule states that "environmental damage should as a priority be rectified at source" and that "the polluter should pay". Although the Maastricht Treaty also introduced the subsidiarity principle, it is worth noticing that the Member States at the same time decided to strengthen the environment and to introduce the "polluter pays principle". In the light of the sub-sidiarity principle, my services are currently examining the possible basis and need for a Community liability. This includes thorough economic and legal studies, yet to be completed. My personal impression is that there is such a need. One obvious reason is that pollution is often a transboundary phenomenon. Another reason is that Community liability is necessary in order to preserve competitiveness within the European Union. Without harmonised rules the companies are maybe given the incentive to do what lawyers call "forum shopping". They may be tempted to look around for countries where "it pays" to pollute!

I know that the discussion on Community environmental liability is difficult and that industry often has expressed deep concerns about its potential impact. Nightmare examples from the United States are often mentioned. However, I think that we are in the fortunate position that we have the possibility to evaluate all the good and bad experiences of other countries and to make our decision on this basis. I can inform you that I have no fixed position on this issue yet – only a first impression. Consequently, I am looking forward to having an opportunity to consider the different elements of the discussion, including, I hope, further input from industry.

Another issue on the agenda is Green marketing. Industry is clearly already aware of this and of its potential benefits. Green clothing and cotton products in general are the most recent examples that I can think of. I am very positive towards the idea of green marketing and the use of environmental eco-labels. However, I am aware that the expression has become overused. No standard or criteria applies to this expression so one should be aware that green marketing can be misleading. A discussion on possible criteria, for example how to evaluate life-cycles of the involved products, is needed.

Another aspect of green marketing is the so called "green auditing". One good example I would like to mention is an incentive called "Better House-Keeping in Industries" which is found in the Environmental Management and Auditing Scheme (EMAS). This better house-keeping scheme serves the dual purpose of raising the awareness of the environmental performance in the industry itself and, at the same time, providing it with a verified "green image". This can be used in marketing of the company but can also allow the company to tackle ineffectiveness from both economic and environmental standpoints. In this respect I am very pleased to see that yearly awards for companies on green audits are increasing. I know that such awards already exist, for example in England – and in Denmark an award will be presented for the first time later this year. I think such incentives are very positive trends.

The Commission has also carried out studies in this field which resulted in a report of 16 December 1994 on Guidelines for the European Union on Environmental Indicators and Green Accounting. This initiative is at present concerned essentially with national accounts. Ultimately, the idea is to translate into a more measurable concept, a progress towards sustainable development. Work has been intensified to develop environmental pressure indicators and indices, environmental satellite accounts to existing economic accounts and, in the long run, integrated economic/environmental national accounts. "Green" accounting should become operational in the next five years. I think industry may obtain benefits from this work. A real reflection of the value of our environmental assets in the economy is essential for the public and policy-makers. We can take a simple example: today, if we destroy a forest and build instead a commercial centre or car park this increases our

GDP in the way it is calculated now. This same kind of thinking has to be reflected in the way industry calculates its profits and losses.

In conclusion, I think that companies which fail to take account of the environment are increasingly likely to be marganilised and ultimately out of business. However, I also think that the whole area of environmental protection and sustainable development raises a lot of challenges and opportunities for industry – the only thing to remember is to THINK GREEN.

Appendix II
An Introduction to the European Environment Agency

David Stanners

Programme Manager, The European Environment Agency

The main duties of the European Environment Agency (EEA) may be summarised as follows:

- to produce objective, reliable and comparable information both for those concerned with framing, implementing and further developing European environmental policy (*e.g.* the European Parliament and the European Commission, especially DG XI), and for the wider European public;
- to help in identifying, preparing and evaluating suitable environmental measures, guidelines and legislation;
- to co-ordinate the European Environment Information and Observation Network (EIONET);
- to publish a report on the state of Europe's environment every three years; and
- to liaise with other relevant national, regional and global environmental programmes and institutes.

It is intended that the EEA shall furnish efficient information, which can be used directly in the implementation of EU environment policy. Priority will be given to:

- air quality and atmospheric emissions;
- water quality, pollutants and resources;
- the state of soil, fauna and flora, and biotopes;
- land use and natural resources use;
- waste management;
- noise emissions;
- chemical substances hazardous to the environment;
- coastal protection, in particular transfrontier.

Multinational and global phenomena will be covered, and the socio-economic dimension must also be considered.

The EEA was established by EU Regulation 1210/90 of May 1990, which entered into force in October 1993 following the decision to locate the Agency in Copenhagen. Its new headquarters were inaugurated on 1 November 1994.

The EEA has an Executive Director, who is designated by the Agency's Management Board. The Board comprises one representative from each member country of the Agency (the Member States of the European Union, plus Iceland, Norway and Liechtenstein), two representatives of the European Commission, and two experts nominated by the European Parliament. The Board receives technical assistance from a Scientific Committee.

The basis for all EEA activities is the multi-annual work programme (MAWP). The 10 programme areas of the MAWP (1994–99) are:

(i)   dissemination and pooling of existing information and know-how;
(ii)   periodical reports on the state of the environment;
(iii) guidelines for reports and assessments;
(iv)   media-orientated monitoring;
(v)   source-orientated monitoring;
(vi)   integrated environmental assessments;
(vii) scenarios for environmental improvement;
(viii) instruments and challenges for environmental policy development and implementation;
(ix)   capacity building of the functions of the EEA and EIONET;
(x)   exchange and dissemination of information.

The responsibility for fulfilment of the MAWP tasks will be shared by the EEA with its other working partners within the EIONET, in order to include existing capacities within the Member States in the work of the Agency. These capacities are:

• National Focal Points (NFP);
• Main Component Elements (MCE);
• National Reference Centres (NRC); and
• designated European Topic Centres (ETC).

The first five ETCs were established in 1994 to address several of the priority areas: *Inland Waters, Marine and Coastal Environment, Air Quality, Air Emissions* and *Nature Conservation*. Two new ETCs were established in 1995: *Catalogue of Data Sources,* and *Land Cover*.

The main working partners of the EEA are the EU Services (in particular the Joint Research Centre and Eurostat) and International Organisations. In addition, the EEA cooperates with countries which are not members of the European Union, under special agreement.

Between 1992 and 1994, the EEA Task Force, which prepared the Agency before it was established in Copenhagen, was working in

140

collaboration with UNECE, UNEP, the OECD, the Council of Europe, IUCN, WHO, and Eurostat – and in cooperation with all the countries of Europe – to report on the state of the pan-European environment.

The final report *Europe's Environment: The Dobris Assessment* (which was published in September 1995) – requested by European Environment ministers during their first "Environment for Europe" Conference, held at Dobris Castle near Prague in 1991 – was presented to ministers at their Third Conference held in Sofia in October 1995. The report forms a basis for developing an environmental programme for Europe, and for raising awareness about environmental problems.

The EEA has now been asked to build on this work, and to report on progress on the main issues identified, as well as to establish and improve a pan-European network. As a first step towards the integration of environmental information systems throughout Europe (depending on additional sources of funding being made available, such as from the EU PHARE and TACIS programmes), the EEA is to provide information and assistance in particular for the extension of EIONET and the Topic Centres on Inland Waters, Air Quality and Air Emissions to PHARE countries, and for the application of CORINE methodologies in other countries. The countries of the Mediterranean Basin and those of Central and Eastern Europe have expressed considerable interest in this cooperation, and some collaborative work has already begun.

With the development of a European information system, the EEA aims to realise three main objectives:

(i) To provide an answer to the "what-is-where question", through the development of a Catalogue of Data Sources.

(ii) To organise information pools, based on existing and ongoing initiatives giving added value through combining different information sources, which focus on "monitoring data" and explanatory material.

(iii) To have an active role in data and information dissemination, focusing on public information and participation, and on the use of emerging new technologies including CD-ROM and public networks.

Appendix III
Examples of Environmental Regulation from the 15 Member States of the European Union

Edited by Bryan Riley
Partner, Watson Burton Solicitors, Newcastle-upon-Tyne

Austria

Kornelia Fritsch-Vallaster
Partner, F Schwank Law Offices, Vienna

Environmental legislation

Austria has adopted a positive attitude towards the environment for many years and already had, therefore, a comprehensive system of environmental laws before it became a member of the European Union on 1 January 1995. In many respects, Austria had even more stringent rules than the EU legislation. Accordingly, the Austrian Government was pleased that it was able to negotiate the "horizontal solution" with the European Union in its Accession Treaty, whereby it can maintain its higher standards – especially product standards – for at least a four-year period with a review process on the EU's side in the interim. Apart from this, Austria has implemented most of the EU legislation.

Austria has enacted an all-encompassing constitutional law in respect of environmental protection. The specific environmental provisions are to be found in a wide range of administrative laws and regulations throughout the Austrian legal system; as Austria is now a federal State, these are issued and enforced by federal as well as provincial authorities. To find the responsible authority it is necessary to look at the relevant law or regulation. Although this may be regarded as cumbersome the eco-federal policy is seen as an advantage in that the provinces can solve the ecological problems at their sources which, in most cases, is more effective.

The Austrian system of environmental law is dominated more by "command and control" than by private engagement. Control is based mainly on strict licensing requirements which involve compliance with conditions attached to the licence, supervision by the authorities and reporting requirements. The legislation is mostly directed at the operators in the sense of "the polluter pays" principle. The use of economic instruments which do not entail direct payment by the polluters to the public authorities, but which may have an effect on environmental policy-making at source, are gaining more and more importance and are now under discussion.

Main areas of environmental legislation

LICENSING OF COMMERCIAL ACTIVITIES: AUSTRIAN BUSINESS CODE

This Code contains provisions regulating the requirement of a plant licence for carrying out commercial activities affecting the environment. Depending on the type of activity involved, its impact on the environment and the wastes generated, an application for a normal or reduced licence has to be made to the responsible authority which is normally the district administrative authority (Bezirksverwaltungsbehörde).

NATURAL RESOURCES: FORESTRIES ACT, MINING ACT AND WATER LAW ACT

Due to geographical circumstances and historical facts, the Forestries Act and the Mining Act have their roots in the middle of the nineteenth century when Austria had already recognised the importance of the protection of its forests and its natural resources. The Water Law Act goes back to 1934.

The preservation of forests and the limitation of emissions of any kind which affect the quality of water (surface and ground water) have especially benefited Austria's environment.

The Mining Act initially dealt mainly with mining licences, but since the amendment in 1994, the interests of neighbours and, in fact, the environment, got greater protection.

A common characteristic and interesting feature of all three laws is that they include special and more stringent provisions for liability, which foresee liability without fault.

AIR: EMISSIONS ACT, SMOG ACT, OZONE ACT, MAINTENANCE OF CLEAN AIR ACT FOR BOILER PLANTS

As a land-locked country bordering on eight countries, imported air pollution is a major problem for Austria and accounts for the major part of acid depositions in the country. In addition, the escalating transport routes through Austria result in increased emission of vehicle pollutants such as nitrogen oxide. Nevertheless, due to stringent emissions marginal values and the fact that only unleaded fuel is allowed, as well as continuous control, the ratio of "air pollutants to GDP" is one of the lowest in the world according to an OECD report. It has to be stated that these laws provide for process-related as well as product-related measures.

Appendix III

WASTE: WASTE MANAGEMENT ACT

The Waste Management Act has been in force since 1990 and contains, after several amendments, the main provisions of the existing waste laws. It regulates the avoidance, recycling and deposition of waste as well as the restriction of importation to, exportation from and transportation of, waste throughout Austria and allows for the legislators to issue all kinds of regulations in pursuit of their goals.

Avoidance of waste has become the leading principle, with the avoidance and recycling of packaging waste receiving particularly high priority. Pursuant to the regulation on packaging the producers and distributors are obliged, without passing on the cost to the consumer, to take back, collect and recycle their products used and brought into circulation. Either they have to comply with this requirement themselves, or become a member of the Austrian Waste Recycling Corporation (ARA) which will undertake the duties instead. Becoming a member, of course, requires payment of fees. The fees are low, with the result that there is no incentive for the producers and distributors to change their attitude and avoid creating waste instead of merely recycling and depositing it.

The Waste Management Act also places companies under an obligation to appoint one employee as the waste agent of the plant.

DANGEROUS GOODS: CHEMICAL SUBSTANCES ACT

The Chemical Substances Act, which is the successor of the Poison Act, has been in force since 1 January 1989. It regulates the marketing of chemical substances, preparations and products and also partly their disposal.

Due to the "horizontal solution" Austria is permitted to retain higher standards than the European Union in this area for at least four years. As these standards are all product related there is a constant conflict between environmental and economic interests.

GENERAL ISSUES: ENVIRONMENTAL INFORMATION ACT AND
ENVIRONMENTAL IMPACT ASSESSMENT ACT

In order to comply with further environmental EU legislation, Austria, as early as 1993 brought into force the Environmental Information Act and, in 1994, the Environmental Impact Assessment Act. Both acts transfer power to the people in the form of granting free access to environmental data stored by the public administration and setting up a forum to object against large projects having considerable effect on the environment, respectively. A study organised by the Ministry for the Environment has shown that even after two years of application of the Environmental Information Act the general public is largely unaware of this law. People ask for information only when they are personally affected.

To implement the EU Regulation on Environmental Management Audit Scheme (EMAS) Austria issued the Regulation on the Accreditation and Supervision of Environmental Verifiers as well as the Organisation of a List of Verified Sites in July 1995. It is worthwhile noting that this EU legislation, which has direct effect in Austria, is no longer based on the "command and control" principle, but allows voluntary participation of companies in the industrial sector.

Enforcement, supervision and intervention

The enforcement of environmental provisions, the supervision of commercial activities and intervention in the case of any breaches are carried out by the various federal, provincial or district authorities referred to in the relevant legislation. These authorities have wide powers, depending on the applicable Act.

These powers include:

- imposition of conditions on licences;
- closing or suspension of operations;
- inspection;
- imposition of recording requirements;
- imposition of notifications/obligations;
- imposition of preventive measures.

Under Austrian legislation, a considerable number of offences and penalties are imposed. They may be of administrative or criminal character, with fines up to ATS 500,000 or imprisonment, although there have been few prosecutions to date.

Liability

In cases of environmental protection, the Austrian legal system grants civil law remedies under the Austrian Civil Code in order to recover damages. The Civil Code also entitles the owners and lessees of real estate to demand the cessation of all their neighbours' activities which result in emissions of waste water, smoke, gases, heat, odours, vibrations, etc in excess of the maximum permissible levels customary in that region which impair the customary use of the real estate in a stricter way regardless of fault. If the emissions emanate from a facility certified by the authorities, it is not possible to seek an injunction. The argument that whenever a licence has been granted by the authorities there is no illegality, makes it especially difficult to obtain damages.

Future legislation

The Austrian Ministry of Justice has already published a draft environmental liability law. This is still the subject of debate as it is very ambiguous with regard to its range of application, the shift of onus of proof towards the polluter, and issues of compulsory insurance etc.

Also under discussion is the use of economic instruments in order to protect the environment, such as taxes on energy. This has become a political issue in that Austrian industry objects to further financial burdens on enterprises and warns of the unbearable pressure of competition.

Amendments may be made to some of the legislation mentioned above in order to comply with EU legislation, but they are not of great importance. One of the most important steps in the EU environmental policy for industry will be the Directive on Integrated Pollution Prevention and Control which will have to be implemented by national law. This Directive will hold the key to the process of harmonisation of standards for industrial plants in the EU Member States.

In the future, as environmental policy has become a transboundary issue, Austria will have to be ready to face the big challenge of the harmonisation of environmental standards by enforcing its higher standards throughout Europe. However, harmonisation might not be practical for all environmental issues due to different problems in different countries.

Belgium

Mario Deketelaere

Professor of Environmental Law, Catholic University of Louvain
Consultant to De Meester, Ballon, Billiet & Co, Brussels

Introduction: constitutional framework, adoption and development of environmental law

Due to a process of constitutional reform, which began in 1970 and was completed in 1993, the Belgian State has become a federal union consisting of three autonomous regions: the Flemish Region, the Walloon Region and the Brussels Region.

As a result of this process of constitutional reform, an increasing number of powers and financial means has been delegated to each of the regions. In addition, the power to adopt and enforce environmental regulations has gradually been transferred from the federal to the regional level.

In particular, the regional legislature has been granted powers over technical environmental standards, waste disposal, hazardous facilities, ground and surface water protection and land use. Only a few environmental areas remain within the authority of the federal legislature: transportation of waste, all aspects of nuclear waste, workers' health and safety regulations, and the formulation of product standards and specifications.

With respect to the enforcement of environmental laws and regulations, the regional authorities have the power to impose a wide variety of administrative sanctions (*e.g.* withdrawal of environmental permit; order to remove waste and/or clean-up of contaminated sites). The municipal and other local authorities also have certain administrative enforcement powers in the environmental field.

The criminal enforcement of environmental laws is controlled at the federal level: public prosecutors may enforce criminal sanctions against violators.

Finally, private parties may bring civil suits in the federal courts to seek redress for violations of environmental law and to seek compensation for environmental damages.

An overview is given of the requirements which companies doing business in Belgium must meet on the environmental level, as well as a survey of the various kinds of liability they may face in this respect.

Regional environmental bodies

The "regionalisation" of the powers with respect to the adoption and enforcement of environmental law has led to the creation and growth of regional bodies and governmental agencies in the environmental field.

Flemish Region

AMINAL

In the Flemish Region, the most important administrative environmental body is the environmental directorate of the Flemish Government, commonly known as "AMINAL" (Administratie Milieu, Natuur, Land en Waterbeheer). It consists of eight departments: general environmental policy, Europe and the environment, environmental permits, environmental inspection, water, land use/management, nature and forests.

OVAM AND VMM

In addition to AMINAL, several specialised, semi-independent governmental agencies have been set up to deal with specific environmental issues:

OVAM (Openbare Afvalstoffenmaatschappij voor het Vlaamse General), the Flemish Public Waste Company, has important powers in the field of waste disposal: development of waste management plans, registration and public clean-up of polluted sites, and receipt of the notification concerning removal of waste, etc).

OVAM also has the power to order the removal of waste and/or the clean-up of contaminated land.

VMM (Vlaamse Milieumaatschappij), the Flemish Environmental Company, carries out various administrative tasks with respect to the pollution of surface water and air: development of water purification programmes, the drafting of annual reports on emission of polluting substances into the air, and the creation of a network for the systematic measuring of water and air quality.

Walloon Region

In the Walloon Region, the most important governmental agency in the environmental field is the Walloon Regional Office for Waste (office régional wallon des déchets), which has enforcement powers with respect to waste disposal, although these are more limited than those of OVAM.

Brussels Region

In the Brussels Region, most of the enforcement powers with respect to environmental issues are exercised by the Brussels Institute for Environmental Management (Brussels Instituut voor Milieubeheer/Institut bruxellois pour la gestion de l'environnement).

Environmental permits and standards

FLEMISH REGION

In the Flemish Region, most of the former permits and procedures for obtaining those permits have been consolidated by the so-called "VLAREM" regulation of 6 February 1991, which implemented the Decree of 28 June 1985 on the environmental permit. VLAREM promotes the concept of a single comprehensive environmental permit and procedure.

Since 1 September 1991 the following permits and procedures were integrated into the "environmental permit" (milieuvergunning):

- the operating permit for hazardous facilities;
- the permit for the discharge of waste water;
- the permit for the disposal of toxic waste;
- the permit for the disposal of non-toxic waste;

VLARAM I contains a list of classified hazardous installations, divided into three classes. Installations of class 1 and 2 need an environmental permit, from respectively the provincial and municipal authorities. For class 3 facilities, notification to the municipal authorities only is required.

The environmental permit covers all aspects of the classified activity which may affect the environment (e.g. operation of the facility, discharges into surface waters, air emission standards, storage of waste, etc).

On 7 January 1992, the Flemish Government adopted the VLAREM II regulation, also based on the Decree of 28 June 1985 on the environmental permit. This regulation, which became effective on 1 January 1993, listed a wide variety of general conditions, to be respected by all the companies operating in the Flemish Region and a large number of specific sectoral conditions for different kinds of activities.

However, the Conseil d'Etat considered that VLAREM II was illegal (judgment of 6 October 1994) and later even nullified the regulation (judgment of 16 March 1995) for a violation of the procedural rules for establishing the regulation because the competent Minister of Environment did not ask the obligatory advice of the Section Legislation of the Conseil d'Etat to be respected by all companies operating in the Flemish Region.

On 31 July 1995, a new VLAREM II regulation was adopted, which came into force on 1 August 1996. In contrast with the nullified VLAREM II, the new VLAREM II also contains provisions which apply to non-classified activities or installations.

Finally, the Flemish Regulation of 23 March 1989 provides that with respect to a number of projects an environmental impact assessment must be carried out before the application for the environmental permit.

WALLOON REGION

In the Walloon Region, the permit for the operation of hazardous facilities is still regulated by the procedures existing under the General Regulations for the Protection of Workers (Algemeen reglement voor de arbeidsbescherming/Règlement général pour la protection du travail – ARAB/RGPT).

Each person who wants to exploit a facility classified as hazardous must apply for an operating permit.

The hazardous facilities are divided into two classes. The operating permit for a class 1 facility is delivered by the provisional authorities, and that for a class 2 facility by the municipal authorities.

In contrast to the Flemish and the Brussels Regions, where the environmental permit is comprehensive, there exists, in addition to the operating permit, a number of other permits and procedures for some specific environmentally harmful activities: discharge of waste water, waste disposal, mining, etc.

The Decree of 11 September 1985 and its implementing Regulation of 15 July 1990 provides that the operating permit for hazardous installations and the building permit with respect to some listed activities must be preceded by an environmental impact assessment.

BRUSSELS REGION

In the Brussels Region, a new regime of comprehensive environmental permit became effective on 1 January 1993. The legal framework of this environmental permit (milieuvergunning) is laid down in the Ordinance of 30 July 1993.

The Ordinance contains a list of classified hazardous installations, which are divided in to three classes: I.A., I.B. and I.I. For the exploitation of all these facilities an environmental permit is required.

Furthermore, the class I.A. facilities – which are the most hazardous – always require an environmental certificate before an environmental permit can be delivered. The certificate prescribes if and under what conditions an environmental permit can be given. An environmental certificate may also be required for class I.B. facilities.

A number of projects are submitted to an environmental impact assessment, which must be carried out before the application of the environmental permit. These projects are listed in the Ordinance of 30 July 1992.

Waste

FLEMISH REGION

By a Decree of the Flemish Council of 14 April 1994, the Flemish Waste Decree of 2 July 1981 was greatly amended. The new Waste Decree became effective on 7 May 1994.

The (Federal) Law of 22 July 1974 on Toxic waste has been abolished for the most part by the renewed decree (as far as it concerns its applicability in the Flemish Region). Consequently, toxic waste (like asbestos and PCBs) is now also regulated under the Waste Decree of 2 July 1981.

The producer of industrial waste must keep and maintain a waste register in which the nature, origin, composition, quantity, destination and manner of useful application or disposal is mentioned. He is also obliged to make a yearly notification to the Public Waste Company (OVAM). Industrial waste must be disposed of or usefully applied in one of the following manners:

- by the company itself, in which case an environmental permit is required;
- by delivery to a permitted waste treatment installation;
- by delivery to a registered waste collector.

Finally, it is prescribed that adequate measures must be provided to prevent any impact on the environment caused by waste during handling and even temporary storage.

If waste is disposed of or abandoned in an unlawful way, OVAM will require the violator to remove the waste. In case the wrongdoer does not fulfill this obligation or if he cannot be found, OVAM will remove the waste and try to recover the costs from the wrongdoer (if he is found).

The international import and export of waste is regulated by the EC Regulation no. 259/93 of 1 February 1993.

WALLOON REGION

In the Walloon Region, waste disposal is regulated by the Decree of 5 July 1985 on waste. It contains rules which are similar to those applicable in the Flemish Region. There is a general prohibition on the abandoning of waste. The operators and persons involved in various kinds of waste disposal activities must obtain a permit or licence.

The (national) Law of 22 July 1974 on toxic waste – regulating the production and disposal of this type of waste – is still applied in the Walloon Region. The international import and export of waste is regulated by the EC Regulation No 259/93 of 1 February 1993.

BRUSSELS REGION

The legislative framework for the disposal of waste in the Brussels Region is laid down in the Ordinance of 7 March 1991 in the prevention and management of waste.

The unlawful disposal of waste is prohibited. Authorities are required to remove unlawfully abandoned waste and to recover the costs of such removal from the wrongdoer.

The Ordinance does not impose a specific permit for facilities involved with waste disposal activities. Instead, specific provisions dealing with the protection of the environment may be inserted in the environmental permit or in the building permit.

The international import and export of waste is also regulated by the EC Regulation No 259/93 of 1 February 1993.

New developments – liability for clean-up costs of polluted sites

Pollution of the soil in Belgium has become so serious as to necessitate property redevelopment.

There are a large number of regulations, on the basis of which, depending on the prevailing situation, the regional and local public authorities are empowered to adopt certain measures arising from soil pollution.

In the Flemish Region, nowadays, the public is debating and demanding soil decontamination. The Public Waste Company (OVAM) has been monitoring polluted sites since the early 1980s and plays a crucial role in the clean-up of contaminated land.

However, until 1995 the legal framework did not allow for systematic clean-up of soil pollution. The absence of clear criteria for assessment and regulations meant that it was only the general principles of proper administration and the duty to take care of the environment imposed by civil law, which provided the necessary legal criteria by which the degree of acceptability of property redevelopments which have been, or are to be, carried out by public authorities, could be judged.

The liability for the costs of redevelopment of such soil was regulated in an inflexible manner. The position of the innocent buyer of polluted soil was not taken into account. Therefore, a specific and comprehensive new piece of legislation was prepared. Recently, on 22 February 1995, the Flemish Council approved the new Decree on Soil Decontamination. The main characteristics of the new decree can be summarised as follows:

- distinction is made between "historical pollution" (which was caused before the entry into effect of this decree, *i.e.* before 29 October 1995) and "new pollution" (which was caused after this decree became effective, *i.e.* after 29 October 1995);
- the Public Waste Company (OVAM) will make an inventory of the polluted soils in the Flemish Region; the data relating to the pollution of the soil will be registered; this register will be used as a guideline for the property redevelopment policy of the public authorities;
- the obligation to carry out a soil redevelopment scheme is imposed upon the actual operator of the ground, both for historical and new pollution;
- the originator of new soil pollution will be held strictly liable for the cleaning-up of the polluted site;
- the general liability regime that applies nowadays remains valid for historical pollution;
- if the operator can prove that he has not caused the historical pollution, he has no obligation to carry out a proper redevelopment scheme and his liability will be restricted to the cost of avoiding any further pollution;
- for the transfer of all land, a soil certificate given by OVAM will be required;
- for the transfer of "risk sites" an exploratory investigation of the soil is compulsory.

Apart from the provisions regarding the setting-up of a register of contaminated sites by OVAM (which will become effective on 29 April 1996) and the delivery of soil certificates by OVAM (enforcement date to be decided by the Flemish Government) the new decree came into force on 29 October 1995. In the Walloon and the Brussels Region there is not yet any specific legislation on soil decontamination.

Study of environmental liabilities

Companies operating in Belgium may incur liabilities in respect of environmental damage either by violating environmental regulations or by causing damage to third parties.

Liability resulting from violations of environmental regulations and/or environmentally related damage to third parties may take one of the following three forms: administrative sanctions and/or criminal sanctions and/or civil liability for environmental damage caused to third parties.

ADMINISTRATIVE SANCTIONS

Administrative sanctions are applied wholly by administrative bodies, without prior intervention of the courts. Apart from criminal sanctions, they may also be imposed on a company.

These sanctions include a wide variety of measures: suspension and/or withdrawal of a permit, closing of the company, removal of dangerous materials, etc. Administrative measures may be imposed by different authorities (the mayor of a municipality, the governor of the province, the environmental department of a specialised governmental agency (*e.g.* OVAM).

For example, the Flemish Environmental Permit Decree of 28 June 1995 provides the following administrative sanctions in case of violation or non-compliance with environmental regulations (*e.g.* VLAREM I and II, terms imposed by the operating or environmental permit):

- suspension or cancellation of the permit;
- mandatory shutdown of the installation;
- cleaning of the installation.

Enforcement of environmental regulations on an administrative level is the exclusive responsibility of the administrative authorities.

The regional administration has recently been reorganised and a large number of official positions are still vacant. Therefore, there is an obvious problem of under staffing. However, it is expected that the administrative authorities will, in the near future, invest substantially more resources in more rigorous enforcement of environmental regulations.

CRIMINAL SANCTIONS

Certain violations of the environmental regulations also entail criminal sanctions.

In the Flemish Region, the new or renewed environmental legislation contains very severe criminal sanctions. When the VLAREM regulations are violated, standards laid down in the Environmental Permit Decree of 28 June 1985 prescribes criminal fines from BF 200 (x 200) to BF 100.000 (x 200) and imprisonment from eight days to one year.

The criminal sanctions provided for in the renewed Waste Decree of 2 July 1981 are as follows: fines from BF 100 (x 200) to BF 10.000.000 (x 200) and/or imprisonment from one month to five years.

It is very important to note that a corporate entity cannot be the subject of a criminal procedure. Criminal action can be enforced only against the physical person who is the author of the environmental offence. Consequently, company managers and directors, as well as company workers, may incur criminal sanctions for violations of environmental regulations.

Although case law illustrates that it is sometimes very difficult to identify the person actually responsible for the offence and a criminal prosecution may therefore not succeed, the criminal liability risk for managers, director and workers is not to be underestimated.

So far, public prosecutors have shown limited interest in the prosecution of environmental violations. However, there is a clear tendency for more severe action in enforcing environmental regulations by criminal prosecution.

For the sake of completeness, reference must be made to a proposal of the "Commission Bocken" which aims to introduce criminal liability for corporate entities. According to this proposal, the company itself will be held criminally liable for environmental offences and may incur severe fines.

CIVIL LIABILITY FOR DAMAGE CAUSED BY ENVIRONMENTAL POLLUTION

Fault or tort liability

Any third party who suffers damage may bring court action against the plant operator based upon tort law or strict liability rules. The starting point of liability for environmental damage in Belgium is fault or tort liability (Art 1382 of the Civil Code). The victim must show that the environmental damage is the result of a fault on the part of the defendant.

Fault

The violation of any statutory provision in itself constitutes a fault. In view of the increasing scope of environmental legislation, this application of the fault criteria is of great importance for the compensation of environmental damage.

Compliance with all of the environmental regulations does not, however, provide any defence and does not protect the polluter against liability.

The potential polluter, in order to avoid liability, must not only observe all statutory provisions, but must also act with due care.

A number of elements appear to be of decisive significance in the application of the general duty to control pollution:

- compliance with state of the art technology (use of best available technology not entailing excessive costs);
- adherence to prevailing professional standards;
- investigation to identify and prevent the risks of pollution to which the activities may give rise.

Environmental damage

Pollution has various negative effects, most of which result in damages of a traditional type which can be compensated: physical injury and death, property damage, loss of amenities, economic damages, moral damages, and pain and suffering.

It is difficult to pursue before a court of law compensation for damage to the eco-system itself – the so-called ecological damages – or to parts of nature which have not been individually appropriated by man, in view of the fact that traditional liability rules are only concerned with individual interests.

Causation

The theoretical definition of the notion of cause is very broad under Belgian law. However, the establishment of the actual link between damage and the alleged polluting event remains a matter of considerable difficulty for the victim.

Strict liability

A number of strict liability rules exist which are of particular importance for the compensation of environmental damage.

The main characteristic of strict liability is that the victim does not need to prove that the damage was caused by the (even rightful) conduct of the defendant. The damage is legally attributable to the liable individual because he bears responsibility for one of the risk factors which contributed to the occurrence of the damage.

First, judicial practice awards compensation for nuisance whenever the use that someone makes of his property causes greater harm to the neighbours than might be gained by the property owner.

According to Article 1384 (1) of the Civil Code the guardian of a defective object is liable for all damage caused by the defect of this object. This provision implies liability in many cases of accidental pollution, but is also relevant with regard to soil pollution.

According to recent case law "any abnormal characteristic feature that can cause damage" is considered as a "defect". With regard to polluted soils, the existence of a considerable concentration of heavy metals may lead to the existence of an abnormal characteristic of the soil and may be considered as an intrinsic defect. Therefore, Article 1384(1) of the Civil Code can provide a basis to recover the costs of property redevelopment from the party who has actual control of the ground.

Article 85 of the Budgetary Law of 24 December 1976 deals with liability for the costs incurred by the civil protection or fire services of cleaning up after a pollution incident. According to this provision, the Government must recover the incurred costs from the owner of the products which caused the pollution.

According to Article 7 of the Law concerning Toxic Waste (22 July 1974), the manufacturer of toxic waste is strictly liable for any damage, regardless of its nature, which may be caused, especially during transportation, destruction, neutralisation or disposal, even if the manufacturer did not initiate the process in question.

Under the new Flemish Decree of 22 February 1995, the operator of a facility classified as hazardous under the Environmental Permit Decree is held strictly liable for the costs of cleaning up new soil pollution.

Denmark

Poul Hvilsted
Partner, Bech, Bruun & Trolle, Copenhagen (Guest Speaker)

Within the concept that environmental regulation denotes either a risk or a challenge to industry it is appropriate to define the two concepts of "risk" and "challenge". A risk is an unforeseeable adverse event which you hope, by all means, to avoid. A challenge is a recognised obstacle which you intend to overcome. The development of Danish environmental law shows that industry must face environmental regulation and see it as a challenge which needs to be met in a responsible manner.

The objective of environmental legislation in Denmark is codified in the Environmental Protection Act of 1991.

Recent developments in Denmark are as follows.

Liability

After a period of legal uncertainty, strict liability was imposed by law in 1994.

The Act on strict liability goes very much along the lines contained in the Green Paper of the EU Commission of 1993. This similarity has implications – any weaknesses in the Green Paper have been adopted into Danish law. A strict liability regime has only come into force as far as the potential environmental impact of specific activities such as metal works, concrete works, chemical production and storage facilities for hazardous chemicals, waste treatment facilities etc are concerned.

Strict liability has not been enacted *ex post facto* and will only be applicable to environmental damage caused by events or acts dated after 1 July 1994. The strict liability rule was enacted to secure legal certainty, with the aim of making environmental damages insurable. However, major areas still remain unclear. This is partly because sections of industrial plant will be governed both within the Act on strict liability and outside of the Act. For years to come, it will remain uncertain to what extent it will be possible to demonstrate the date of the activity which caused environmental damage.

It is an obvious weakness – as was the Green Paper – that the extent of strict liability was not defined by way of substances rather than activities.

For activities not defined in the Act of 1994 and for environmental damage caused by acts prior to 1 July 1994, a regime of culpable negligence remains in force. This means that the injured party (primarily the public) needs to demonstrate the cause, *culpa*, extent of damage and the non-expiry of statutory limitation. This has proved to be very difficult. A Supreme Court verdict recently endorsed a state of the art defence. Another recent Supreme Court verdict has held the 20-year statutory limitation absolute, meaning that if the cause is dated more than 20 years prior to the damage, or the discovery of the damage, this in itself will imply dismissal.

Consequently, Danish law appears to apply the "polluter pays" principle; in reality, however, implementation is extremely difficult.

Environmental approvals

Ever since the adoption of the first Environmental Protection Act in 1974, certain types of potential environmental impact activity would need prior administrative approval before their commencement.

The approval system has, over the last 20 years, become increasingly sophisticated and, in 1993, activities already in operation in 1974 were subject to environmental approval. In the period until the year 2000, new approval procedures will be developed, with the objective that all environmental impact activities will be regulated by environmental permits by the year 2000.

According to regulatory mechanisms today, the permit will contain a very detailed description and regulation of the business (see below) using, to an increasing degree, standardised limit values.

CONTENTS OF APPROVAL

- Location
- Processes and technical facilities and arrangements
- Emissions to air (composition of compounds, origin and limit values)
- Emission to surroundings
- Noise emission (limit values DbA)
- Waste water (volumes, limit values of compounds and disposal methods, possible recipient quality, monitoring and control)
- Other waste (volumes storage, transport and disposal methods)
- Storage facilities of substances (tank facilities, technical requirements such as chemical resistance ability)

- Self control and monitoring
- BAT programme
- Risk management
- Reservations (certain limits in time/scope)

Over the years, the administrative enforcement has been strengthened. In general, the enforcement obligation rests with the local municipality and, obviously, qualitative differences do exist. It appears, however, that a more uniform level has been reached securing equal treatment for industry.

Taxes

The most efficient instrument to regulate and change behaviour has not, surprisingly, been the introduction of taxes or "green fees" as they are known in Denmark (much to the discomfort of the golfers). A broad variety of taxes do exist.

The most important taxes concern taxation on the use of raw materials and the disposal of waste. A general water discharge tax has proven extremely effective in regulating the water consumption of the general public.

In 1993, a CO_2 tax was introduced, levied on the part of industry whose processes create CO_2. This tax was special as it established a clear relationship between the revenue of taxation and the redirection of funds from the industry which, therefore, introduced facilities whereby the CO_2 emission would be reduced.

A new package of environmental taxes has just been presented in Parliament *inter alia* the increase in the application area of CO_2 tax.

The introduction of taxes does cause dramatic changes to the competitiveness of certain types of industry, for which reason it has created much opposition. In general, Danish industry, however, has responded constructively to the use of taxes, partly owing to the fact that such taxes may be passed on to the customers. It is, nevertheless, of the utmost importance that the European Union quickly and effectively restores equal opportunity rights of business and competitiveness by introducing harmonised laws on taxes to cover all the European Union.

Environmental impact assessment

The EU directive on the obligation to execute environmental impact assessments whenever deciding upon major projects influencing the physical conditions of the environment, has proven to be an efficient and successful instrument to avoid environmental blunders.

Currently, there is litigation on compliance with the directive as regards the decision to build a bridge from Denmark to Sweden. In addition to this, future litigation is anticipated to ascertain the qualitative criteria in such assessments.

Contaminated land

Over the years, one of the most controversial issues in the environmental law discussion in Denmark has concerned contaminated land.

Contaminated land is defined as areas polluted from past activities by polluters who have abandoned the land or, for other reasons, cannot be held liable for the pollution.

In 1977, it was revealed, by chance, that a herbicide company, Cheminova (a manufacturer of DDT) had buried large quantities of poisonous waste in the ground at its previous site situated just outside Copenhagen and only 200 metres from one of the largest drinking water reservoirs supplying the city. Cheminova had vacated the premises in 1953 to move to another site in Denmark.

This revelation, among others, lead to the enactment of the Contaminated Land Act in 1981, which provided for registration of old contaminated sites. After registration, it is a public responsibility to perform clean-up operations.

To date, some 3,000 sites have been registered and it is expected that some 7,000 may still remain. At the rate of the present allocation of public funds to this area, it may take some 125 years before the last site has been cleaned up at the expense of the public.

The Act also provides for voluntary clean-up to be performed by the owner, if he is not willing to observe the restrained usage of his property for an undeterminable period of time.

In the years 1990–93, 460 sites were cleaned up and 370 of those were voluntary clean-ups. These figures will show that, in practice, contaminated sites have become the burden of the owner, who has had nothing to do with the pollution. Also lenders will be hit by this state of affairs, realising the potential take-over of contaminated sites, which can only be resold at reduced value due to the pollution.

A discussion in legal theory, concerning whether any owner of real estate is liable to prevent pollution from spreading to the ground water level and/or neighbouring land, is ongoing. A recent Supreme Court verdict has ruled that, in the case where the pollution derives from a facility which the owner does not use, then he will not be liable. Another question would arise if the facility was in actual fact used by the present owner, even though the pollution may have occurred during a previous ownership.

Concluding remarks

Danish environmental law does show a tendency towards stricter regulation and more efficient enforcement. This will inevitably imply heavy costs and investments to be carried out by industry to cover pollution control and pollution reduction arrangements. Some taxes will hit industry even though these "green fees" will relate more to the environmental impact of the individual.

A few years ago, environmental law was regarded as a somewhat suspicious field in which to practice as a lawyer, now it is an important element of business law. Lawyers in Denmark are called to assist both public authorities and private clients in deciphering the complex rules, although these rules are becoming clearer.

In the author's own experience, environmental law now plays an important part in the traditional area of due diligence, and it is now seen – which was unthinkable some years ago – that environmental matters may be crucial to any transaction, be it a company purchase or an asset deal.

Finally, it must be emphasised that, in the future, compliance with environmental regulation may be a burden for industry, but at the same time, it will become a parameter for commercial success. What you make, how you make it and what to do with what you make will increasingly become a concern of the general public, and responding responsibly to that concern may become the decisive factor for customers.

England and Wales

Michael Conaghan
Partner, Lawrence Jones Solicitors, London
Lewis Denton
Solicitor, Davies Wallis Foyster, Manchester and Liverpool

EU-LEX also has two other UK Member firms practising Environmental law, whose partners helped to edit this report – Lewis Denton of Davies Wallis Foyster, Liverpool and Manchester and Brian Riley of Watson Burton, Newcastle.

Like other European countries, until recently, the approach in England and Wales to the safeguarding of the environment was piecemeal, dealing with environmental problems as and when they arose, with the enforcement of environmental legislation being divided between a multiplicity of authorities including, amongst others, local authorities, waste regulation authorities, the Inspectorate of Pollution and the National Rivers Authority.

The Environmental Protection Act 1990 and the Environmental Act 1995 have made fundamental changes to that approach and the following is a brief summary of some of those changes.

- The establishment of the Environment Agency, which will take over the functions and powers of waste regulation authorities, the Inspectorate of Pollution and the National Rivers Authority and certain functions of local authorities. The Agency will be operational from April 1996.
- In the case of certain of the more polluting industrial processes to be found in the fuel production, metal production, chemical, waste disposal and other similar industries, the substitution of the previous separate pollution regimes relating to part of the environment (*i.e.* land, water and air) by an integrated system of pollution control. For instance, whereas previously a chemical factory might have required separate licences for emissions into the air and into water, the factory will now require a single authorisation relating to all emissions into any part of the environment (whether air, water or land) and the emission limit for any particular substance will be set by reference to the total amount of that substance emitted by the factory in any of the three mediums.
- A duty to clean-up "significantly" contaminated land is imposed upon the polluter in the first instance but, where the polluter cannot be found, the duty is imposed upon the current owner or occupier of the

contaminated land. Local authorities will be responsible for identifying significantly contaminated land in accordance with statutory guidance to be issued by the Government. Draft guidance has now been issued for consultation and it is expected that the guidance in its final form will be issued mid-1996. It is important to note that there is no time limit as to when the contamination occurred; a duty to clean up contaminated land can exist however long ago the land became contaminated. In assessing the extent of the clean-up, the local authority must act reasonably and must take into account the cost which is likely to be involved and the seriousness of the harm/pollution.

- The extension of the controls upon the deposit of waste to the whole waste cycle, including the production and transportation of waste. With the exception of householders, every person in the waste management chain is subject to a statutory duty of care to prevent the escape of waste, to transfer the waste only to an authorised person or for an authorised transport purpose, and to ensure that others involved in the management of the waste do not commit certain offences, including managing waste without a licence.

Finland

Mika Alanko
Attorney-at-law, Bützow & Co Ltd, Helsinki

Like other Scandinavian countries, Finland regards itself as an environmentally friendly country with high standards of environmental conservation and protection. To some extent this claim can be justified even though in various fields there is still a lot of work to do.

The first Nature Conservation Act was enacted as early as 1923. It has been partly amended several times, but the basic structure has been maintained. The first Acts on pollution control were not enacted until the 1960s. Within the last 35 years environmental legislation has expanded remarkably: *e.g.* Water Act (1961), Waste Management Act (1978), Air Pollution Control Act (1982), Noise Control Act (1988), Act on Environmental Civil Liability (1994) and Act on Environmental Impact Assessment (1994).

Already a party to the EEA Treaty (in force on 1 January 1994) Finland has adopted the majority of the EU environmental legislation. Some fields were already harmonised before that (*e.g.* chemical legislation), some fields needed only adjustments, but the waste legislation was totally reformed, partly due to Finland's recent membership of the European Union.

In the following some recent developments within the environmental field of law are discussed.

Civil liability

The application of general civil liability rules on environmental damages has proved to be problematic from the claimant's point of view. The burden of proof of cause and culpability and the amount of damage has often proved to be overwhelming.

In order to promote the judicial protection of the victims of pollution and nuisance, Finland, a few years after Sweden, Norway and Denmark, enacted an Act on Environmental Civil Liability based on a strict liability principle. The Act came into force on 1 June 1995.

The scope of application of the new Act is broad. No list of fixed activities or substances limits the scope of the Act and it encompasses, in principle, all non-contractual damage caused by stationary activities, provided that they result from pollution of water, air or soil or from nuisance like noise, vibration, radiation, heat or smell. Some specially regulated damages, like nuclear damage, are not, however, included.

The Act is not retroactive. In practice this means that when environmental damage is detected, a major issue is whether it has been caused before or after 1 June 1995. From industry's point of view, it is of the utmost importance to have clear documentation of the emissions after the above-mentioned date in order to have some defence against possible claims based on strict liability.

The new Act includes a lot of detailed issues which need to be clarified by court precedents. However, it is likely that future development will prove to be similar to that in Sweden, where a similar Act has been in force since 1986; no high court precedents will, however, be obtained as companies are reluctant to go to court as defendants in an environmental damage case.

At the end of the day, it can be less damaging to a company to settle claims outside the courts rather than to find itself in a long court battle with a lot of negative publicity and maybe irreparable damage to its image.

Contaminated land

In 1988 the Government decided to assess the extent of polluted land areas in Finland. As a result of this assessment, some 10,400 sites were listed as suspected polluted areas. Had all small and minor sites been included, the list would have included some 25,000 sites. The clean-up costs were estimated to be FIM5.4 billion.

Fortunately, there is no great obligation to clean up all the contaminated sites fit for re-use as they are still designated unused land areas. The pressure to restore these sites comes, however, from the possible risks to ground water and public health.

The new Waste Act, which came into force on 1 January 1994, clarified the rules regulating liability questions about clean-up costs. The Waste Act is not, however, retroactive, which means that the Waste Management Act 1978 is applicable to the sites contaminated before 1 January 1994.

Both above-mentioned Acts are based on the "polluter pays" principle. If the polluter cannot be found or if he escapes the clean-up liability, the Acts have slightly different rules. According to the Waste Management Act 1978, there is a possibility that an existing landowner or even a tenant could be held liable for the clean-up costs even though he would not have known or would not have had anything to do with the pollution caused before the piece of land was purchased or leased. However, according to

172

the Waste Act 1994, a landowner or tenant can be held liable only if he has consented or been aware of the polluting activity on his site or if he knew or should have known about the contamination while acquiring or leasing the piece of land. The clean-up liability can also be avoided if it would be considered to be unreasonable.

The rules in the Waste Act 1994 have strengthened the importance of including environmental considerations when purchasing a piece of land. The stricter rules regarding contamination before the beginning of 1994 have put some pressure on companies to inspect their land in order to detect possible contamination. The results of these studies can effectively be used in a liability dispute between a landowner and the authorities.

Environmental impact assessment (EIA)

One aspect of the impact of membership, first of the EEA Treaty and finally of the European Union, was the enactment of the Finnish Environmental Impact Assessment Act in 1994. The Act is designed to meet the requirements of both the EU Directive on Environmental Impact Assessment (85/337/EEC) and the Convention on Environmental Impact Assessments in a Transboundary Context (signed on 25 February 1991 in Espoo, Finland).

The EIA is necessary when the type of activity or installation is included in a list which is a combination of the obligatory lists of the Convention and the Directive, with a supplement for Finnish environmental conditions. The EIA may also be required on a case-by-case basis, depending on whether the project would have significant environmental impacts.

If an EIA is required, no environmental permit can be granted before the EIA procedure is concluded. The permit authorities are not bound, however, to an environmental impact statement (EIS), but they are obliged to explain how the EIS has been taken into account in the permit decision.

Criminal liability of a legal body

According to the traditional Finnish criminal system, criminal sanctions have only been imposed on private persons. After a long preparation of a legislative proposal, the Finnish Penal Code was amended in Spring 1995. A new section regarding the criminal liability of a legal body (corporate fine) was included in the Penal Code. It came into force on 1 September 1995.

According to the amendment, a corporate fine can be imposed on a legal body for a crime committed during the course of business activity. The imposed fine may vary between FIM5,000–5,000,000.

A corporate fine is possible only when such sanction has been pre-scribed for that crime in the Penal Code. In the explanatory part of the Government's proposal to the amendment it has been stressed that environmental crimes would be one of the main applications of the new fines.

As the level of the fine can be very high, it is to be expected that it will increase the willingness of legal bodies to comply completely with their environmental obligations. As the amendment has been in force only a few weeks, it remains to be seen what kind of role the corporate fine will play in the Finnish criminal court practice.

Concluding remarks

From industry's point of view the expanded environmental legislation has created new challenges and risks. Thus, it is of utmost importance that risk assessments regarding production and transactions also contain environmental considerations.

Even though the new legislation has increased the environmental considerations, the risks and challenges are manageable due to reasonably clear legislation. In addition, the traditional administrative approach, where authorities are willing to discuss various matters openly during a permit application procedure, eases the management of environmental challenges.

France

Laurence Rager
Avocat, Custax & Legal, Paris

Introduction

As in other industrialised countries, French environmental law is derived from a large number of laws passed in the nineteenth and twentieth centuries. Concerns for public health and for the expansion of agriculture and industry are behind this legislation and are at the root of the law relating to forestry, mining and classified installations (installations classées), establishments officially listed because of the danger or risk they pose to the environment.

Although combatting industrial nuisance is still an extremely important part of French environmental law, it has been reinforced since the 1970s by legal measures aiming to protect nature for its own sake. This objective is not enshrined in the Constitution, but the Law of 10 July 1976 (No 76.629, known as the Loi Nature) remains the key text in this field. It acknowledges that the environment in general, and nature in particular, are "of general interest" and institutes the procedure of environmental impact assessment.

Regulations covering town and country planning and the listed building regime complete the legal framework. The French regulatory system is accordingly focused on three main areas as follows:

- the fight against pollution and nuisance;
- the protection of the natural and historic heritage;
- controls on planning and development.

As a result, sources of environmental law are extremely diverse.

There are a few major laws:

- the Loi Nature (10 July 1976);
- the Classified Installations Law (19 July 1976);
- the Law of Water (3 January 1992);
- Law on Waste (13 July 1992);
- Law on Quarries (4 January 1993);
- Law on Reinforcement of Environment Protection (2 February 1995).

The subject is dominated by administrative regulations intended to uphold public order, health and safety. This explains why French environmental law is mainly administrative in character. Nevertheless, adherence to administrative norms must be combined with compliance with civil and criminal standards. French law is characterised by the independence of its administrative jurisdiction from its civil and criminal jurisdictions (la jurisdiction judiciaire). Consequently, the absence of an administrative lawsuit does not preclude recourse to civil or criminal proceedings.

Environmental administration

Although European legislation is already an extremely important part of national environmental law, environmental administrators still play a key role in drawing up and enforcing environmental norms. The environmental administration is made up of civil servants and contractual agents working for public authorities at both the state and local levels.

Endowed with powers which are especially vulnerable to the vagaries of political reality, the environmental administration (which dates from the establishment of a specialised ministry in 1971) encompasses a highly diverse mixture of administrative bodies. Moreover, the allocation of responsibilities between local authorities and the state is extremely confusing.

We would classify local and national authorities under the following rules.

NATIONAL ADMINISTRATION

The state assumes five main responsibilities with regard to the local authorities:

• drawing up of legal norms;
• powers of regulation, supervision and punishment;
• determining the available finance;
• arbitration and mediation;
• collaboration in the fulfilment of common objectives.

At the national level, the following bodies operate:

• the Water Division;
• the Industrial Environment Division;
• the Clean Technology and Waste Division;
• the Task Force on Product Regulation;
• the Commission of Major Risks.

There is also a task force on noise and a research and information division (le service de la recherche, des études et du traitement de l'information sur l'environnement (SRETIE)) and a specialised environmental inspection division (la mission d'inspection spécialisée de l'environnement (MISE)).

LOCAL ADMINISTRATION

Regional level

An Environmental Directorate (la direction régionale de l'environnement (DIREN)) has been established in each region and is supported by the Directorate for Industry, Research and the Environment (la direction régionale de l'industrie, de la recherche et de l'environnement (DRIRE)). These bodies enforce the legislation relating to water, protection of sites, nature, architecture, environmental impact assessments and advertisements, and handle requests for permission for works within these categories.

Within the DRIRE, inspectors of classified installations are employed to identify relevant installations which are neither authorised nor declared, to take part in inquiries prior to authorisation and to devise technical standards with which the operator must comply. They must visit classified installations regularly, report any breach of the regulations and monitor even unclassified industrial, craft and commercial operations which are liable to cause atmospheric pollution.

Departmental level

The Prefect and his staff are at the heart of departmental administration. As the representative of the state within the Department, the Prefect is concerned with all proceedings in the environmental field. He has regulatory powers and must uphold the law. Although competent in practically every area, he is principally involved with combatting noise, classified installations, mining of quarries, spreading of pesticides, prevention of manmade and natural hazards and, more generally, the protection of nature. He also plays a key role in public inquiries governed by the Law of 12 July 1983. The Prefect is helped in his functions by services concerned with infrastructure and with agriculture and forestry (la direction départementale de l'equipement (DDE) and la direction départementale de l'agriculture et de la forét (DDAF).

Communal level

The process of decentralisation in 1983 granted the communes considerable autonomy in certain areas of planning and infrastructure development. These include the grant of planning permission, the preparation of the development structure plan (POS), the creation of enterprise zones (zones d'aménagement concerté), and controls on posters and hoardings.

Communes also have major obligations in the field of environmental health and waste collection, treatment and disposal. They can regulate noise by means of local by-laws, subject to the administrative control of the Prefect.

SPECIALISED AUTHORITIES

The environmental administration in France includes a large number of specialised agencies which are autonomous public bodies. These are as follows:

At the national level

- the French Institute for the Environment (IFEN);
- an environmental and energy conservation body (l'agence de l'environnement et de la maîtrise de l'énergie (ADEN);
- the National Institute for Industrial Environment and Risk (INERIS).

At the local level

- the water authority for each basin (les agences financiéres de bassin (AFB)).

Advisory bodies

Advisory bodies consist of the following:

- the High Committee for the Environment (le haut comité pour l'environnement);
- the General Council for Classified Installations (le conseil supérieur des installations classées);
- the National Council for Noise (le conseil national du bruit);
- the Commission for the Assessment of Chemical Substances Harmful to the Environment (la commission d'evaluation de l'ecotoxicité des substances chimiques);
- the Departmental Commission on Quarries (la commission départementale des carriéres).

Commercial activities covered by environmental legislation

The regulatory framework is structured around three phases of commercial activity. The setting up of a business or industrial plant is subject to planning controls, and its operation is covered by technical regulations, and specific provisions relating to the manufacture of certain categories of products.

Appendix III

Planning permission must be obtained for any construction or modification of a building. It is granted by the mayor (marie) in the name of his commune or the state, which process takes on average eight to 12 months for major building works and two months for minor construction.

The grant of planning permission takes environmental concerns into consideration on several counts.

The application can be rejected or granted subject to special conditions if the construction is liable to result in environmental damage or endanger public health and safety. An appeal from the refusal of planning permission lies with the administrative judge.

Planning permission must comply with the development or structure plan (plan d'occupation des sols (POS)) if one exists. The POS includes an analysis of the environment and divides the territory of the commune into zones reserved for specific purposes. In the absence of a POS, the provision restricting construction in rural areas comes into play (Art L 111-1-2, code de l'urbanisme). Nonetheless, permission can still be granted for buildings and installations unsuited to built-up areas.

The application for planning permission must usually contain an environmental impact assessment (étude d'impact écologique (EIE)).

REGULATION FOR INDUSTRIAL PROCESSES

Commercial activities liable to damage the environment are principally governed by the Law of 19 July 1976 on classified installations. This applies to any stationary installation operated or owned by any natural or legal person, public or private (Art 1), which threatens any danger or nuisance. It is drafted widely to include both established and potential hazards. An official list (nomenclature) specifies which categories of installations and processes are covered: there are approximately 500,000 classified installations in France at present.

The Prefect is competent as regards classified installations, which are subject to different procedures of authorisation or declaration depending on the gravity of the threat they pose to the environment. The less dangerous category must be declared before being put into operation; mandatory conditions for each category of installation are set out in standard orders (arrêtés).

Where an installation is subject to authorisation, the application for authorisation must contain an environmental impact assessment, information relating to health and safety, and the conclusions of the mandatory public inquiry which lasts at least one month (Law of 12 July 1983).

The applicant can request that confidential information of a commercial or industrial nature should not be divulged. A final decision is usually given after five to seven months, together with "customised" technical specifications. An authorisation is granted for an unlimited period, but a new one will be necessary if significant modifications are undertaken.

In addition, a risk assessment and an emergency plan are required for particularly dangerous industrial processes within the terms of the Seveso Directive on major industrial hazards, which was incorporated into French law by the Law of 22 July 1987. Such installations are subject to a more stringent regime. More specifically, restrictive conditions of use (servitudes) can be imposed around such installations at the request of the operator, the Prefect or the mayor. The operator is liable to compensate owners and others with an interest in property for direct and proven damage caused to their property. Inspectors of classified installations are responsible for ensuring that operators comply with all relevant technical and legal regulations.

REGULATION OF PRODUCTS

Specific provisions of environmental law apply to the marketing of certain products:

- chemical products (Law of 12 July 1977);
- insecticides (Law of 22 December 1972);
- chemical fertilisers (Law of 13 July 1979);
- waste (Law of 15 July 1975 modified by Law of 13 July 1992).

Liability and remedies

ADMINISTRATIVE LIABILITY

Contentious environmental matters involve not only planning applications and classified installations but also cases arising from specialised environmental laws relating to atmospheric pollution (Law of 2 August 1961), water (Law of 16 December 1964 and 3 January 1992 and its reduction in applications), waste (Law of 15 July modified) and the laws relating to chemical products. In such cases, liability may be incurred by the administrative authority on the one hand or the operator on the other.

Remedies of operator

The operator can institute proceedings within a period of two months for judicial review (le recours en annulation et le recours de plein contentieux) of administrative decisions, authorisations, supplementary orders and special regulations imposed on installations subject to declaration (Art 14, Law of 19 July 1976).

Liability of operator

The operator commits a criminal offence for certain breaches of the Planning and Rural Codes (code de l'urbanisme et code rural) and other environmental legislation (imprisonment and fines). The Law on classified installations makes it an offence not to comply with administrative regulations or the technical conditions applicable.

Operating without the requisite authorisation or declaration is punishable by two to twelve months' imprisonment and/or a fine (Art 18, Law of 19 July 1976).

Criminal offences within planning law are relatively effective since they permit communes or associations to claim damages within the criminal proceedings (se constituer partie civile). Damages thus awarded against the operator can be extremely heavy.

CIVIL LIABILITY

Civil litigation, the province of the juge judiciaire, was dominated for a long time by cases involving interference with the neighbourhood (troubles de voisinage). Although still important, this area has become less significant compared to cases arising from the new concept of ecological damage (dommage écologique). The question therefore arises as to the legal basis upon which a company or business may be sued for environmental damage.

INSURANCE

Once found liable, companies are bound to compensate victims of their pollution. The operator may insure against civil (but not criminal) liability for pollution, risk of which is inherent in every industrial process. Both operational insurance (l'assurance responsabilité civile (RC) exploitation) and specific policies against environmental damage (assurance des risques d'atteinte à environnement) are available.

RC operational insurance and RC directors' insurance (assurance RC chef d'entreprise) protects the company against general civil liability under Article 1384 of the Civil Code. However, in 1970 exclusion clauses were inserted against damage caused by atmospheric pollution and water, extended in 1974 to exclude other categories of harm to the environment from noise, fumes, radiation and modification of the temperature. This inspired the creation of specific insurance coverage for pollution risks in the form of a supplementary clause appended to the RC directors' insurance policy. However, the sum assured is often insufficient to guarantee compensation for all damage sustained by the victims.

Operators may take advantage of ASSURPOL which offers the only commercial policy providing higher coverage (FRF165 million per incident of pollution). ASSURPOL is an economic interest grouping comprising 70 French and foreign insurance or reinsurance companies which was set up to cover the risk of environmental damage of French territory, including its overseas colonies, and in the Principality of Monaco.

The development of new technologies will increase the need for companies engaged in polluting activities to obtain adequate insurance.

Green products

For frankly commercial reasons, green or eco-products have proliferated without ever being legally defined.

The authority responsible for setting scientific standards (AFNOR) has created a label, "NF-Environnement", which guarantees that every aspect of the product's manufacture has respected the needs of the environment (the cradle-to-grave principle).

Standardised technical regulations, reviewable every three years, have already been drawn up for certain categories of product (*e.g.* paints and varnishes) and cover packaging, electric batteries, rubbish bags, cosmetics, lubricants and gas heating appliances.

Effective environmental protection depends on good relations between businesses, government, environmental defence associations and the public, and therefore upon access to relevant information.

The Law of 2 February 1995 institutionalises an associations' participation.

Conclusion

The sources of environmental law remain very diverse. However, the jurist's task should be facilitated by the publication of an Environment Code (Code de l'Environnement), which is being elaborated.

France disposes of a particularly complete body of laws.

A law on atmospheric pollution is being elaborated and will be the last piece of this legislative jigsaw.

The question of the elaboration of an environmental norm being then solved, there remains the question of its effective application.

Germany

Jochen Köster
Partner, Benkelberg, von Stein Lausnitz & Partner, Halle-Saale

It is very difficult to keep a summary of current German environmental legislation short so only the latest developments are covered in this area, which – as a legal discipline – is still in its infancy.

German and European legislation

German environmental legislation, like European legislation in general, has adapted itself to the more integrated, multi-media approach.

In former days, environmental provisions were made to avoid specific dangers in certain sectors. Now the idea of taking care of the environment as a whole and of preserving it for following generations is widely accepted.

Additionally, as the relevance of European environmental provisions increases the similarities between German environmental law and European environmental provisions also increase.

Simplification of administrative measures generally

The length of all legal proceedings in Germany, including the amount of time it takes for an investor to obtain approval for a new venture, has often been criticised. Now, there is some hope for the future. The Government has recently commissioned a panel of independent experts to consider and make proposals to simplify and accelerate administrative procedures. This Commission was led by the former Vice President of the Federal Administrative Court. The Commission's 200-page report was delivered at the end of 1994. This report, in addition to dealing with administrative provisions generally, also covers matters of environmental interest.

There are more than 100 suggestions and proposals made in the report for the revision of the provisions of numerous acts, which cannot all be quoted here. Therefore, only the Commission's main aim and some of their more important environmental proposals are discussed.

The main aim of the Commission was to maintain the high German standards of protection of the environment and, at the same time, to accelerate the administrative procedures and make them more flexible, so that they could react to the special new demands of sustainable industrial development.

One of the Commission's proposals was to suggest that if an investor/applicant obtains a full approval for a new development, he must accept that if, in the future, new environmental controls are imposed, his site will become subject to such controls. Alternatively, he can obtain full approval one step at a time, taking the next step only when he has satisfied the environmental requirements of the appropriate authorities.

Another idea was that the investor gets only a non-specific permission, and is thus entitled to manage the details but, on the other hand, is subject to regular control and monitoring.

A further proposal was that the investor could make greater contribution to the procedures by which he obtains approval for such a venture, such as settling any potential environmental problems himself with people likely to be affected by his actions.

Another proposal was that the investor may take a speculative approach and run the risk that the full approval will be partly or totally withdrawn by the authorities after the new plant or industrial process has been set up. Alternatively, he may obtain a conditional approval at the outset and then apply for a full operational consent once the new plant or process is ready for operation. The risk, in the latter case, is that, at the date of the original conditional approval, it will not be foreseeable whether the authorities will grant a full operational approval.

The last proposal was the possibility of the installation of a project manager. This would mean a qualified civil servant being made responsible for ensuring that speedy procedures are implemented and would therefore be exempt from other tasks.

We have to wait and see which of these suggestions will become transformed into law and whether they will then be judged to be effective or not, by those who have to use them.

Some more concrete recent developments are as follows.

Liability for damage caused by emissions: the Pollution Act

This Act came into force in January 1991, two years before the Maastricht Treaty and Article 130r. It provides that the operators of certain dangerous works or plant – which are listed in an appendix – are liable for damage caused by emissions from their premises. It is not a question of negligence having to be proved. The liability is strict and absolute.

The statutory limit of the liability is DM160,000,000,000,00. The authorities can refuse approval to operate such a plant if the operator does not provide a security for the potential compensation costs. Such a security can be in the form of a bank guarantee, or insurance.

Environmental information

Germany has recently revised the Environmental Information Access Directive in July 1994. As far as third parties were concerned, the previous provisions governing restriction of access to information during the process of approval were a potential source of conflict and were regarded as being too limited.

Kreislaufwirtschaftsgesetz

Directly translated, this means the "Economy of circulating goods" Act. This legislation, introduced to encourage goods to be recycled and re-used, was promulgated in October 1994 and will come into force in October 1996. It is the successor to the Waste Disposal Act. It rules that those who cause the waste (producer and consumer) are to be responsible for the disposal of the waste; the responsibility of the state is remarkably reduced.

The principle of the obligation placed upon producers of goods by the Act is that a producer, who does not comply with the disposal of waste provisions of the Act, will not be allowed to sell or market his goods (or what remains of them).

Bodenschutzgesetz

Directly translated, this means "the Care of the Soil" Act. The object of this Act is to avoid detrimental changes to the soil and to take precautions to prevent such changes. Detrimental emissions are to be avoided as far as possible. Impending detrimental changes should be averted and contaminated ground must be de-contaminated.

For many years now, the authorities in Germany felt the need for an Act which would provide detailed provisions on the responsibilities and the extent to which a responsible person should be liable in respect of decontamination of contaminated land and on the standard of clean-up. The existing provisions were not created for such tasks and are not sufficient. There is often great uncertainty about what standard of clean-up the authorities can demand. The problem took on more importance and became more urgent, when land and sites within the former GDR were taken into consideration.

The former GDR

As part of the unification agreement, a procedure whereby the investor could be given exemption from liability for the remediation of contaminated land was enacted.

The authorities can decide to what extent (if any) the exemption applies to an individual site or applicant. This point is important because, although the period during which applications for such exemptions could be made has already expired, anyone who has such an exemption, or who has applied for, and is granted, an exemption in the future, can transfer that exemption to successive owners of the land. However, any transfer of an exemption has to have the prior approval of the authorities.

The law on environmental crime

Although this area of law is only on the fringes of what can be described as "environmental" law, these provisions are of great importance to managers in industry and authorities.

The provisions on environmental crime were bundled in the Criminal Code in 1980. They have recently been revised, with the revised provisions becoming effective on 1 November 1994.

The provisions are now further differentiated. To cause certain kinds of pollution of the soil has now become a crime. Furthermore, the maximum term of a prison sentence has been extended from three to five years and, in severe cases, from five to 10 years.

It is not yet clear whether the courts will impose such severe prison sentences. In the past, judgments imposing prison sentence were the great exception, but, in the future, because of the growing public perception of environmental crime, harsher punishments could result.

Greece

Dimitris Zepos
Partner, Zepos & Zepos, Athens

The cornerstone of Greek environmental legislation is Article 24 of the Greek Constitution of 1975. According to its first paragraph, "The protection of the natural and cultural environment is an obligation of the State. For its protection the State has the obligation to adopt special preventive or repressive measures".

In this respect, the Greek State has adopted a number of legislative acts concerning the environment, the most important of which are law 360/1976, re "Urban Planning and Environment", law 743/1977, re "the Protection of the Maritime Environment", law 947/1977, re "Residential Areas", law 1377/1983, re "Expansion of Urban Planning, Residential Development and Relative Regulations" and law 1577/1985, re "General Construction Regulations".

In 1986, the Greek legislature attempted to unify the fragmented provisions regarding the protection of the environment by adopting law 1650/1986. This law serves today as the major legal foundation for the protection of the environment in Greece.

Law 1650/1986

According to law 1650/1986 (L.1650), private or public works are, at the discretion of the Minister of Environment, Urban Planning and Public Works, categorised, as far as their impact on the environment is concerned as follows:

1st category:	Works and activities which, due to their nature and scale are likely to have a severe impact on the environment. On such works and activities, special terms and limitations may be imposed, for the protection of the environment.
2nd category:	Works and activities which, without posing serious threat to the environment, must be subject, for the protection of the environment, to general terms and specifications provided for by regulatory acts.
3rd category:	Works and activities which have an insignificant impact on the environment.

The criteria for determining in which category a work or activity must fall, are as follows:

- the nature and importance of the work or activity;
- the nature and quantity of pollutants emitted;
- the existing possibilities of preventing such emissions;
- the risk of a serious accident caused by the operation of a plant and the need for the implementation of restrictions for the protection of the environment.

Before commencing any work or activity falling within the above-mentioned categories, a special approval of the terms regarding the protection of the environment is necessary. In this respect, the preparation and submission of a study on the impact of the works or activities on the environment is a pre-requisite.

For works and activities falling within the 1st category, approval on environmental grounds is granted by the Minister of Environment. For certain works falling within this category, such approval may also be granted by the local Prefect who is also competent to approve the environmental terms for works and activities falling within the 2nd category. For the works and activities falling within the 3rd category, approval on environmental grounds is granted by the competent mayor or community head.

The above-mentioned authorities who are competent to approve the environmental terms have also been assigned the task of checking the correct implementation of the said terms, while the Ministry of Environment has jurisdiction to control the correct implementation of the environmental terms all over Greece.

The authority for such control is also granted to the Environmental Quality Control Units (KEPE) which are formed by a decision of the competent prefect.

Air pollution

Law 1650 provides that specific measures and restrictions may be adopted, following a relevant joint Ministerial Decision, for works or activities which may have a negative impact on the quality of the atmosphere. Such measures and restrictions may include *inter alia*:

- for industrial, agricultural, drilling, commercial, tourist activities etc, the use of specific raw materials and fuel, the implementation of anti-pollution technology, the determination of marginal quantities of exhausts and the setting of time-schedules;

- for vehicles and machinery, the marginal quantities of exhausts, technical specifications, the of gas or improved fuel, traffic limitations;
- for the storage, distribution, transportation and marketing of fuels and explosives, the implementation of measures aiming to reduce exhausts and to apply specific security measures;
- for central heating installations, marginal quantities of exhausts, the use of specific fuel, the use of smoke-collectors;

Furthermore, Presidential Decree 1180/1981 sets the permissible quantities of polluting substances in the atmosphere.

Water pollution

Law 1650 provides that specific measures and restrictions may be adopted, following a relevant joint Ministerial Decision, for works and activities which may have a negative impact on the aquatic environment.

Since the enactment of this law, a number of Ministerial Acts regarding the protection of the acquatic environment have been issued, most of them in compliance with EC Directives 76/464, 82/176, 84/156, 84/491, including *inter alia* the following:

- Council of Minister Act 144/1987, re protection of the acquatic environment from the pollution caused by certain dangerous substances (Hg, Cd and HCH);
- Ministerial Decision 18186/271/88, re measures and restrictions for the protection of the acquatic environment and determination of the marginal quantities of dangerous substances in liquid waste;
- Ministerial Decision 26857/553/88, re measures and restrictions for the protection of the underground waters from certain dangerous substances;
- Ministerial Decision 55648/2210, re measures and restrictions for the protection of the acquatic environment;

It should also be noted that according to the provisions of law 1739/1987, re management of acquatic resources and other provisions, a licence for the operation of an industrial plant using water during the production process may not be granted before a special permit is obtained from the competent department of the Ministry of Industry, Energy and Technology.

Land contamination

TOXIC AND DANGEROUS WASTE

Specific areas where the deposition of toxic and dangerous waste is permitted, are designated by Joint Ministerial Decisions. By a joint

Ministerial Decision, the use of pesticides and fertilisers which may cause a danger of contamination may be restricted or forbidden.

SOLID WASTE

Specific areas where the deposition of solid waste is permitted are designated by a decision of the competent prefect.

The competent authorities for the management of solid waste are the local governments. Entities producing, disposing or managing solid waste which may be hazardous to the public health or to the environment must keep a relevant record. The unauthorised deposition of solid waste in the natural environment or within civil areas is forbidden.

Ireland

Andrew O'Rorke

Partner, Hayes & Sons, Dublin

Irish people, like all other European Nationals, have in the past half-century or so become more conscious of the need to care for the environment in which they live. World-wide problems have been of concern in Ireland, such as global warming and catastrophes like the Chernobyl disaster in Russia. Within Ireland, there were more local problems which contributed to this growing concern such as severe smog in most urban areas and accidents such as the fire in the Whiddy Refinery some years ago.

There have, however, been legislative provisions concerning the environment in Ireland predating this, for example the Public Health (Ireland) Act 1878 which covered a general ambit such as water and atmospheric pollution. With this recent awareness of the environment, however, has come an upsurge in development relating to the law in this area.

A testament to this is the fact that in 1988 Ireland had its first major environmental court case, *Hanrahan and others* v *Merck, Sharp & Dohm*, ending in a decision of the Supreme Court, the final Court of Appeal. The plaintiff farmers claimed that emissions from the defendants' chemical factory had caused damage to their health and their live stock and interfered with the enjoyment of their properties. The plaintiffs pleaded trespass, negligence, nuisance and the rule in *Rylands* v *Fletcher* (1886) ER 3 HL 330. In the Supreme Court, the case was decided in favour of the plaintiffs simply on the grounds of nuisance. The case was much discussed in Ireland, both for the facts giving rise to it and for the manner in which the court approached it. The decision has proved to be a much criticised one as many claim that it is based more on the sympathetic attitude of the court to the plaintiffs than on any sound legal reasoning. It remains, however, Ireland's first real landmark environmental decision.

There is also the prospect of the Irish courts handing down another extremely significant decision. Several women living in County Louth, on the east coast of Ireland have commenced proceedings against British Nuclear Fuels, the body responsible for the running and maintenance of the nuclear power plant in Sellafield, on the west coast of England. The plaintiffs are claiming damages for physical harm allegedly caused by nuclear radiation emanating from the plant. The plaintiffs' plan is to introduce evidence to the effect that the incidence of cancer in their area was much higher than that of anywhere else in Ireland, a fact which they attribute to the nearby nuclear plant. It will be interesting to see how the court deals with the issue of causation in this case, as in the *Hanrahan* case the High Court and the Supreme Court took very different approaches as to the requirement that it be proved that the damage caused to the plaintiff was as a result of an act or omission of the defendant.

Much of the development in Irish environmental law has been due to the influence of membership of the European Union. Many of the EU Directives have supplemented to great effect pre-existing Irish legislation. For example, Irish water pollution legislation contained mostly in the Local Government (Water Pollution) Acts concentrated on providing mechanisms for pollution control, but was silent on the precise standard to be obtained. Now, however, the EU Directives provide a precise, scientific figure which, when utilised in conjunction with the existing Irish legislation, can be observed.

Irish planning legislation has always required consideration to be taken of environmental factors.

The key piece of legislation was the Local Government (Planning and Development) Act 1963 which allowed for planning permission to be refused to development of land on various grounds relating to potential damage to the environment.

Directive 85/337/EEC has made a large impact on planning and development in Ireland however. This Directive was substantially implemented in Ireland when the Local Government (Planning and Development) Regulations 1990 came into force on 1 February 1990. The Directive requires that an assessment of the possible effect to the environment of any development likely to have a significant effect must be carried out before permission will be given to the development. The implementation of the Directive ensures, more comprehensively than pre-existing Irish legislation, that a certain amount of forethought will be used in dealing with environmental problems, so that attempts can be made to prevent problems arising rather than merely dealing with them after they have arisen.

A further example of the European influence on pre-existing Irish legislation is in the area of atmospheric pollution. Traditionally, Ireland has enjoyed relatively pure air outside of the cities and isolated industrial areas. However, in recent times the quality of air in the cities has steadily decreased. This led to the Air Pollution Act 1987 which reformed and updated the previous law relating to air pollution in Ireland. This Act, as in the area concerning water pollution, provides for European standards to be applied to pre-existing Irish mechanisms of pollution control.

Although much of the problem in urban areas has been eliminated due to a prohibition on burning bituminous coals which came into force in

1990, there is still concern about air pollution from industrial areas. In particular, the area of Ringaskiddy, County Cork has been the subject of many reports and investigations due to fears about declining air quality in the area. Within that small area located in the extreme south of Ireland, are situated processing plants for some of the biggest international, chemical and pharmaceutical companies, which gives rise to large amounts of air pollution. A report carried out by the Minister for State at the Department of the Environment in 1991, however, concluded that air quality in Ringaskiddy was not significantly affected by industrial activities. This conclusion was borne out by various other reports carried out by other bodies subsequently. Concern is still voiced, however, about the levels of pollution in similar industrial areas around the country.

Perhaps the most significant environmental legislation introduced in Ireland in recent times was the Environmental Protection Agency Act 1992. Rather than provide specific provisions regarding enforcement of pollution control or particular standards regarding pollution control, the significance of this Act lies in the establishment of the Environmental Protection Agency. The aim of this body is to formulate general policies towards tackling environmental problems in Ireland and to co-ordinate the activities of local authorities and other inferior bodies. This Act provides for a more efficient system of environmental control by overseeing the various bodies which, to date, had worked alone rather than in harmony. Significantly, the Act allows for the imposition of obligations on public authorities which previously were not subject to the same controls as the private sector. Local authorities, since the introduction of this Act, are no longer exempt from the general obligation to obtain planning permission for their developments, to obtain a licence for the discharge of sewage and trade effluents to waters or to obtain a permit for the disposal of wastes.

The Act represents an attempt by the Irish Government to take a larger view of environmental problems rather than tackling specific problems as they arise. By taking an overview of the legislative provisions already in existence regarding the environment, great progress can be made and the efficiency of these provisions can be greatly improved. The establishment of this overseeing body is the major development in Irish environmental law.

It is encouraging to see the Irish Government taking an aggressive approach to the conservation and care of the environment. By so doing, the Government has taken great heed of the First Programme of Action of the European Community on the Environment which enunciated some principles to be borne in mind by Member States. Among these were a few basic propositions some of which were paraphrased by the leading Irish *Environmental Law* textbook as "Prevention is better than cure" and "Environmental effects should be taken into account at the earliest possible stage in all decision-making processes". Membership of the European Union has, in this way, greatly aided Ireland's attitude to tackling environmental problems through legislation. Legislation such as the Local Government (Water Pollution) Acts and the Public Health (Ireland) Act 1878 was geared towards problems which had already arisen and provided a scheme, at times largely ineffective, for damage limitation. The European influence has imported into Irish law the attitude that damage can be prevented before it even arises.

A microcosm of this can be seen in the area of marine pollution. The Oil Pollution of the Sea Acts 1956 to 1977 and the Sea Pollution Act 1991 allowed for compensation to be paid to anyone who had suffered pollution damage. The Sea Pollution (Prevention of Oil Pollution) Regulations 1994 now oblige any person who controls a harbour to provide facilities for the disposal of oily residues and other substances. This is an example of preventative measures being taken rather than measures dealing with pollution after the fact.

We are now conscious of environmental protection in Ireland. The increasing awareness amongst people of damage being done to the environment has led to the willingness of ordinary citizens to enforce their rights and protect their environment. Separately Ireland, with its large reliance on its picturesque scenery and numerous lakes and rivers for tourism purposes, has now an economic interest in preserving its environment.

The influence of the European Union has led to a much more aggressive approach being taken, resulting in a greater consciousness of the importance of this area. The hearing of such a high-profile case as *Hanrahan* and the publicity concerning the Sellafield Nuclear Plant provide proof of this and it also provides impetus to future potential litigants, to enforce or protect their rights.

Italy

Dr Natalia Barbera
Studio Deberti Jacchia, Milan

Environmental problems in Italy originated from the industrial development, which accelerated in the 1950s, using the territory and natural resources without taking into consideration compatibility or environmental impact.

Clear examples of such inconsiderate environmental management are: pollution of water and soil arising from industrial waste, atmospheric pollution especially in large urban and industrial areas, as well as disasters linked with hydro-electric plants.

Until the mid-1970s the responsibility for coping with environmental disasters was assigned by the law to local health departments. The objective of such legislation was mainly to protect people's health from environmental risks.

Finally the Legge Merli, 319/1976 introduced into Italian law the concept of "environment" as an independent and autonomous entity to be protected. This idea is also reinstated in the DPR 915/1982 on waste disposal.

Unlike Spain, Portugal and Germany, the Italian Constitution does not include any articles which cover protecting the environment. This was partly covered by the interpretation of Articles 2, 9 and 32 of the Italian Constitution which cover man's rights, land and health as an inalienable right.

The following regulations have been issued: Law No. 319/1976 on the protection of water quality, DPR 915/1982 on waste disposal, DPCM 28 March 1983 on air quality, and L. 361/1985 on specially protected areas. The above Acts represent the first significant set of laws which introduce the concept of environment into Italian Law.

Such regulations take into account the concept of environment as a relevant issue of general interest.

Until the appointment of the Ministry of the Environment in 1986, different government authorities were in charge of the environment. These were Public Works, Agriculture and Forests, Merchant Navy, Transport, Industry, Trade and Craft, Health, Cultural and Environmental Heritage, Internal Affairs, Scientific Research, Southern Italy and Tourism.

The purpose of creating the Ministry of the Environment was to unify various authorities, which worked at cross purposes with each other.

In recent years the Ministry of the Environment has had to deal with environmental emergencies which have previously been ignored, such as waste disposal, export of hazardous waste, programmes for the abatement, control and prevention of pollution from industrial sources, drainage of contaminated sites, protection of ground water quality from pollution caused by agriculture and industry, and lack of water drainage systems even in the most developed cities.

The source of the Italian statutes specifically applicable to certain areas of environmental regulation was EU law, and not national law.

Italy has adopted the following measures in order to come into line with its European partners and to comply with European standards:

- regulation on waste (Law No. 441/1987, Law No. 475/1988);
- regulation on protection of air quality (DPR 203/1988: the 1990 guidelines to limiting emissions and the 1991 measures for air control and clearance systems);
- regulation on the preventive measures for the environment from industrial hazards (DPR 175/1988: requirements for security by industries of 1989);
- regulation on environmental impact assessment (DPCM 377/1988);
- regulation on river basins and soil contamination (Law No. 183/1989);
- regulation on the protection of the Adriatic sea against pollution (Law No. 283/1989);
- regulation on the quality of drinking water and the protection of water from hazardous substances (Law No. 71/1990);
- regulation on the prevention and limiting of noise pollution (DPCM 1 February 1991).

Specific provisions, statutes and regulations applicable to certain areas of environmental regulations

Although certain rules are contained in prior legislation, most environmental regulation originates from EC Directives which have been implemented in the last few years. Each year a large number of environmental regulations are introduced into Italian law to implement EU Directives in accordance with the "EC Statute" (Legge Comunitaria), an annual statute whereby the Government is delegated the power to implement a number of EU Directives in various fields.

AIR QUALITY

Air pollution is governed by the Presidential Decree No. 203 of 24 May 1988, implementing EU Directives 80/779, 82/884, 84/360 and 85/203.

This law states that construction plans for new plants must be filed with the relevant regional authority.

Accordingly, regions must in turn verify that the plans include the necessary precautions to prevent pollution and that the emissions are within the limits fixed by the Decree of the Prime Minister of 12 July 1990. Regions are entitled to lower the limits of the emissions, if a specific case arises. In such a case the authorisation must specify the maximum emissions allowed in the authorised plant and the start-up date for the plant.

If the authorisation is infringed the region can warn or suspend the working of the plant or, at worst, revoke the authorisation, in case the company does not comply with its requests.

Infringements of emissions limits and failure to obtain the required authorisation carry criminal sanctions.

The emissions of gas, steam or smoke in a public area or private area of common use, which may harm, disturb or contaminate any entity, are caught under Article 674 of the Criminal Code. This provision is deemed applicable in cases of infringement of DPR 203/1988.

In addition to DPR 203/1988 other statutes have been issued regarding specific aspects of air quality such as workers' health protection, petrol, etc.

The Decree of the Ministry of the Environment of 12 November 1992, provides general requirements to prevent air pollution of large urban areas and measures to improve air quality. This decree implements the provisions on urban mobility adopted by the European Union in the Green Book on Urban Environment.

NOISE POLLUTION

Legislative decrees have implemented EU legislation fixing common product noise standards such as noise from domestic machines, noise generated by hydraulic or cable digging machines, bulldozers and mechanical shovels, permissable sound level of lawnmowers and permissable sound level of power cranes.

WASTE

Waste disposal is governed mainly by Presidential Decree No. 915 of 10 September 1982 (DPR 915/1982), implementing EU Directives 75/442, 76/403, and 78/319, and by Law No. 475 of 9 November 1988.

DPR 915 divides waste into three categories:

- urban waste;
- special waste;
- toxic and dangerous waste.

The list of products and substances in each category is contained in an Annex appended to DPR 915 and also in the DPR 915 "Implementation Provisions". The regions may also issue statutes and regulations implementing DPR 915.

Each stage in the disposal of toxic and dangerous waste must be duly authorised by the regional authorities. Authorisation must be granted for temporary storage, treatment, transportation and final disposal.

As regards the authorisation of waste disposal the implementation provisions prescribe, upon the authorised operator, the duty to verify that any transfer of such waste is only to an authorised person.

Authorisation infringements are punishable by imprisonment or with a fine. In case of repeated violations or risks to the public health and/or environment, suspension or withdrawal of the authorisation is applicable.

Law No. 475 imposes duties, upon whoever deals with waste disposal, to notify every year to the regional authorities the quantity and quality of waste produced or treated during the last year. This Law also provides for the creation of a register of those entities authorised to carry out waste disposal services.

RECYCLING WASTE

This law has been the source of much debate and several of its provisions have been declared unconstitutional by the Italian Constitutional Court.

After several amendments and reiterations, the last regulation on this matter is contained in the Decree No. 66 of 9 March 1995.

The scope of the Law is the recycling of waste, previously defined as secondary raw materials. This complies with the requirements laid down by EU Directives (91/156 and 9/689).

RISK OF SERIOUS ACCIDENTS

Presidential Decree No. 175 of 17 May 1988 implemented EU Directive 82/501 on the risks of serious accidents related to certain industrial activities.

Under this regulation, companies using the substances listed in the Annexes appended to the Decree are obligated to notify the Ministry of Health and the Ministry of Environment. Such notification should give detailed information on the kind of activity carried out in the plant and also on the safety systems, etc.

In case of failure to observe the prescriptions provided by this regulation, the monitoring authority has wide powers such as closing the plant. Criminal sanctions are also applicable.

198

WATER QUALITY

Law No. 319 of 10 May 1976 (the "Merli Law") as amended, regulates water pollution and discharges into water and/or soil. Under such law different authorities are invested. The state plays a co-ordinating role, indicates the general criteria for the proper use of waters and lays down the general technical rules. The regions prepare regional plans for water purification, supervise the control of discharges, and co-ordinate the activity of other local entities. The provinces register all private and public discharges and ensure compliance with the requirements of the proper use of the waters. Local municipalities control discharges.

This Law classifies discharges in relation to the private or industrial origin. Any discharge must be authorised and must comply with the maximum pollution limits set down by the Law.

Authorities responsible for environmental matters

NATIONAL PROVINCIAL AND LOCAL REGULATION

Jurisdiction over environmental matters is divided between the state, regions, provinces and municipalities. This gives rise to problems since statutes are sometimes not clear on the scope of the powers of each authority.

The President of the Council of Ministers and the Ministry of the Environment are the most important authorities in issuing administrative regulations relating to the environment under the powers granted to them by statute. Interpretative documents issued by administrative authorities are not binding, although clearly such interpretations may be relevant to ascertain the authorities' position on a specific point.

Apart from the environmental statutes and regulations issued by the state, regions and some provinces have regulatory powers upon delegation by the regions.

Regional and provisional statutes cannot contradict national law, but can introduce stricter requirements for the benefit of the environment. Provinces and municipalities are mainly in charge of monitoring the observance of environmental regulations and may intervene to ensure this.

THE NATIONAL AND REGIONAL ENVIRONMENTAL AGENCIES

The Decree of 4 December 1993, No. 496 which became Law No. 61 of 21 January 1994 filled the gap concerning the monitoring of the environment, created by the referendum abolishing the existing law regarding the jurisdiction of the local health authority.

This Law appoints the National Environment Agency to perform many functions. These include environmental protection and monitoring, as well as technical and scientific issues such as standards and compatibility limits, eco-labelling, eco-audits, risks of serious accidents and environmental assessments.

The Agency is the national referee of the European Environment Agency (EEA). Therefore the national agency is considered a useful instrument for the environmental information network throughout Europe, set up by the European Agency, in order to promote cooperation among the members of the European Union as regards the quality of, pressure on and vulnerability of the environment.

Furthermore, it states that regions shall appoint the Regional Environment Agencies to take over responsibilities previously held by the health authorities.

Under this Law the agency at regional level is considered the central character of local environmental policies. Past experience, in fact, has shown that the regions are the most suitable institutions to understand local demands as regards the economic and social issues of the area. The national agency will be in charge of co-ordinating the policies of the regional agencies policies, through checks, support, and assessment of the programmes implemented by the latter, according to the subsidiarity principle.

The appointment of these agencies at national and regional level, linked with the European Agency and provided with an efficient information system supporting the tasks of those entities, will produce a designed improvement in this field. In fact, based on relevant and up-to-date data, through efficient, continuous and systematic control, programmes are easy to establish and maintain.

Current situation

According to an OECD Survey (end 1994), comparing the environmental policies of the various industrial countries, with reference to the different areas of environmental regulation, the Italian scenario is not encouraging.

QUALITY OF AIR

The level of sulphur monoxide (Sox), nitrogen monoxide (Nox), and carbon dioxide (CO2) per gross domestic product unit (GDP) is per person below the average of the other OECD countries.

In the late 1970s a large reduction in Sox emissions took place. However Nox, CO2, and CO have increased beyond the growth of gross domestic product.

Italy has ratified international treaties on climate change and supports the European Union aim of settling CO2 emissions at the 1990 level by 2000.

However, in Italy this is affected by many weaknesses such as:

- lack of air-quality monitoring (especially in the south);
- defective harmonisation of monitoring processes and methods;
- delay in communicating and publishing relevant data;
- the quality of air programmes and the emissions audit from local authorities;
- according to DPR 203/1988 (regulation on air quality) which have not yet been completed;
- the self-auditing system, under DPR 203, infringes the European Directive on Industrial Atmospheric Pollution, which necessitates prior authorisation.

Furthermore, the pollution from transport increased heavily between 1970 and 1994, much more so than in other developed countries.

WASTE

Apart from an efficient control of cross-border transport of hazardous waste by Italian authorities, treatment and waste disposal are not adequate. An unofficial survey shows that more than 5,000 contaminated industrial sites need to be drained.

WATER

As regards sewage, only 50% of Italian cities have treatment plants. Furthermore, 90% of these plants do not work efficiently, if at all, and are used only for primary sewage treatment.

In order to comply with the Directive 27/1991 which requires, by 2005, secondary sewage treatment for any basin with over 10,000 inhabitants, the Italian Government is obliged to serve the demand of 53 million inhabitants which would incur an expense of Lira 19,000 billion.

The "Galli Law" 36/1994, provides measures to implement the above Directive, through a programme. However, such a programme is unlikely to be realised as the funds provided by a three-year plan are insufficient.

Institutions acting in the Italian environment scenario

INDUSTRY

In the past, Italian industry was liable for trade of hazardous waste and for many environmental disasters such as Seveso, Manfredonia, Priolo, and Massa Carrara. Currently, it is more considerate as regards environmental challenges. Companies like Ferruzzi-Montedison, Fiat, Eni and Enel have invested large amounts of money in protecting the environment in compliance with the sustainable development demands.

ENVIRONMENT ASSOCIATIONS

These associations aim at awakening public interest in environmental issues and at drawing them to the attention of the appropriate governmental institutions.

MINISTRY OF THE ENVIRONMENT

This plays a co-ordinating role, supported by public opinion and environmental associations.

New statutes and perspectives

The Draft Directive on Integrated Pollution Control aims at harmonising the principles of granting, monitoring and renewing mandatory pollution permits to all types of industrial installations.

This Directive considers pollution as a global environmental issue without any consideration to the specific areas affected. Such a global view has not inspired Italian legislation either at the national or at the regional level. However, two exceptional statutes, although not yet put into practice, should be mentioned:

- Law No. 70 of 25 January 1994 which provides measures to facilitate the fulfillment of environmental regulations, health and public safety obligations and to implement an environmental management and auditing scheme;
- Law No. 36 of 5 January 1994 which regulates on water resources.

Law 70/1994 implements EU Regulation 1836/93. The Regulation establishes a system for the evaluation and improvement of the environmental performance of industrial activities. The "eco-management and audit schemes" also provide for informing the public on the results of the environmental audits carried out. The performance should be constantly improved by the economically viable use of "the best technologies available". Mandatory audits are not required. Companies may register any industrial activity under the scheme and then perform the audits accordingly.

Unfortunately, the Decrees implementing Law 70/1994 have not yet been issued. This law assigns the relevant functions as regards eco-audits to the same authority, which is in charge of eco-labelling matters (not yet appointed). It also establishes controls by public authority. The auditors' tasks are assigned to the certification bodies. Special exemptions as regards the participation of small and medium-sized enterprises, which are dominant in Italy, are granted through programme agreements with the associations representing the category.

Basically, as this system demands full cooperation between the enterprise and the public authority involved, it would be convenient to overcome the hurdles of the current law as regards authorisation procedures; otherwise the eco-management and eco-audit may become a further procedural burden on the business community shoulders.

Galli Law No. 36/1994 aims to create a new management system concerning production processes through the clearance of the relevant procedures. It supersedes the previous regulation's narrow view concerning the mere control of discharges. This is inspired by a global view of water management with regard to the whole water cycle, *i.e.* from supply to sewage and recycling.

Furthermore, it overcomes the territorial and numeric split in different authorities and provides efficient bodies with the appropriate dimension to grant an efficient, workable and economic water service.

The Galli Law encourages companies equipped with treatment plants to recycle sewage through tax concessions by reducing water supply charges and by granting financial facilities to realise those treatment plants.

Conclusions

As stated before, through a global approach to the environmental issues and a simplification of the different jurisdiction and procedures of the various authorities, Italy will catch up Europe's front-runners.

A draft universal law on global environment protection might simplify and rationalise the current statutory mess.

Rather than complying with the EU Directives with a defensive attitude, Italy will be able to follow a policy which considers the environment as a relevant factor of the economy. Such a strategy will be increasingly important to successfully compete at an international level.

Luxembourg

Nathalie Gattoni
Economist, GEDELUX SA
Serge Bernard
Lawyer, Etude Roland Michel

Just one of the consequences of the continued unification of Europe is the free circulation of goods and services, and it is necessary to question the impact that this has on the development of environmental law in Luxembourg, the smallest country of the European Union.

In fact, when considering the subject of environmental legislation in Luxembourg the country's size is significant. This, and its location, play an important role from the point of view of waste treatment, as well as pollution, which does not acknowledge frontiers.

Regionalism

Luxembourg is bordered by large countries which are well-equipped to deal with the prevention and control of damage to the environment. It has therefore been easy to transport waste out of Luxembourg to countries with the necessary infrastructure for the management of waste without thinking of future developments.

There is currently no national landfill site for industrial waste in Luxembourg; neither is there any plant equipped to process, treat or recycle special waste products. In consequence, there is a one-way traffic of this waste to other countries of the European Union.

The proximity of the bordering regions of Saarland and the Rheinland (Germany), Lorraine (France), as well as the Province of Luxembourg (Belgium) creates, on the one hand, an enormous number of opportunities for an inter-regional community, but, on the other hand, generates problems owing to the diversity of each of these regions and, most particularly, the diversity of their legal systems.

In this way, when dealing with the management of the environment, the legal and administrative authorities depend on their national and regional governments. Lorraine, for example, is directly controlled by Central Government in Paris; the Land of Sarre, on the other hand, has important legislative authority and the Grand Duchy is totally self-governing. The administrative structure of each region distinguishes itself clearly from the four others and each administrative area has different legal statutes. The situation, and collaboration, becomes ever more complicated in ratio to the number and regional diversity of those involved. One major problem in the framework of federal management of waste is its classification and encoding.

There is no harmonisation in this matter and, as a result, waste management on an interregional level becomes difficult to achieve. For example, with the exception of Wallonia, all the four regions have their own lists of waste.

These lists define the zone in which monitoring and control can be legally administered. As far as the scope and structure of these lists is concerned, they are not comparable either to each other or with the current work of the European Union. However, the Grand Duchy and its four frontier regions offer a single industrial infrastructure which covers the whole territory. These regions are isolated somewhat from their country as a whole and do not have sufficient size to justify a complete recycling and waste elimination programme on their own. This would however be possible for the five regions as a whole.

Systems and Acts of environmental law in Luxembourg

Apart from internationally recognised standards and those set out in the Constitution, internal environmental controls are regulated principally by law, the grand ducal decree and ministerial rule.

Some important environmental structures such as the Agence de l'Energie were created by law.

The development of environmental law in Luxembourg is not as recent as one would think. The law of 21 June 1976 was probably the first environmental law and concerned the prevention of pollution and control of noise. However, progress since 1976 has been rapid and continuous.

EXAMPLE: WASTE MANAGEMENT

The legal framework of waste management in Luxembourg is based on the law of 17 June 1994. The object of this law is primarily the prevention and the reduction of waste before processing. It is interesting to note that the concept of prevention appears also in the legislation of the four above-mentioned regions, but with varying importance.

The law of 17 June foresees a national and regional plan for the management of waste up to 1997 and introduces the principle of responsibility without fault for whoever produces waste products, and also defines the authorities' role and their duties when managing waste.

It is equally important to mention the grand ducal decree of 1 August 1988 relating to dangerous waste products (later modified by the grand ducal decree of 16 March 1994), the law of 9 May 1990 relating to dangerous, unhealthy and inconvenient structures, as well as the law of 27 June 1993 relating to the national landfill site for non-household or similar waste.

In order to put in place integrated systems of waste management, the Ministry of the Environment created the company, GEDELUX SA, and the "Campaign Superdrëckskescht".

GEDELUX SA

This company, which was funded jointly by the state and the Federation of Industries (51% state/49% industry), was created by the law of 10 August 1991 and is designed to put into action the prevention, treatment and elimination of industrial waste.

The Government has entrusted the company in particular with the conception and management of the national landfill site for non-household or similar waste at Haebicht. This landfill site allows the Government to aim at a ban on the transport of the majority of industrial waste, according to the European directives.

THE CAMPAIGN SUPERDRËCKSKESCHT (SUPER DUSTBIN) 1 + 2

The first campaign was financed by the Ministry of the Environment and is directed at households. The second campaign, directed at small and medium enterprises, is financed by participating companies. Both campaigns are put into practice by the Administration of the Environment, which has as an objective, to collect special waste which is part of household and similar waste, as well as to inform and advise the population on the subject of reducing waste.

A look at the future

Although the legal and administrative authorities on the subject of management of the environment may differ from one region to another, the regions have no interest in acting independently. The advantages of cross-border cooperation remove problems which can occur either from an environmental or from an economic point of view. Administrative structures should, however, be adapted to the demands to correspond to the global perspective of the environmental problems as well as guarantee the cooperation of the various authorities.

The advantages, but equally the problems of this inter-regional collaboration, could serve as a European pilot study, if not a prototype for the creation and development of a European legislative model.

Finally, it is apparent that the conflicts of interest in this area of law and the environment are generally resolved by a consensus, which is all the more powerful for being motivated by a desire to comply with the laws of nature.

The Netherlands

René Bakers
Partner, Thuis & Partners, Heerlen/Naastricht

Emergence of environmental law

Eighteen years ago I applied for a job with a large legal firm. I was asked in which branch of the law I would like to specialise. When I replied that I thought that environmental law was set to take off and would, in the near future, also be an interesting area, commercially speaking, on which to focus, the idea was greeted with a great deal of scepticism. The firm hired someone else. Since then, environmental law has become extremely important in the Netherlands, generating a lot of work both inside and outside the legal profession.

Environmental scandals

In 1980, the general public in Holland was shocked for the first time by an environmental scandal. In that year, in the small town of Lekkerkerk, it emerged that a brand new housing estate had been built on top of seriously polluted soil. The result was that the polluted soil had to be dug out from under the houses and replaced by clean soil. The cost was $100 million. At the time, the public and the Government thought that this was an isolated incident, and, because of this, financial resources were made available to tackle it directly and adequately. The authorities have since realised that there are many more problem areas, where the soil under existing buildings and housing estates is polluted.

The situation with industrial sites is even worse. It was recently calculated that it will cost at least $75 billion to clean up known pollution in industrial sites. A process has therefore been set in action, which is now unstoppable. In 1983, interim legislation was passed on soil pollution, which made it compulsory to clean up the soil whenever pollution was discovered, and imposed liability for the costs involved on those using the land. This law was in fact retrospective, without any time limit.

Pre-legislation pollution

Thus, in principle, even very old pollution, dating from a period when nobody had the slightest idea that certain processes were extremely harmful to the environment, also came under the scope of this law. However, the Supreme Court later limited the time-frame for liability so that, generally speaking, only pollution occurring after 1 January 1975 is subject to this law. Liability for pollution which occurred before that date would only be exacted if the polluter ought to have been aware of the authorities' concerns about it, either as a result of the authorities' instructions or the polluter's own expertise.

Since then, many new laws have been passed, including the Environmental Control Act and the Soil Protection Act. One of the most practical aspects of the new legislation is that it requires that an environmental impact statement be drawn up for every major project. This means that no major project can go ahead and no permit can be granted for such a project unless a comprehensive report has been drafted to show the effect that the project will have on the environment. Not only do these environmental impact statements cost investors a lot of money, they also take up time, leading to delays in the completion of projects.

Complex environmental legislation

An important and complicating factor is that environmental legislation is not a body of laws: rather, it can be found in various areas of the law. For example, there are environmental provisions in administrative law, private law and criminal law.

In addition, laws relating to nature and land conservation and public health also contain environmental provisions. We can see, therefore, that environmental provisions extend into all areas of the law, the result of which is that environmental legislation as a whole, often combined with urban planning regulations, has become extremely complex and the lawyers who are experts in these areas can be said to be real specialists.

A recent and very interesting court case was one which involved a pharmaceutical company, Philips-Duphar. The dispute centred on the contamination of a site where pesticides were dumped in the years before 1970. Philips-Duphar referred to these substances as "herbicides". Philips-Duphar had used the site to dispose of, among other things, 10,000 x 200 litre containers of pesticides. Eventually, the Supreme Court ruled in favour of Philips-Duphar. According to the ruling, Philips-Duphar may well have been aware that the authorities would be concerned about this pollution before the crucial date mentioned (1 January 1975) but Philips-Duphar would not necessarily have realised this before 1970.

It was further held that it did not matter whether it was their own land they polluted or someone else's – in this case, the city of Amsterdam's dump site. It could be said that this jurisprudence clearly determined the extent to which the liability provisions are retrospective.

Since then, greater clarity has been achieved with regard to the future. Until recently, there was another problem: the extent of residual pollution, and therefore the extent of the clean-up, depended on the purpose for which the land was used. The standards governing a housing estate were much stricter than those governing the clean-up of an industrial site. However, on 1 January 1995, the "ALARA principle" was generally adopted. This means that pollution must be reduced to a level where pressure on the environment must be "as low as reasonably achievable", *i.e.* that the effects of any pollution must be reversed as much as possible, irrespective of the future use of the land.

Positive news for industry

There is also positive news for industry, which is as follows:

(i)   Tax laws grant a right to keep funds in reserve for cleaning up pollution, provided that a concrete plan has been developed or a company has actually been ordered to do so by the authorities or a court; in other words, a writ has been served demanding payment of the costs. This tax allowance is extremely advantageous when proceedings drag on for many years. Where a high rate of interest is applied, it is possible that the advantage in terms of liquidity becomes so great that it eventually outweighs the disadvantage of paying the costs. The tax authorities are thus very generous to industry on this point.

(ii) In reality, it now appears that stringent environmental legislation generates a huge number of jobs and calls for a huge amount of new investment, which can help to revitalise the economy. For example, the first large-scale "coal gasification" plant in the world has been brought into service.

(iii) In practice, it has also become apparent that where consumers are aware of the pollution caused by a particular product, it has a considerable effect on their purchasing behaviour, and manufacturers are forced to make environmentally friendly products. A good example of this phenomenon is the manufacturer's switch to aerosol cans that do not use CFCs as a propellant.

(iv) The way in which Holland treats the environment and environmental legislation is seen as an example for other countries, which
are coming more and more to realise that they will have to draw up
regulations to cover environmental issues. This has led to the export
of legislation and clean production methods, which is of great
importance to the economy.

Political demands versus environmental policy

The great fear which has always existed, that tough environmental measures would cause countries to price themselves out of the market, has
proved to be unfounded.

However, there is the constant danger that polluting industries will be
shifted from Holland to countries with less-stringent environmental
requirements. It is not clear that Dutch industrialists and the multi-
nationals are taking their responsibilities in this area seriously enough.

I have had my doubts ever since I heard the Chairman of the Board of
Azco-Nobel saying that his company would continue to produce CFCs
until their production was banned. I am not so sure about Dutch politicians either. As soon as unemployment begins to worsen, they lose interest
in the environment and strict compliance with the regulations. At the end
of the day, it is people's attitudes which are the deciding factor, and not
regulations. My many visits to Denmark and the contacts I have made
there, have convinced me that, in many ways, the Danes have developed
the right attitude towards the environment.

Even the Dutch have something to learn from the Danes!

Portugal

Carlos Alexandre Matias and Joäo de Pihno
Partner, António Marante & Associados – Sociedade de Advogados, Porto

General legislation

(i) Articles 52 and 66 of the Portuguese Constitution

Portuguese law gives everyone the right to demand in the civil courts a decision to stop any environmental damage and to give indemnities to the victims. This is the rule. In spite of having or not having a proper interest, a person can ask the court to give a decision about an environmental problem, as if the problem were his own – any individual can proceed in the name of all citizens.

*(ii) Environmental skeleton legislation
(Lei de Bases do Ambiente – Law No. 11/87 of 11 April)*

This is the most important law on the environment in Portugal. It gives to the Instituto Nacional do Ambiente, a non-executive authority, general powers of control and the duty to inform citizens about their rights. This law also gives important definitions of pollution, both water and air-borne.

The law previews almost all crimes against nature and the environment, except those which are included in the Penal Code. What is new is that, for the first time, companies can be held criminally responsible, and not, as in the past, only individuals.

*(iii) Legislation on Environmental Defence Associations
(Lei das Associacóes de Defesa do Ambiente – Law No. 10/87 of 4 April)*

This law gives important powers to environmental associations to control the public authorities and the administration. These associations are free from taxes and other costs and have the right to receive a contribution from the state itself.

What is important, is the impartiality of this kind of association.

*(iv) Legislation on Environmental Impact of Construction
(Lei de Avaliaçao do Impacte Ambiental – D.L. No. 186/90 of 6 June)*

Under this law all the construction projects that impact on the environment are subject to approval by the competent authority in the region.

213

Other important legislation

(i)   Water

(a)   D.L. No. 70/90 of 2 March

This law created the Instituto Nacional de Àgua (INAG) and reviewed all the penalties for those who do not respect the controls on emissions into water (rivers). This legislation chiefly affects factories and all other industrial plants with a potential for pollution.

(b)   D.L. No. 74/90 of 4 August

This law gives to certain public authorities, the power to control and prevent the contamination of water. National and local authorities enforce the control. It also governs the composition of Portuguese drinking water.

(c)   Port No. 624/90 of 4 August, Port No. 808/90 and Port No. 810/90 of 10 September

This law regulates sewage water and the levels of discharge of both industrial and private effluent.

(d)   D.L. No. 468/71 of 5 November and D.L. No. 87/87 of 20 February

This law regulates all river land and gives power to certain authorities to take measures to prevent the well-known "chenas" – flooding.

(ii)   Air

(a)   D.L. No. 255/80 of 30 July

This law gives to the Secretaria do estado do Ambiente the power to establish the limits of air pollution in the biggest cities of Portugal.

(b)   D.L. No. 29/87 of 20 March

This law regulates the limit of pollution elements in the air.

(c)   D.L. No. 352/90 of 9 November

This law creates the Direcçao Geral da Qualidade do Ar, which has all the competency to produce information about air pollution, to verify the quality of the air and to take special measures to avoid excessive pollutants in the air.

(iii)   Waste

(a)   D.L. No. 343/75 of 3 July

This law gives local authorities power to authorise (or not) the location and construction of shelters, parks, junk shops, sports, etc.

(b)　D.L. No. 216/85 of 28 June

This law regulates the use of industrial and non-industrial oils and fuel oils and forbids the spreading of oil without authorisation.

(c)　D.L. No. 488/85 of 25 November

This law regulates the collection of waste and its elimination.

(iv)　Noise

(a)　D.L. No. 251/87 of 25 June

This law lays down the general rules regarding noise in schools, residential areas, hospitals, factories, traffic, etc. It also governs the maximum levels of noise allowed on construction sites and for machines.

(b)　D.L. No. 292/89 of 2 September

This law regulates the penalties for those who do not respect the law on noise pollution.

(c)　Port No. 879/90 of 20 September

This law gives to the Instituto Português da Qualidade the power to list the products which are able to produce noise.

Enforcement

The above summarises the main legislation that controls damage to the environment in Portugal.

It can be seen that Portugal has similar legislation to most other countries of the European Union. However, enforcement of these laws is more difficult to ensure. There are few cases where individuals or companies have actually been prosecuted for damage to the environment but it is likely that, as the Portuguese consumer, like other European consumers, becomes more demanding about his right to a clean environment, prosecutions will result and enforcement of environmental legislation will become more prevalent.

Spain

Felix Vilaseca

Partner, Bufete Roig Aran, Barcelona

Sources of Spanish environmental law

In Spain, protection of the environment is governed by Articles 45, 148 and 149 of the Spanish Constitution. Such protection falls within the scope of criminal law by virtue of the provisions of Article 347 of the Penal Code and has been developed by multiple national and regional laws. The responsibility of developing and applying environmental regulations is assumed by the autonomous regional governments and the municipal authorities.

The majority of the directives of the European Union on this matter have been incorporated into the national legislation and, thus, are fully applicable in the majority of cases – although their enforcement or the requirement that the Administration should enforce them is still very deficient. It is, perhaps, in the most industrialised areas like Catalonia and the Basque Country where the directives are applied most.

Priorities of the environmental policy

The priorities of the environmental policy are as follows:

- the fight to prevent land wasting;
- the quality of water and optimisation of its use;
- the treatment of wastes;
- the quality of the environment.

These environmental priorities cause legislation to concentrate on the protection of the environmental impact of new activities: saving and recycling water consumption, as well as recycling and reduction of waste residues.

All industrial projects, whether agricultural, stock-raising or urban, which have an object which comes within the aforementioned objectives may apply for official grants. The sectors which most profit from grants are chemicals and energy, with a total of 70% of investments and grants during the period from 1990 to 1994. Of these investments 50% have been allocated to water purification, 25% to the treatment of waste residues and 16% to the purification of atmospheric emissions.

Protection of the environment

Environmental legislation regulates the system of offences and specific penalties, which vary from fines, to the closing down of the premises in question.

In addition, risk liability is deemed to exist when resulting from the creation of a severe and tangible danger, as well as for negligence, the "iuris tantum" of which is presumed and is punishable in accordance with the provisions of Articles 1902 and 1908 of the Civil Code. This liability may extend to the administration which granted permission to carry out the activity causing the damage or which has failed to control an activity causing damage to the environment.

The environment is also protected by Article 347 of the Penal Code, although its application requires that there exists a voluntary act, *mens rea* or inexcusable negligence which creates a dangerous risk for people's health or severely prejudices environmental conditions.

Penalties vary between fines and imprisonment, in addition to repairing any damage caused.

It should be remembered that Spanish courts are very restrictive when it comes to assessing damages.

A recent judgment of the Supreme Court, regarding a criminal charge laid by the Prosecutor in respect of discharging toxic waste into a river, is worth noting. According to this judgment the facts did not amount to the commission of an offence contained in the Penal Code because, when the waste was being discharged the river was already very polluted and the new discharges could not, therefore, create severe damage to the environment because it had already suffered deterioration prior to the said discharges of waste taking place.

This notwithstanding, prosecutors are increasingly active and there are even those which specialise in offences against the environment, punishing acts deemed to degrade the environment, as befits an industrialised country, and thereby forcing those companies which contaminate most, either to move to developing countries or to convert into non-contaminating companies or into companies with a very low contamination factor.

Measures to deter the discharge of contaminating agents

Spanish legislation establishes the obligation for industrial companies (Decree-law 2/91 concerning industrial waste applicable to Catalonia) to

218

declare the volume of industrial waste generated during the previous year and the process used to treat or store it. Companies are also required, should it be the case, to name the specialist company to which they entrust this treatment or management, all of which allows the autonomous regional administration to keep control of waste-dumping operations and to penalise those carried out without such due control or which infringe the applicable law.

Unfortunately, there are a great number of highly contaminating small companies which, albeit on a small scale, escape this type of control, which is designed more for large solvent companies with a sense of responsibility.

Consequently, National Quality Plan No. II for 1994–97, which has been devised by the Ministry of Industry and Energy, is specially aimed at small and medium-sized businesses.

Independently from the penalties applicable in cases of offences arising out of the discharge of toxic waste into watercourses, Spanish legislation (Decree-law 849/86) establishes, as a method of assessing the cost of making good the damage caused, the evaluation of the cost of treating the waste which would have been necessary to avoid the contamination produced, thus obtaining a daily figure which is claimed from the company in question until such discharges are suspended or they remedy the excessive degree of contamination with respect to the maximum permitted by law.

While proceedings for administrative penalties become statute-barred after two months, the obligation to return things to their original state or to repair the damages caused is statute-barred after 15 years.

The European Commission has commenced proceedings against Spain for failing to comply with the provisions of Directive 76 of 4 May 1974 in Algeciras Bay, as a pressing measure to reinforce compliance with environmental regulations in Spain.

Where solid wastes are concerned, in spite of the fact that the regulations are well developed, there are very few legal dumps and very few companies legally authorised to treat and purify these wastes, with the result that sometimes it is almost impossibly expensive to comply with the law.

Conclusions

In Spain, as in the other EU Member States, the citizens and the administration are becoming more aware of the need to conserve and protect the environment.

This is mainly evidenced in those regions where there are higher cultural and economic levels (Catalonia and the Basque Country) and which are more industrialised. Their *per capita* income is also higher than in the rest of the regions of Spain. This awareness creates a tendency in the consumer to look for non-contaminating products and companies as opposed to those which offend against the surrounding environment.

Companies are taking advantage of this popular reaction in order to modernise and create products which, from the beginning, are not contaminating, commencing with the consumption of harmless raw materials as opposed to those which suggest an aggressive risk for nature. Therefore, in all of their processes, the level of contamination and of dangerous or toxic wastes will be minimal, with all the advantages which such a policy has for their country.

Sweden

Lena Eriksson
Associate, Engström & Co, Malmö

Sweden is a country blessed with an abundance of nature's beauty. Forests and lakes are to be found practically everywhere in our elongated country – even in the cities. Naturally we, as well as most modern countries today, have laws to protect and care for the environment.

The two major laws in Swedish legislation today are the Environment Protection Act (Miljöskyddslagen (1969:387)) and the Environmental Damage Act (Miljöskyddslagen 1986:225)).

The Environmental Protection Act controls any activity that is considered environmentally hazardous. It covers activities on real estate, permanent plants and operations that cause disturbances in the neighbourhood. Examples of such disturbances are water pollutants, air pollutants and noise. Activities of a more specialised and grave nature require special permits. These permits are applied for to the National Licensing Board for Environmental Protection. Before applying, the party must have performed an environmental impact assessment which should be attached to the application for a permit. As an example the planned bridge connecting Malmö with Copenhagen in Denmark has been the subject for discussion. An impact assessment has been made and that is an important part of the future for this vast project.

In cases where the activities cause only limited or local disturbances no permit is required; however, the local environmental authorities must be made aware of the proceedings.

Any party about to undertake any kind of environmentally hazardous activity is required to implement certain safety measures and accept restrictions in order to minimise the risks. The precautionary measures required must be the best known technology in use today, anywhere in the world. However, the costs for the use of such technology and safety measures have to be weighed against the project, the hazards and the company as such. Conditions in a permit for the activity remain in force for 10 years but may be subject to revision at an earlier date should unforeseen disturbances occur or new technology be developed that may substantially alter present conditions.

Every environmentally hazardous activity is subject to supervision by a supervisory authority, which is entitled to gain access to plants and other installations and carry out checks necessary for the purpose of the supervision. Anyone responsible for environmentally hazardous activities is required to submit a yearly environmentally report to the county council authorities. The report must contain an account of which measures have been taken to fulfill the conditions laid out in the official permit.

Infringement regarding the provisions of the Environmental Protection Act or regulations issued pursuant to the Act makes the party liable to a fine or up to two years' imprisonment.

The second of the main environmental acts is the Environmental Damage Act. This Act applies to claims for indemnity after the damage has been done. In order to be able to make any claims for indemnity the damage must emanate from a building, land or installation on a site. It also applies to use of water-catchment areas or an installation in water.

This Act also covers a wide range of on-site applications.

It covers forestry, farming, building roads, building a house or simply living in a house. The owner of a house is responsible for any activity on his grounds whether it involves air pollution, stench or noise.

If the owner of a house digs around his own house and thereby causes a neighbouring house damage, this also falls within the application of the Act.

The Environmental Damage Act also contains special provisions on environmental damage insurance. To be able to cover indemnity in some cases five major insurance companies have together formed an Environmental Damage Consortium with insurance terms and conditions approved by the Swedish Government. For those engaged in environmentally hazardous activities, contributions to this insurance is mandatory.

As stated in the insurance provisions, indemnity is payable to a claimant for bodily injuries or for material damage which is covered by the Act itself. Indemnity is paid in cases where the claimant is entitled to indemnity but cannot get such indemnity paid or cases where the damage is done but it proves impossible to establish who is responsible for causing it.

Natural resources

The main law regarding the protection of natural resources is the Act on the Management of Natural Resources etc (Lag (1987:12) om hushållning med naturresurser m.m.). This Act is constructed with a long-term view in mind and its main target is to promote a sound management of land, water and the general environment from ecological, social and economical aspects. The Management Act is one of the basic considerations in all general planning legislation, covering conservation as well as development interests. The Act is also applicable when decisions are taken under other statutes, for instance the Planning and Building Act (Plan och bygglag (1987:10), the Water Rights Act (Vattenlag (1983:291)), the Environmental Protection Act and the Nature Conservation Act (Naturvårdslag (1964:822)), to name a few. It is also one of the Acts responsible for co-ordination in cases where conflicting interests have to be considered. In the Act there are references to a number of areas in Sweden about which certain considerations must be taken. Certain river areas are regulated in regard to power generation, including coastal areas sensitive to development and other areas of great natural value. The Act also protects certain areas from over-development instead of trying to protect the existing societies. Many fishing sites that have housed fishermen and their families for centuries are situated in exceptionally beautiful coastal areas. In order to allow the residing population to stay on and not allow the area to become a high-cost vacational area restrictions have been made regarding building new houses etc.

The term "everyman's right" is embodied in the Nature Conservation Act and allows everyone the right of way across even private property. The countryside is a public asset and should as such be available to all provided, naturally, that due consideration and care is taken. This is a far-reaching right but, unfortunately, it has been misinterpreted by many who do not understand the age-old customs in Sweden.

No one may take branches or trees that are alive and growing. It is permitted to pitch tents and camp in many areas but the owner's permission is usually required and, although the use of the land as such is permitted, the use of living trees and drilling for fossils is not. It is also permitted to use beaches and forests for recreational purposes. This "everyman's right" is one of the reasons why building in coastal areas is regulated in a very strict manner.

The Act covers the conservation of areas such as national parks, nature reserves and threatened plants and animal species. Special permits are required for any noticeable intervention in the natural environment.

Activities such as stone and gravel quarrying and land drainage require a permit. This is also applicable to activities such as lowering or draining a lake.

The Act on Sweden's Exclusive Economic Zone (Lag (1992:1140) om Sveriges ekonomiska zon) is a new Act which came into force in January 1993. Its origin is to be found in the United Nations Convention of the Law of the Sea of 1982. Though the UN Act never came into force the material in the Act is considered to have a common law basis. The boundaries for the exclusive economic zone have been determined in detail and are to be found in a special ordinance. This Act protects marine life and the environment. It does not in any way infringe the rights of free shipping or any of the acknowledged principles of international law. It does however lay down requirements for permits and how to apply for such permits regarding utilisation of certain natural assets and also the right to carry out certain research involving the marine environment.

Waste disposal

The Waste Collection and Disposal Act (Renhållningslag (1979:596)) has, over the last few years, brought Swedish society closer to a fully developed "eco-cycle-orientated" society. Waste management must take place in such a manner as to enable the re-use or recycling of material whenever possible in order to save natural resources and raw materials. Where household waste is to be disposed of it is the responsibility of the local authority, and can amount to recycling, compostation or finally disposing of the waste.

An amendment in Spring 1993 added a producer responsibility. In the future it is possible to impose an obligation upon anyone who, in a commercial sense, manufactures, imports, sells or gives rise to waste, to make sure that the waste is taken care of in an appropriate manner (*e.g.* recycling or permanently disposing of the waste), whether in the process of manufacture or by way of packaging a product.

A certain product that has an inherent waste problem is the beverage industry. There are Acts covering beverage containers, whether PET or aluminium. The system for recycling of both kinds is well-developed and in order to induce people to participate in this campaign a deposit sum is charged whenever any kind of beverage in stores is purchased.

Batteries and the use of mercury, lead and cadmium are also a hazard to the environment. Charges based on the amount of metals used in the batteries are to be levied in order to finance the disposal of used-up batteries.

The Vehicle Emissions Act (Bilavgaslag (1986:1386)) is targeted to prevent environmental damage through, mainly, exhaust fumes.

Approved cars, trucks and buses are divided into three categories, each classification being made in accordance with the emissions from that type of car. Economic control operates through differentiated sales taxes for the three classes.

Nuclear safety and protection against radiation

Progress means having to deal with legal problems covering new ground. Nuclear power is still in developing stages and new problems occur constantly.

Appendix III

In Sweden today there are three nuclear power plants located in Barsebäck, Ringhals and Forsmark, sharing a total of 12 reactors.

Even though these plants have operated for a number of years there is still no definite decision as to the location of the waste products storage area. The right to self-government in certain areas means that practically every county in Sweden has used its veto against placing the waste site on its territory.

The Act on Nuclear Activities (Lag (1984:3) om kärnteknisk verksamhet) regulates safety in connection with nuclear activities. The Act is not limited to the operation of nuclear power plants but applies to all possible handling of nuclear substances and waste products. Strictly speaking, no handling of nuclear material is allowed without permission. Every attempt is made to prevent the proliferation of nuclear weapons.

The owners of nuclear power plants are responsible for the storage of waste products and, as that particular issue has not yet been finally decided, the companies pay an annual charge to the state. The money is collected in a fund in which assets are used to compensate the owners for costs regarding research and handling of nuclear waste, as well as other costs involved with the running of a nuclear power plant.

Today it is forbidden, without special permission, to store nuclear waste from foreign countries on Swedish soil. Such a permit will not at present be issued.

Appendix IV
An Example of Environmental Regulation in Central and Eastern Europe: Hungary

Dr Károly Bárd

Partner, Eörsi & Partners, Budapest

The Hungarian Parliament (in which the Government has a stable 72 member majority and can therefore pass legislation as it wishes) is likely to pass new laws on the protection of the environment shortly.

This new legislation, in so far as its philosophy, form and content are concerned, follows closely the format of the European Union laws. The new legislation will provide a framework upon which future implementing decrees will be hung. Such decrees will be issues at both Government and ministerial level and will be used in conjunction with other laws affecting the human environment, such as energy, mining, fishing, forestry, agriculture, hunting, building, regional development and water development.

The present law is not to blame for the present state of the environment in Hungary. The uncontrolled industrialisation of the country, together with a lack of financial resources for the handling of waste and the implementation of pollution prevention measures, have caused the present situation. Additionally, the former Hungarian economy was dominated (95%) by large state-run companies, farms and cooperatives, which generated very heavy resistance to any suggestions of an efficient enforcement of the environmental legislation then in place.

Nevertheless, it is hoped that the new Act will be a good innovation and will be effective both now and in the middle and long-term future, as well as providing changes and introducing new subject matter and methods of dealing with these new areas.

For the long term, it is important to review the regulations concerning the environmental protection information systems, which includes a historical review of pollution within Hungary. All this information will one day be registered in the Land Register – a development which should provide a more secure base for the planning of new projects in the future. However, it is unlikely that this will come about within this century.

For the near future, the provisions which require the payment of contributions by industry for the use of environmental media must be noted. The scheme requires the payment of sums to compensate for damage caused to the environment by virtue of the industrial processes being used. The sum payable is calculated on the basis of the number and type of emissions to various environmental media, the cost of the goods after production and the cost of the import and/or turnover of raw materials used in the industrial process concerned. In effect, this is a fee payable for damage created to the environment, by virtue of an industrial process being allowed to take place. Many other countries are familiar with such contributions, which are aimed at promoting environmental protection; and those in Hungary are assessed only on the basis of guidelines set out in legislation passed by the Hungarian Parliament.

Another important element of the new law, which is to be immediately effective, is the provisions requiring environmental impact assessment studies. Such studies, which deal with direct and indirect effects, are described within the legislation itself. They will become part of the specific licensing procedure on environmental protection. The studies and assessments are to be carried out by duly nominated officials but at the request of the user or future user of the environmental media within a given area.

For lawyers, one of the most important issues is, naturally, the liabilities imposed by any specific legislation. However, in this respect the new legislation does not effect any changes. Nearly all the present laws on environmental protection, as well as the proposed legislation, provide for strict liability for environmental pollution and are identical to provisions given in the Civil Code.

The characteristics of this liability are that the polluter is strictly liable for all the pollution caused. There was a small mistake in the recent *Financial Times'* environmental liability report, which indicated that the new legislation in Hungary would introduce strict liability only for certain damage – this is wrong. The Hungarian legal system will impose strict liability for all types of damage to the environment by way of pollution, irrespective of the severity of the pollution caused. There are very few exemptions from strict liability. (Only one other area of Hungarian law has such strict liability, this being the liability of an employer who has caused or is responsible for an infringement of the Health and Safety Regulations.)

Besides paying for any damage caused, a polluter must also pay certain fees, which are set out in regulations. These are not criminal sanctions, which also exist, but are separate and distinct.

The two obligations to pay compensation and fees are independent of each other and can either work in tandem or individually. The new legislation provides for the purchase of permits, which set out permitted tolerance levels of pollution. Any infringement of these tolerance limits results in the payment of an additional penalty fee. However, compensation for damage caused by pollution is also payable, irrespective of the tolerance levels set out in the permits. Even the slightest incidence of pollution (even if it is under the tolerated level contained in the permit), can lead to an obligation on the part of the polluter to pay compensation if damage is proved. The liability of several polluters is fully joint and several.

When it comes to dealing with environmental offences, the practice of the courts in Hungary is still in development; however, we are quickly learning new methods and approaches, which come mainly from the United States. A person who causes damage has to pay all the costs associated with that damage in an unlimited sum, whether that damage is material or otherwise. For example, it is the case that the owner of a dog that is killed by environmental pollution could claim moral damages, even though his loss is, in some respects, immaterial. Moreover, if only one polluter can be identified, he will be responsible for paying full damages, even though it is obvious that other unidentified polluters were also involved. All types of evidentiary techniques are accepted in the courts, as is the use of statistical data for production turnover etc in the calculation of the damage payable caused by several polluters.

According to the new legislation (except under criminal legislation), unless otherwise proved, an owner or user of real estate, in which an activity is being carried out, is liable for any contravention of the regulations. The burden of proof is on the owner or user of the real estate to prove that he did not cause the pollution. The person suffering damage can require the administrators of environmental protection to enforce his claim against the polluter, and a central environmental protection fund has been created by the new legislation from which third parties can obtain redress for damage caused.

What therefore can be recommended for a new investor starting his activity on Hungarian soil? Not to underestimate the problem but to avoid dramatisation, it must be said that the state of the Hungarian environment is poor. It is recommended that the above-mentioned official impact assessment studies, even though not obligatory, are carried out before applying for the necessary licences and permits under the new legislation. It is general practice when entering into contracts with sellers of goods (be it for the state or the municipality), to oblige them to carry out these impact assessments (which will include the sinking of test bore holes, as well as other methods of investigation).

In 1995 the Hungarian Parliament passed a new privatisation law which will accelerate the privatisation procedures and development in Hungary. If the seller is not ready to undertake this impact assessment or can only undertake a part of the assessment, it is best that the purchaser pays for it himself. It should be appreciated that it will be an authorised expert or expert body, advised by the authority itself, which carries out the impact assessments and this can, to a very broad extent, both accelerate and facilitate the whole procedure. There are dire consequences for those that carry out only a partial impact assessment study as any pollution that is later found to exist on the site will generate additional costs, especially if the seller did not give a full guarantee for the latent damage. A fixed sum therefore should be included which covers, either totally or partially, the cost of unexpected environmental protection measures and/or the increased cost of an investor's insurance policy to cover these risks. The municipalities in Hungary are already giving these guarantees. The Hungarian insurance industry does offer third-party liability insurance cover for pollution-related damage but this basically only covers damage of an accidental nature.

In the drafts of the new legislation it was suggested that there should be an obligatory third-party property insurance for pollution. However, this has not found its way through to the latest draft. This may, in the future, be brought forward by the Hungarian Parliament.

Finally, the situation in Hungary is worse than in Western Europe. Pollution is a phenomenon of our age that we have to live with. However, it is not because the legal means and techniques to minimise this danger are not available.

Index

Index

Index

Index

Index

Index

Index

Index compiled by Kim Harris

243